CRITICAL INSIGHTS

Magical Realism

CRITICAL INSIGHTS

Magical Realism

Editor
Ignacio López-Calvo
University of California, Merced

SALEM PRESS
A Division of EBSCO Information Services, Inc.
Ipswich, Massachusetts

GREY HOUSE PUBLISHING

The Manchester Library
The Bishop's School
La Jolla, California

Copyright © 2014 by Grey House Publishing, Inc.

All rights reserved. No part of this work may be used or reproduced in any manner whatsoever or transmitted in any form or by any means, electronic or mechanical, including photocopy, recording, or any information storage and retrieval system, without written permission from the copyright owner. For information, contact Grey House Publishing/Salem Press, 4919 Route 22, PO Box 56, Amenia, NY 12501.

∞ The paper used in these volumes conforms to the American National Standard for Permanence of Paper for Printed Library Materials, Z39.48-1992 (R1997).

Library of Congress Cataloging-in-Publication Data

Magical realism / editor, Ignacio López-Calvo, University of California, Merced. -- [First edition].

  pages ; cm. -- (Critical insights)

Edition statement supplied by publisher.
Includes bibliographical references and index.
ISBN: 978-1-61925-413-8

  1. Magic realism (Literature)--History and criticism. 2. Latin American literature--History and criticism. 3. Comparative literature. I. López-Calvo, Ignacio. II. Series: Critical insights.

PN56.M24 M34 2014
809.915

LCCN: 2014947173

PRINTED IN THE UNITED STATES OF AMERICA

Contents

About This Volume, Ignacio López-Calvo ... ix

On Magical Realism as an International Phenomenon in the Twenty-First Century, Ignacio López-Calvo ... xvi

Critical Contexts

Theories of Magical Realism, Erik Camayd-Freixas ... 3

Magical Realism and Its Discontents, Juan E. De Castro ... 18

Magical Realism and Subaltern Studies, Maggie Ann Bowers ... 35

Magic and Realism in History: Magical Realism vs. the Fantastic Today, Gene H. Bell-Villada ... 49

Critical Readings

When Magical Realism Loses Its Spell: Revisiting Gabriel García Márquez's *Of Love and Other Demons,* Rudyard J. Alcocer ... 67

The Plague of Modernity: Macondo, Inc. and the Branding of "Magical" Latin America, Martín Camps ... 84

History, Ehtnography, and Magical Realism in Marcio Veloz Maggiolo's *The Diffuse Biography of Sombra Castañeda*, Fernando Valerio-Holguín ... 97

The Construction of the Magic and the Role of Popular Religion in the Caribbean Context, Ángel L. Estévez ... 113

The Unbearable Weight of Being in Daniel Galera and Rafael Coutinho's *Cachalote,* David William Foster ... 131

Underdogs and Beautiful Lies: Magical Realism in the Second World, Nicholas Birns ... 146

Proliferation: The Case for Magical Realisms from Oyeyemi's *The Icarus Girl*, Kim Anderson Sasser ... 162

Panthers and Jaguars: Realism and Responsibility in Salman Rushdie's *Shame*, Rachel Trousdale ... 178

The Shadow of Magical Realism in José Luis Cuerda's 1980s films, Ignacio López-Calvo ... 193

Resources

Additional Works on Magical Realism	213
Bibliography	217
About the Editor	221
Contributors	223
Index	229

Dedication

To my friend Luis Sanz Sevillano

About This Volume

Ignacio López-Calvo

The present volume revisits what is perhaps the most influential literary movement to come out of Latin America and the Caribbean: magical realism. The essays review past and current criticism of magical realist works around the world, analyze seminal as well as lesser known magical realist literature and film, and update the theoretical discourse addressing this literary and cultural mode. Several essays explore the origin of the term "magical realism" and point out the differences among pure fantasy, surrealism, and magical realism. Others look at the peculiar combination of a mostly European, realistic, rational worldview (including its concept of time) and the mostly non-European acceptance of supernatural, magical, irrational, or carnivalesque events as part of everyday life, which has been interpreted as a subversive, postcolonial reaction to Eurocentric views. As will be seen, some critics argue that this magical realist approach to reality, which is often associated with a "primitive," indigenous, or "Third World" consciousness and opposed to Western modernity, endows everyday reality with a deeper meaning that unearths the mystery behind things. Together, these essays provide an updated look at magical realism's relevance in the twenty-first century.

After the introduction to the volume, Erik Camayd-Freixas compares the different theories of magical realism in their historical context and explores methodological guidelines for its continued study. Coined in 1925 to describe German post-expressionist painting, the term "magical realism" reappeared with new meanings in Latin American literature after 1940. In 1949, continues Camayd-Freixas, Alejo Carpentier formulated his influential concept of the Latin American "marvelous real," referring to the cultural syncretism arising from the clash of primitive and modern, Western and non-Western belief systems, and giving "magical" or "marvelous" realism more of an anthropological dimension. Also influential was

Jorge Luis Borges' use of modernist techniques in developing a new brand of "fantastic literature." With the "Boom" of the Latin American novel (1967–1984), the term "magical realism" became so popular and so widely used to describe almost any form of non-realist literature that many critics proposed to discard it altogether. Then, Todorov's systematic study, *The Fantastic* (1970), showed what magical realism was not, leading to more rigorous and restricted definitions of the term, which favored its anthropological dimension. Finally, in the 1990s, as magical realism was called into question by post-colonial studies, its use in Latin American narrative declined, but its success had already been influencing writers across the world to adapt magical realism to their own cultural experience and national traditions. As a result, claims Camayd-Freixas, in the twenty-first century, magical realism is being theorized once again as a literary mode capable of many different manifestations.

In the following essay, Juan E. De Castro analyzes the underlying reasons for the simplistic identification of Latin American literature as necessarily magical realist by US cultural circles, the editorial consequences of this prejudice, the parallel existence of Spanish-language magical realist writers in the region, and the exoticization necessarily present in their style of writing. He also wonders about the reaction against magical realism of two groups of young Latin American writers in 1996, "The Crack" and the McOndo group, particularly considering that magical realism was far from the hegemonic mode of writing for their Boom predecessors (only Gabriel García Márquez, in some of his novels and stories, can be classified as a magical realist). In turn, Maggie Ann Bowers explores the relationship between magical realism and subaltern studies, following a chronological coterminous development of the rise of magical realism as an internationally recognized genre and the work of the subaltern studies groups in both India and the Americas. Her analysis examines the radical possibility in both the disruptive qualities of magical realist narratives in relation to authoritarian discourse and the development of subaltern studies in providing alternative accounts of authoritarian history. Ultimately, it considers the identification of the subaltern magical realist text beyond the context of the indigenous and colonized, ethnically-defined subject, moving back towards that of a Gramscian European underclass.

Closing the section on critical contexts, Gene H. Bell-Villada's essay explores the differences between magical realism and the fantastic. As he explains, whereas in magical realist narratives something magical or supernatural occurs in an everyday setting and characters simply accept it as part of life rather than as something shocking, in the fantastic, unreal events inevitably elicit hesitation in the reader, who cannot decide whether the supernatural events are "really happening" or are somehow illusory. Bell-Villada affirms that magical realist texts by García Márquez, Carlos Fuentes, Toni Morrison, William Kennedy, Cristina García, and José Saramago, among others, are both realistic and magical, moving beyond both these traditions by fusing and building on both.

Moving on to essays focusing on magical realism in particular literary works, Rudyard J. Alcocer examines Gabriel García Márquez's *Del amor y otros demonios* (*Of Love and Other Demons,* 1994), arguing that the novel's relatively modest popular reception as well as the tensions in its critical assessments can be attributed to its problematic relationship with the magical realist style. Alcocer concludes that while it expresses the magical realist style to a certain degree, it does not do so sufficiently. As a result, by not creating a "coherent" magical realist world in the novel, the isolated instances of the style that do take place seem forced and misplaced. Adding to the study of García Márquez's novels, Martín Camps first draws from the ideology of *macondismo*, which considers magical realism as a product to sell the idea of a Latin America distanced from the civilization of Europe and North America. In this sense, he adds, magical realism represents a colorful "wrapping paper" to translate contradictory realities in Latin America. Camps mentions the recent approval of the tourism slogan "Colombia, realismo mágico" (Colombia, magical realism) to advertise Colombia to the world, which constitutes the first time a literary style has intersected with a tourism strategy. In his view, the slogan was probably chosen because magical realism contains the seal of the developing world, the site of magic and primitivism. His essay focuses on *One Hundred Years of*

Solitude from the perspective of the process of modernization that is initiated once José Arcadio Buendía tries to connect the small town of Macondo to the world. Macondo becomes a poetic representation of Latin America's struggles to incorporate modernity, a dystopic project that eventually destroys the town.

Fernando Valerio-Holguín switches from the continental Caribbean region to the islands to frame the Dominican Marcio Veloz Maggiolo's *La biografía difusa de Sombra Castañeda* (*The Vague Biography of Sombra Castañeda*; 1980) within the magical realist mode, the ethnological novel, and what Seymour Menton called the "new historical novel." He analyzes the relationship between history, ethnography, and magical realism in this novel and explores that which makes it different from other works in the same genre: the search for cultural identity through the simultaneous and trans-epochal presence of the white, black, and indigenous races, as well as the European, African, and Indigenous cultures in the Republic Dominican. This approach, argues Valerio-Holguín, distances the author from the official culture's monoglossia. Ángel L. Estévez continues with the study of Marcio Veloz Maggiolo's works with his exploration of the relationship between *vodou* and magic in three Caribbean novels: Alejo Carpentier's *The Kingdom of this World*, Mayra Montero's *Del rojo de su sangre* (*About the Red in Your Blood*), and Marcio Veloz Maggiolo's *El hombre del acordeón* (*The Man of the Accordion*). He first explains the nature of magic in Hispaniola Island (Haiti and Dominican Republic) and then examines how each of the authors has adopted magical realism as a discursive modality to dive into the concept of Otherness. As part of the construction of its argument, references are made to specific historical events, which each author recreates, offering his/her own (re)interpretation of certain historical, social, and political realities that have often been the source of friction between the two nations sharing the island.

In the last essay dealing with Latin American works, we move from the Caribbean down to South America and to a different literary subgenre. David William Foster studies the potential presence of magical realism in Daniel Galera and Rafael Coutinho's graphic novel *Cachalote* (2010), one of the most sophisticated Brazilian texts of that genre. The stories of six non-intersecting individuals are recounted against the backdrop of mysterious and unexplained occurrences that contextualize the burden of the human condition, which they experience with a mixture of despair and disconcertedness. The title of their novel, which means "sperm whale" in Portuguese, refers to the appearance of such an animal in a couple of the texts. But the whale, especially when it becomes beached, stands as an icon for the unfathomableness of life. Coutinho's artistic representations are somber and threatening and correlate forcefully with Galera's spare and often alarming verbal narrative.

Nicholas Birns demonstrates the crucial role of magical realism in the evolution of Canadian, Australian, and New Zealand literatures to world rank. As the subaltern literatures of the Anglophone world, these bodies of writing felt, similar to Latin American fiction, neglected by metropolitan tastemakers, even though they were composed in a world language. Magical realism liberated them from the taint of provincialism, paradoxically by telling stories of a strongly national and quirky nature, as in the Australian novelist Peter Carey's tales of glass churches and outlaws, subversive dwarfs and tellers of tall tales. No single Canadian magic realist eminence emerged to equal Carey, but feminist and regional writers used magical realism to help constitute an idiom that was not just emulative of or provincial with respect to British models; meanwhile, New Zealand writers, such as Maurice Shadbolt, used magical realism to explore the past conflicts with that nation's indigenous people, the Maori, and as late as 2013, Eleanor Catton used fantastic elements in her novel *The Luminaries* to include Maori and Asian migrants in the New Zealand community. In the 1990s and after, though, the appeal of magical realism generally waned, as writers from Canada, Australia, and New Zealand felt they could compete on global terms and rejected the magical realism mode as quaint and sentimental. In the work of an indigenous Australian writer like Alexis Wright, however, magical realism still remained a powerful, if not unaltered, contributor to her groundbreaking novels *Carpentaria* and *The Swan Book*. Magical realism had played its role in helping make the previously minor literatures of the subaltern English–speaking world seem major.

Kim Anderson Sasser maintains that the Nigerian-British Helen Oyeyemi's *The Icarus Girl* (2005) and the Cuban Alejo Carpentier's *The Kingdom of this World* (1949) should be considered as comprising a unique strain of magical realism characterized by a double positioning of magic. According to Sasser, these two novels represent one of many types of magical realisms that have arisen throughout the literary mode's history, including ethnographic or formalist, postcolonial or First World, territorial or global, African or British, magically saturated or sparse. She argues that, due to these diverse manifestations, we should pluralize the term, magical realisms, to respond to increasing critical arguments for a broader understanding of this literary mode. While still valuing the mode's Latin American and postcolonial usages, the pluralization offers a more nuanced understanding of what that seminal phase, as well as subsequent phases, are doing with the integration of narrative magic and literary realism. Sasser proposes to revise the mode this way, making space for innovative ways of conveying current, twenty-first century concerns, as has been achieved by Oyeyemi, arguably the youngest in a new generation of magical realist authors.

Rachel Trousdale argues that, in his 1983 novel *Shame* and his 1987 travel book *The Jaguar Smile*, Salman Rushdie stages a debate between realistic and fantastic fiction, giving fantasy an unequivocal win. Realism, he suggests, constrains an author's freedom of speech, limits a book's possible subject matter and, most importantly, misrepresents its own statements of "truth," which are actually colored by their placement in narrative and the language of genre. On the other hand, fantastic literature, by foregrounding its own unreality, forces authors to take moral responsibility for the content of their texts and readers to take responsibility for interpreting them. Closing the volume is my essay on José Luis Cuerda's version of Spanish comedic magical realism in his 1980s films and how it was used for social criticism. In the essay, I explore the influence of Latin American magical realism, as well as an earlier version of magical realism "made in Spain," in the absurdist and "surrealist" humor present in his films *Total* (1983); *El bosque animado* (*The Living Forest*, 1987); and *Amanece que no es poco* (*Dawn is Breaking and That Is Something*, 1988).

On Magical Realism as an International Phenomenon in the Twenty-First Century
Ignacio López-Calvo

> "I used to be more popular in the old days, bigger, so to speak, in Macondo than in McOndo."
> (Junot Díaz, *The Brief Wondrous Life of Oscar Wao*)

At a 2013 literature conference in Incheon, South Korea, I had an interesting conversation over breakfast with the writers Kole Omotoso, from Nigeria, and Syl Cheney Coker, from Sierra Leone. They coincided in their reaction to reading Gabriel García Márquez's *One Hundred Years of Solitude* (1967): "What I read there was no different from everyday life in my home country," both agreed. Less interesting, however, was the reason we began talking about García Márquez: I happened to mention that my field was Latin American literature. As many of my colleagues, I am used to having to talk about magical realism to people outside the field whenever I mention what I do for a living. I also tend to cringe when I see that, inevitably, magical realism has to represent Latin America (hence homogenizing its rich variety of genres, styles, and themes) in world literature college syllabi; when I see yet another tropicalized book cover of a Latin American novel that has nothing to do with the Tropics; or when I read book reviews on Latin American literature that express surprise at Latin American novels not dealing with magical realism, as can be observed in the *New York Times*' Nicole LaForte's opening sentence: "Alberto Fuguet's latest novel has no metaphysical butterflies, no levitating grandmothers, no flying carpets—indeed, none of the fantastic imagery that is most commonly associated with Latin American literature" ("New Era . . ." n.p.). This perception, of course, has to do with how Latin American literature has been positioned in international marketing campaigns.

As is well-known, literary magical realism began in Latin America with three pioneers who, influenced by 1920s and 1930s French surrealism, developed their own narrative modes: the Guatemalan Miguel Ángel Asturias, who juxtaposed European rationalism with indigenous pre-Columbian knowledge; the Venezuelan Arturo Uslar-Pietri, who "considered magic realism to be a continuation of the 'vanguardia' modernist experimental writings of Latin America" (Bowers 14); and the Cuban Alejo Carpentier, who fused it with Afro-Cuban culture, myth, and religion. In his essay "De lo real maravilloso americano" ("About the [Latin] American marvelous real"), the last part of which would become the prologue to his novel *El reino de este mundo* (*The Kingdom of this World*, 1949), Carpentier termed it "lo real maravilloso americano" (the [Latin] American marvelous real):

> in Haiti, where I found myself in daily contact with something that could be defined as the marvelous real. I was in a land where thousands of men, anxious for freedom, believed in Mackandal's lycanthropic powers to the extent that their collective faith produced a miracle on the day of his execution. (86–87)

Carpentier would later extend the presence of the marvelous real in Haiti to the rest of the continent, where an inventory of its cosmogonies had not been done yet: "Because of the virginity of the land, our upbringing, our ontology, the Faustian presence of the Indian and the black man, the revelation constituted by its recent discovery, its fecund racial mixing [*mestizaje*], America is far from using up its wealth of mythologies" (88). However, Amaryll Chanady has refuted this "territorialization of the imaginary," which she considers essentialist, claiming that Carpentier was using "the concept of the marvelous real as a marker of difference in Latin American discourse of identity rejecting European influence" (137). Several essays in this volume demonstrate, indeed, that, having become an international literary phenomenon, the reach of magical realism goes well beyond the borders of Spanish-speaking countries.

Critical of what they saw as the mindless application of surrealism in France, Asturias and Carpentier substituted Sigmund

Freud's unconscious by Maya and African worldviews respectively, in an attempt to move beyond the Eurocentric gaze and grasp the essence of their respective countries' cultures. Even though neither author had a Maya or African ethnic background, they sought to incorporate the marginalized, albeit influential, subjectivities of non-Western communities in their respective countries. European modernity became, then, challenged by alternative subaltern and racialized knowledges. Carpentier argued that, in a heightened state, a writer could capture the mystery behind things, that is, elements of the miraculous within ordinary things. According to him, in contrast to surrealism, "improbable juxtapositions and marvelous mixtures exist by virtue of Latin America's varied history, geography, demography, and politics—not by manifesto" (Zamora & Faris 75). This way, he highlighted the coexistence of Western rationalist worldviews with non-Western, ethnicized thought systems in Latin America and the Caribbean basin. As Maggie Bowers explains,

> Having been witness to European surrealism, he [Carpentier] recognized a need for art to express the non-material aspects of life but also recognized the differences between his European and his Latin American contexts. He used the term 'marvellous realism' to describe a concept that could represent for him the mixture of differing cultural systems and the variety of experiences that create an extraordinary atmosphere, alternative attitude and differing appreciation of reality in Latin America. (13)

A new version of magical realism was then popularized worldwide by the Colombian García Márquez, particularly thanks to the success of his masterpiece *One Hundred Years of Solitude*. But in the 1980s, he and other Latin American authors who popularized this mode of narration[1] began to distance themselves from it. As their followers copied their style, in some cases blatantly, some critics' respect for it faded away. In fact, today, some dismiss magical realism as a market strategy or a fashionable literary practice that, at one point, became commodified for mass consumption and turned into cliché. Then, the reader may wonder, why publish another volume on magical realism now? In spite of this criticism, it is still worth revisiting—from a fresh perspective—the state, influence, legacy, evolution in the last decade, and international reach of Latin American narrative's most influential export.

Defining magical realism is not an easy task, among other things because, as can be seen in the "Additional Works" section in this volume, the term has been used to describe the works of many different authors and works set in very different contexts. The tenuous borders between magical realism and the fantastic have created numerous disagreements among critics as well, mainly because there is a tendency to label any text dealing with fantastic, inexplicable, or supernatural as magical realism. The confusion began with Ángel Flores' article "Magical Realism in Spanish American Fiction," where he identified Jorge Luis Borges with magical realism. As is well known, Luis Leal later corrected Flores, clarifying that Borges had not started the magical realist movement. These limits become particularly blurred when we deal with authors such as Borges and Julio Cortázar, who resorted to both literary modes. For instance, while Borges has been traditionally associated with the fantastic, critic Seymour Menton argues, in "Jorge Luis Borges, Magic Realist," that part of his literature can be better understood as an example of magical realism. For this same reason, Lois Parkinson Zamora, in her essay included in *Magical Realism: Theory, History, Community*, states: "I begin by tracing the nineteenth-century U.S. romance tradition with the help of two twentieth-century Latin American magical realists, Gabriel García Márquez and Jorge Luis Borges, in order to show the tendency of both romance and magical realism to archetypalize itself" (499). As seen, in this case, Borges is unproblematically associated with the magical realist tradition, even though the distortion of reality and the imagined worlds of some of his short stories, for example "La lotería en Babilonia" ("The Lottery in Babylon") and "La biblioteca de Babel" ("The Library of Babel"), have little to do with this literary mode. The same can be said about Cortázar's short stories "La caricia más profunda" ("The Deepest Caress") or "Continuidad de los parques" ("Continuity of the Parks"), among many others. Perhaps because of the frequent association between Latin American literature and magical realism, there is a widespread tendency to associate too many Latin American texts with it.

Magical realism is generally understood as a mode (some critics consider it a genre) of literary narration or visual arts that appeared in the mid-twentieth century, where elements that seem magical or unreal are blended within an otherwise mundane and realistic narrative or setting. These fantastical events—telekinesis, clairvoyance, levitation, apparitions—emerge naturally from everyday reality and characters often see them not as something extraordinary, but as just another aspect of everyday life. In the words of one of the main experts on this literary mode, Wendy B. Faris, magical realism:

> combines realism and the fantastic so that the marvelous seems to grow organically within the ordinary, blurring the distinction between them. Furthermore, that combination of realistic and fantastical narrative, together with the inclusion of different cultural traditions, means that magical realism reflects, in both its narrative mode and its cultural environment, the hybrid nature of much postcolonial society. (1)

Erik Camayd-Freixas, in his essay included in this volume, has also tried to identify the common denominator of most magical realist narratives:

> the single characteristic on which critics agree is that magical realism makes the extraordinary seem commonplace and vice versa. This is dependent on the non-conventional point of view of the ("naïve" or "unreliable") narrator, and on naturalizing devices such as the extremely detailed and matter-of-fact description and narration of a rationally implausible event.

The impressive 1995 volume *Magical Realism: Theory, History, Community* is a comprehensive attempt at exploring this influential narrative style in world literature. Its editors, Lois Parkinson Zamora and Wendy B. Faris, deny the notion that it is an exclusively Latin American phenomenon, as implied by Carpentier, García Márquez, and others. Instead, they present it as an influential international narrative mode as well as a major component in postmodernist fiction. Their collection of essays opens with translations of several foundational texts, such as "Magic Realism: Post-Expressionism" (1925) by German art critic Franz Roh, who coined the term to make a distinction between the 1920s post-expressionist European painting style and surrealism. It is followed by translations of two foundational essays by Alejo Carpentier—"On the Marvelous Real in America" (1949) and "The Baroque and the Marvelous Real" (1975), which deal with Latin American literature—and by two of the first critical studies on magical realism in Latin American literature: the often quoted "Magical Realism in Spanish American Fiction" (1955) by Ángel Flores and Luis Leal's response to it, titled "Magical Realism in Spanish American Literature" (1967). In the last paragraph of his essay, Leal makes his similarly oft-quoted statement: "In magical realism key events have no logical or psychological explanation. The magical realist does not try to copy the surrounding reality (as the realists did) or to wound it (as the Surrealists did) but to seize the mystery that breathes behind things" (123). Other essays in the collection address different theorizations on magical realism and the presence of this narrative mode in works by international authors, including the Latin Americans Carpentier and Isabel Allende. In one of the opening statements in their introduction, Zamora and Faris argue that "magical realism is especially alive and well in postcolonial contexts and is now achieving a compensatory extension of its market worldwide" (2). If that was the case in 1995, can we still defend this statement today? Or has this literary tradition faded away in some regions? Two decades later, this book seeks to build on Zamora and Faris' collection of essays, analyzing the evolution of this "attitude toward reality" (121; to use Leal's phrase) until our days as well as its manifestations in different cultures.

Román de la Campa has criticized the fact that *Magical Realism: Theory, History, Community* takes the links between magical realism, post-modernity, and post-colonialism for granted. He also points out the lack of attention to contemporary Latin American criticism on the topic, since the volume only includes articles written by Ángel Flores and Luis Leal several decades earlier. Indeed, after acknowledging the importance of criticism by contemporary Latin Americanists ("It is true that Latin Americanists have been prime movers in developing the critical concept of magical realism and are still primary voices in its discussion" [Zamora & Faris 2]), their contribution is largely ignored in the volume. De la Campa laments, in particular, the failure to engage recent criticism of magical realism carried out by young Latin American writers, such as the ones who participated in the literary anthology *McOndo*. Addressing this lacuna, our volume includes several original articles by Latin Americanists, who discuss the criticism by Latin American authors of the McOndo and Crack groups, among other writers.

But does magical realism still matter? I believe it does. A case in point is Junot Díaz's celebrated novel *The Brief Wondrous Life of Oscar Wao* (2007), which mocks the tradition of magical realism in Latin American writing, while concomitantly becoming part of it.[2] Not only do we have the *fukú* curse that has damned the protagonist's family for generations (the typical situation in magical realist texts where characters accept something "magical" or illogical as part of everyday life), but Díaz ends up resorting to the same tropical exoticism, violence, sensualism, cult of Third-World underdevelopment, superstitions, mythical legends, popular folklore, and distortion of time that has often characterized Latin American magical realism. It seems clear, therefore, that magical realism still casts a shadow over the continent's writers, even though, in the 1990s, the McOndo group (formed by the Chileans Alberto Fuguet and Sergio Gómez, the Bolivian Edmundo Paz Soldán, the Peruvian Jaime Bayly, and the Colombian Santiago Gamboa, among others) and other earlier, 1980s-era voices began to reject categorically its heritage throughout the continent. As Nicholas Birns explains in his essay for this collection, at one point, international critics began to expose the formulaic and contrived nature of some blatant imitations of the magical realism's masterpieces. Although magical realism is no longer a major frame of reference for many contemporary Latin American authors, the fact that they consider it an influence to avoid is still significant. Fuguet, for instance, distanced his writing from magical realism, proclaiming in 1997 that, unlike García Márquez's ethereal and imaginary Macondo, his world:

> is something much closer to what I call "McOndo"—a world of McDonald's, Macintoshes and condos. In a continent that was once ultra-politicized, young, apolitical writers like myself are now writing without an overt agenda, about their own experiences. Living in cities all over South America, hooked on cable TV (CNN en español), addicted to movies and connected to the Net, we are far away from the jalapeño-scented, siesta-happy atmosphere that permeates too much of the South American literary landscape. ("I am not . . ." n.p.)

The McOndo authors openly embraced American popular culture and tried to register its pervasive influence on Latin American societies. More in tune with a contemporary urban or suburban world influenced by globalization, consumerism, and mass media than with the cultural exoticism and essentialism that tropicalizes Latin America, these writers rejected the expectations from some US and European publishers, critics, and readers. Fuguet, for example, complained about the purported expectations of the University of Iowa's International Writers Program and the *Iowa Review*, whose editor dismissed one of his short stories for not being "Latin American enough": "but the flying *abuelitas* and the obsessively constructed genealogies didn't seem to fit in my work . . . Add some folklore and a dash of tropical heat and come back later. That was the message I heard" ("I am not . . ." n.p.). The 1996 short-story collection *McOndo* attempted, therefore, to close the chapter on magical realism, which they considered a cultural caricature and a misrepresentation of contemporary Latin America, as Fuguet complained in an interview with Nicol LaForte: "I'm a really big fan of Márquez, but what I really hate is the software he created that other people use . . . They turn it into more of an aesthetic instead of an ideology. Anybody who begins to copy 'One Hundred Years' turns it into kitsch" ("New Era . . ." n.p.). Tellingly, however, the other leader among the McOndo writers, Edmundo Paz Soldán, has retracted from earlier declarations against magical realism, stating in a 2005 interview with Claudia M. Milian Arias:

> We were very young and naïve and maybe that is why our response to the exoticization of Latin America through the immense popularity of magical realism was so visceral. . . . Today, it is very clear, for many of us, that it is naïve to renounce such a wonderful tradition of political engagement on the part of the Latin American writer. And I also think that McOndo just wants to carve out a space for itself and does not want to deny the importance of magical realism in the Latin American literary tradition. (141)

Paz Soldán has also acknowledged the mistake of replacing one stereotype with another, that is, that all Latin Americans enjoy an urban life. On the other hand, the critic Wilfrido H. Corral has harshly criticized the purported worldview behind the McOndo writers' protest:

> As to their affinity with "postmodern neoliberalism" reflected in their supposedly apolitical attitude, disdain for Marxism, celebration of individualism, technology, the urban and developed, it can be affirmed that the McOndists are located in the very center of the political and cultural mainstream in Chile and Latin American, rather than on its margins. They form part of the social and literary establishment and are comfortably settled within the sociopolitical system of their country. Rather than as García Márquez's rebel and disillusioned children, they must be seen as the obedient offspring of neoliberalism and of an existentialist and intimate literary tradition that has been being written in the continent for decades.[3]

For their part, the Mexican writers of the Crack Generation of the mid-1990s (Jorge Volpi, Ignacio Padilla, Eloy Urroz, Pedro Ángel Palou, Ricardo Chávez Castañeda, and Vicente Herrasti) also rejected magical realism, but this time, that of post-Boom writers, such as Isabel Allende and Laura Esquivel. They reacted, through their *Manifiesto Crack* (*Crack Manifesto*, 1996), published a month earlier than *McOndo*, not against García Márquez and the Boom writers of the 1960s and 1970s (as is often believed), but against writers whom they considered their epigones of the 1980s. They saw in the Chilean Roberto Bolaño (whose Santa Teresa in his last novel, *2666*, is considered by Corral a "sort of anti-Macondo, which is representative of today's Latin American city")[4] a better model to follow and the "missing link," to use Ignacio Padilla's words. Crack authors no longer felt the need to look for a Mexican or Latin American identity, often choosing European settings for their literary works. Camayd-Freixas has also rejected the second-wave iteration of magical realism: "a second opportunity for Magical Realism in Latin American fiction has seemed at least precarious since 1967: excepting *Siete lunas y siete serpientes* (1970) by the Ecuadorian Demetrio Aguilera-Malta, most are watered-down versions, like Isabel Allende's *La casa de los espíritus* (1982), Vargas Llosa's *El hablador* (1987), and Esquivel's *Como agua para chocolate* (1990)" (Camayd-Freixas 584–85).

Along these lines, in an interview with Edmund White, Colombian writer Juan Gabriel Vásquez, inevitably talking about his 2013 *The Sound of Things Falling* (a realist crime novel about Colombia's drug wars) in comparison with *Hundred Years of Solitude*, states:

> I want to forget this absurd rhetoric of Latin America as a magical or marvelous continent. In my novel there is a disproportionate reality, but that which is disproportionate in it is the violence and cruelty of our history and of our politics. Let me be clear about this. . . . I can say that reading "One Hundred Years of Solitude" . . . in my adolescence may have contributed much to my literary calling, but I believe that magic realism is the least interesting part of this novel. I suggest reading "One Hundred Years" as a distorted version of Colombian history. ("Requiem for the Living" n.p.)

As seen, rather than being indifferent to magical realism, Vásquez reacts against it in his novel, declaring the magical inadequate for the re-creation of the tragic sociopolitical reality of contemporary Colombia. At least he refuses to consider the magical as the only way to understand Latin America, a continent whose recent history he considers more tragic than magical.

Along these lines, in his essay on the Peruvian José María Arguedas' *El zorro de arriba y el zorro de abajo* (*The Fox from Up Above and the Fox from Down Below*, 1971), Alberto Moreiras ventures to propose a date when magical realism died. He describes this narrative mode as "a technical device within the larger and more encompassing apparatus of transcultural representation" (85) and as "the dominant manifestation of literary transculturation in contemporary Latin American times" (93). According to Moreiras, transculturation and literary transculturation, as defined by Ángel Rama in *Transculturación narrativa en la América Latina* (*Narrative Transculturation in Latin America*, 1982), are a critical response to western modernity that "is meant to counter the colonialist 'whitening' of Latin American culture" (86). He, therefore, associates both magical realism and transculturation with the crisis of modernity and the clash between two modes of knowledge in Latin America: a European, Eurocentric, and hegemonic rationalist worldview and a semi-peripheral, subaltern, and ethnicized knowledge coming from people of pre-Columbian or African descent. For the Spanish critic, however, Arguedas' novel closes magical realism and anthropological ethnofiction because "it is revealed to be inexorably dependent upon the subordination of indigenous cultures to an always already Western-hegemonic machine of transculturation: to modernization itself" (Moreiras 101). In his view, Arguedas' eventual suicide, which is announced in the text, ultimately embodies "a violent conflict of cultures that will not be mediated away" (Moreiras 103). In the end, magical realism cannot mediate between cultures, because it "is an impossible scene of emancipatory representation staged from a colonizing perspective" (Moreiras 104). In any case, as can be observed in our collection of essays, this decline or death of magical realism pointed out by Moreiras may have been limited to Latin America, as it has continued to flourish in other regions of the world.

What is most relevant about Moreiras' article to this volume, however, is that magical realism is understood in the context of the struggle between subaltern, ethnicized, non-western conceptualizations and the hegemonic imposition of western modernity in Latin America. Bowers coincides in this appreciation of magical realism, since, in her view, it offers "a way to discuss alternative approaches to reality to that of Western philosophy, expressed in many postcolonial and non-Western works of contemporary fiction" (1). Magical realist cultural production is thus seen as a tool for questioning Eurocentric views, as it endows non-Western worldviews with additional agency. Zamora and Faris have likewise noted magical realism's counter-hegemonic nature: "Magical realist texts are subversive: their in-betweenness, their all-at-onceness encourages resistance to monologic political and cultural structures, a feature that has made the mode particularly useful to writers in postcolonial cultures and, increasingly, to women" (6). Rather than as the worn out literary cliché inherited by 1980s epigones (as described by McOndo and Crack authors), then, it is seen by these critics as a liberating tool for ethnicized groups and women who defend their own heterogeneity, particularly in postcolonial contexts.

More importantly, magical realism has had a central role in extending the privilege and recognition of the "world's republic of letters" (to use Pascale Casanova's term) from hegemonic cultural, political, and economic centers to the periphery. As Casanova points out,

> there exists a 'literature world,' a literary universe relatively independent of the everyday world and its political divisions, whose boundaries and operational laws are not reducible to those of ordinary political space. Exerted within this *international literary space* are relations of force and a violence peculiar to them--in short, a *literary domination* whose forms I have tried to describe while taking care not to confuse this domination with the forms of political domination, even though it may in many respects be dependent upon them. (xii)

It is important to remember that, in part thanks to magical realism, literary texts from culturally "peripheral" regions of the world, from "minor" languages and literatures, have finally been incorporated to the "world of letters." For decades, magic realism's aesthetics, politics, and language struggled for dominance with (or at least for sharing the value and legitimacy of) other international literary modes and genres. While its literary capital has clearly diminished over the years (due to overuse, poor imitation by epigones, literary annexations, publisher exploitation, marketing campaigns, and other reasons exposed in this volume), it has, undeniably, left an indelible mark in literary history.

Faris, in *Ordinary Enchantments*, adds to the view of this literary mode as an effective decolonizing tool: "Magical realism radically modifies and replenishes the dominant mode of realism in the West, challenging its basis of representation from within. That destabilization of a dominant form means that it has served as a particularly effective decolonizing agent" (1). Yet, as mentioned, this implicit political impetus to celebrate alternative modernities in so-called Third World societies may become diffused whenever US and European marketing campaigns tropicalize magical realist narratives, turning them into a sort of exoticizing celebration of underdevelopment in settings that are reminiscent of the stereotypical banana republic. As Bowers warns, "It seems that unless the reading public are aware of colonialism, its attitudes and its aftermath, then the possibility to take an exotic or escapist approach to magical realist narratives will remain" (123). On the other hand, the criticism that reduces all types of magical realism to a literary formula celebrating pre-modern innocence and irrationalism may stupefy its potential decentering subversiveness. Ultimately, the postcolonial affirmation of non-Western thought as a form of resistance to hegemonic cultural impositions becomes simplified into a nostalgia for underdevelopment, superstition, and magic. From this perspective, our volume sets out to re-evaluate the mark that magical realism has left on Latin American and world literature, including the last two decades after the publication of *Magical Realism: Theory, History, Community*.

While acknowledging the importance of the reception, appropriation, and adaptation of magical realism in other parts of the world, this volume pays particular attention to Latin American cultural production and criticism. However, it is clear that there are other magical realisms outside Latin America. In this context, Camayd-Freixas poses the question: "Can the international phenomenon be meaningfully called 'Magical Realism' or does it belong to the broader, more diffuse tendency called 'primitivism'?"

(586) To which he answers: "I see no contradiction between the delimitation of a Latin American core and the intercultural possibility of other *regional* cores of Magical Realism, all with shared affinities, each with net peculiarities, and, above all, each both eccentric and central in its own right" (Camayd-Freixas 586). Together, the essays on Latin American literature and those on other international literature unveil a fluid intercultural dialog among magical realist writers, often between peripheral or semi-peripheral literary traditions (without the need to find an intermediary in the cultural centers of European and North American metropolises), which has contributed to extend the magical realist literary tradition until our days.

Notes

1. Magical realism has been considered a "mode" rather than a literary genre because this style or technique can be used across literary genres and film.
2. For more information, see my essay "A postmodern plátano's Trujillo: Junot Díaz's *The Brief Wondrous Life of Oscar Wao*, more Macondo than McOndo" (*Antípodas* 20 [2009]: 75–90).
3. "En cuanto a su afinidad con el 'neoliberalismo post-moderno' que se refleja en su actitud supuestamente apolítica, desdén por el marxismo, celebración del individualismo, de la tecnología, lo urbano y lo desarrollado, se puede indicar que los macondistas se han ubicando en pleno centro del *mainstream* político y cultural de Chile y de América Latina y no en sus márgenes. Forman parte del *establishment* social y literario y están instalados cómodamente dentro del sistema sociopolítico de su país. Más que como hijos rebeldes y desencantados de García Márquez, deben ser vistos como hijos obedientes del neoliberalismo y de una tradición literaria existencialista e intimista que desde hace décadas se viene escribiendo en el continente" (Corral 47–48).
4. "Especie de anti-Macondo, representativa de la ciudad latinoamericana actual" (71).

Works Cited

Arias, Claudia M. Milian. "McOndo and Latinidad: An Interview with Edmundo Paz Soldán." *Studies in Latin American Popular Culture* 24 (2005):139–49. Web. 28 March 2010.

Bowers, Maggie Ann. *Magic(al) Realism*. New York: Routledge, 2004.

Camayd-Freixas, Erik. "Reflections on *Magical Realism*: A Return to Legitimacy, the Legitimacy of Return." *Canadian Review of Comparative Literature/Revue Canadienne de Littérature Comparée* 23.2 (Jan. 1996). 580–89.

Carpentier, Alejo. "On the Marvelous Real in America." *Magical Realism: Theory, History, Community*. Eds. Lois Parkinson Zamora & Wendy B. Faris. Durham, NC: Duke UP, 1995. 75–88.

Casanova, Pascale. *The World Republic of Letters*. Trans. M. B. DeBevoise. Cambridge, MA: Harvard UP, 2004.

Chanady, Amaryll. "The Territorialization of the Imaginary in Latin America: Self-Affirmation and Resistance to Metropolitan Paradigms." *Magical Realism: Theory, History, Community*. Eds. Lois Parkinson Zamora & Wendy B. Faris. Durham, NC: Duke UP, 1995. 125–44.

Corral, Wilfrido H. *Bolaño traducido: nueva literatura mundial*. Madrid: Ediciones Escalera, 2011.

De la Campa, Román. "Magical Realism and World Literature: A Genre for the Times?" *Revista Canadiense de Estudios Hispánicos* 23.2 (Winter 1999): 206–19.

Faris, Wendy B. *Ordinary Enchantments: Magical Realism and the Remystification of Narrative*. New York: Vanderbilt UP, 2004.

Flores, Ángel. "Magic Realism in Spanish American Literature." *Magical Realism: Theory, History, Community*. Eds. Lois Parkinson Zamora &Wendy B. Faris. Durham, NC: Duke UP, 1995. 109–17.

Fuguet, Alberto. "I am not a magic realist!" *Salon.com*. 11 Jun. 1997. Web. 29 May 2008.

_____ & Sergio Gómez, eds. *McOndo*. Barcelona: Mondadori, 1996.

García Márquez, Gabriel. *One Hundred Years of Solitude*. New York: Perennial Classics, 1998.

LaForte, Nicole. "New Era Succeeds Years of Solitude." *New York Times.* 4 Jan. 2003. Web. 22 Sept. 2013.

Leal, Luis. "Magical Realism in Spanish American Literature." *Magical Realism: Theory, History, Community.* Eds. Lois Parkinson Zamora & Wendy B. Faris. Durham, NC: Duke UP, 1995. 119–24.

López-Calvo, Ignacio. "A postmodern plátano's Trujillo: Junot Díaz's *The Brief Wondrous Life of Oscar Wao*, more Macondo than McOndo." *Antípodas* 20 (2009): 75–90.

Menton, Seymour. "Jorge Luis Borges, Magic Realist." *Hispanic Review* 50.4 (Fall 1982): 411–26.

Moreiras, Alberto. "The End of Magical Realism: José María Arguedas' Passionate Signifier ('El zorro de arriba y el zorro de abajo')." *The Journal of Narrative Technique* 27.1 (Winter 1997): 84–112.

Rama, Ángel. *Transculturación narrativa en la América Latina.* Mexico City: Siglo XXI, 1982.

White, Edmund. "Requiem for the Living. *The Sound of Things Falling* by Juan Gabriel Vásquez." *New York Times' Sunday Book Review.* 1 Aug 2013. Web. 22 Sept. 2013.

Zamora, Lois Parkinson, & Wendy B. Faris, eds. *Magical Realism: Theory, History, Community.* Durham, NC: Duke UP, 1995.

CRITICAL CONTEXTS

Theories of Magical Realism
Erik Camayd-Freixas

The term "magical realism" was coined by art critic Franz Roh in 1925 to describe German post-expressionist painting. It was independently applied to literature for the first time, with a diverging meaning, by Italian novelist Massimo Bontempelli in 1927 to characterize modernist fiction. While, soon, the concept was virtually forgotten in Europe, it was resurrected in Latin American literature, again with varying meanings, starting in 1940. By the mid 1970s, it had become very popular in the context of the so-called "Boom" of the Latin American novel (1967–1984). Thereafter, as magical realism declined in Latin American fiction, it was picked up by many different national traditions of world literature and continues to enjoy a successful afterlife. This has further expanded the already varied conceptions of the term, making its definition one of the most challenging and interesting theoretical problems in contemporary literature.

Franz Roh published his 1925 book *Nach-Expressionismus, Magischer Realismus: Probleme der neuesten Europäischen Malerei* (*Post-Expressionism, Magical Realism: Problems of the latest European Painting*) at the height of the modernist avant-garde movement in Europe and the beginning of a new tendency in German art, marked by a post-World War I return to a rather blunt realism (Arnason 317–23). Roh coined the oxymoron "magical realism" to describe this new style. Two years earlier, another German art critic, Gustav Hartlaub, had proposed a competing term: "new objectivity" (*Neue Sachlichkeit*). Roh sought to define post-expressionism as a synthesis of two opposing tendencies: impressionism and expressionism. On the one hand, the impressionism of Van Gogh and his contemporaries emphasized external objects and the effect (or *impression*) they have on our senses. For instance, an impressionist painting up close may look like a conglomerate of dotted brush strokes, but as we retreat, realistic figures begin to take shape. On the other hand, the expressionism of Emil Nolde, Ernst Kirchner, and the followers of Edvard Munch established the predominance of the subject, or inner self, over the object. The expressionists sought to project their emotions and existential angst onto the objects they depicted, thereby deforming them. They considered such distorted figures to be more "real" and humanly relevant than our proportionate everyday perceptions because they embodied the emotions that the subject *expressed* upon the world. Franz Roh believed that this tension between subject and object was a universal dichotomy in art. Today, postmodern critics shun such broad "universalist" or "essentialist" generalizations. Yet for Roh, this subject-object dialectic was finally resolved in the synthesis of the new post-expressionist "verism" of his contemporaries, such as painters Max Beckmann, Otto Dix, and George Grosz.

Roh's rationale for calling this new type of realism "magical," as opposed to "mystical," was scarcely convincing, given the spiritual connotation of a "primitive" belief in the supernatural, which the word "magic" had acquired with the rise of ethnology and anthropology. In contrast, Roh meant the "wonder" that the constant movement of atoms and molecules should generate the sensation of concrete objects. He was drawing from Husserl's phenomenology, introduced in 1913. Edmund Husserl suspended in brackets the old impasse of whether the world is fundamentally matter or spirit, noting that our perception of phenomena is the only given fact from which to approach reality. This became the philosophical foundation for Roh's theory of post-expressionism. But the critic did not persist in the use of the term magical realism; he occasionally employed "ideal realism" instead, and later opted for Hartlaub's competing term, "new objectivity." Meanwhile, in European painting, as post-expressionism intersected French surrealism as well as Russian and Italian futurism, leftist artists became associated with "new objectivity," while right-wing fascist sympathizers were more closely identified with Bontempelli's "magical realism." The increasingly negative overtone that fascism and fascist art accrued during the 1930s contributed to the term's waning popularity in Europe (Guenther 33–73).

In 1927, Roh's work on magical realism was translated into Spanish and published by the influential *Revista de Occidente*, directed by José Ortega y Gasset. Given the diffusion of Spain's premiere cultural journal among the literary circles of Buenos Aires, Mexico City, Havana, and other centers of culture in Latin America, it is presumed that his concept of magical realism may have enjoyed a certain currency across the Atlantic. Nevertheless, the first Latin American literati to use the term in writing (Usigli 1940; Lins 1944; Uslar 1948; Portuondo 1955) make no mention of Roh and use the term with totally different meanings, to include poetic-lyrical-symbolic realism and psycho-existential realism. With this first acceptation of the term in Latin America, writers sought to transcend traditional realism, naturalism, and regionalism by *internalizing* the narrative point of view through techniques such as the interior monologue and the then popular "stream of consciousness." They narrated from inside the protagonist's mind in order to express, either a poetic view of the world and the self, or else a psychological and existential search for authenticity in a lurid world, viewed through the distorting prism of an alienated individual, who nevertheless succeeded in exposing disquieting existential truths.

Notwithstanding this literature's vague affinity with post-expressionism, Enrique Anderson-Imbert (1956) and Luis Leal (1967) would be the first to point out Roh's forgotten paternity, at a time when the term "realismo mágico" had already become, in its own right, a commonplace of Latin American letters. With few exceptions (e.g., Seymour Menton), the prevailing view among critics is that Roh's concept, and German post-expressionism for that matter, have very little to do with Latin American literature (González Echevarría 25–27).

A more direct connection, however, may be found with Bontempelli's original literary version of *realismo magico*. In 1926, Massimo Bontempelli founded the literary journal *900 (novecento)*, which circulated in Italy and France, bringing together modernist figures, like James Joyce, Virginia Woolf, Rainer Maria Rilke, Max Jacob, and Blaise Cendrars. Purportedly without any knowledge of Roh, Bontempelli proposed his own avant-garde literary formula:

"*precisione realistica e atmosfera magica.*" This formula—normalizing a supernatural atmosphere by describing it or narrating it in precise realistic detail—remains, to this day, a core technique of magical realism. In addition, Bontempelli urged his fellow writers to become primitives with a past. "Adam and Eve had no past"—he contended, alluding to the surrealist ideal of a return to the primal. "We cannot be Adams again: *Siamo dei primitivi con un passato*" (Bontempelli 188). Being "primitives with a past" meant returning to one's national traditions, archetypes, and foundational myths—a very meaningful proposal for the young Latin American writers who were flocking to Europe at the time, and who would launch, a few years later, their own magic-realist proposals. Venezuelan essayist Arturo Uslar-Pietri, who had met Bontempelli in Paris and joined the debates of *900* in Italy, was a key contact. He would soon befriend Guatemalan Miguel Ángel Asturias and Cuban Alejo Carpentier in Paris, where all three contributed to Asturias' journal *Ensayo* and Carpentier's journal *Imán*.

Significantly, Bontempelli's proposals had very different cultural and political implications in Europe as opposed to Latin America. In a European hegemonic context, the idea of evoking a pure national archetype, so dear to fascism, was eventually hijacked by the Third Reich. By the end of the 1920s, Bontempelli, like other Italian futurists, had become an active fascist, leading to a rupture with many of his former literary friends. Yet in 1938, as political conditions deteriorated and it became evident that fascism was going too far, Bontempelli was expelled from the fascist party for refusing to take over a university post that had belonged to a Jewish professor. In a Latin American post-colonial context, on the contrary, that same search for national archetypes led to reclaiming indigenous traditions (in the case of Asturias' Latin American highlands) and neo-African culture (in the case of Carpentier's Caribbean basin). After their European experience, both Asturias and Carpentier became active Marxists. By 1949, Asturias had become the first Latin American novelist to describe his own work as magic-realist, based on his surrealist interpretation of the "primitive" Mayan psyche; whereas Carpentier had launched his own concept of *lo real maravilloso americano* ("the American marvelous real"), inspired by Cuban *santería* and Haitian *vodou*. Henceforth, magical realism has remained primarily a countercultural and counter-hegemonic literary style.

According to Carpentier (1949), the marvelous resides in the cultural reality of Latin America itself, by virtue of the continuous clashes of disparate belief systems (European, indigenous, African) over five centuries of tumultuous history, and the hidden syncretism generated by such clashes. The task of the artist is not to create the marvelous through any technical means, but rather to perceive and bring forth the hidden cultural and historical marvels that have long been waiting to be discovered. Due to this radical negation of artificiality, Carpentier refuses to recognize any "-ism" or literary style other than the (neo-) Baroque, precisely because of the Baroque's capacity for accepting and incorporating onto itself the most varied cultural elements. Following Carpentier, and yet admitting the role of technique, Haitian novelist Jacques Stephen Alexis (1956) opted instead for the term "réalisme merveilleux."

A second moment in the development of the term in Latin American literature came with the early attempts at a more precise critical definition. Initially, this took the form of a debate between critics Ángel Flores and Luis Leal. Flores (1955) took a formalist approach, describing the term as an "amalgamation of realism and fantasy" distinguished by its preoccupation with style, precision and succinctness, a tight and logical plot, the transformation of everyday life into the awesome and unreal, the intemporal fluidity of the narrative, the rejection of sentimentality and lyrical effusions, and the predilection for the new and the surprising (112). These traits, however, characterized modernist fiction as a whole and, therefore, were lacking in specificity. Flores cited as early precursors a wide array of authors of non-realist fiction, such as Gogol, Dostoyevsky, Hoffman, the Grimm brothers, the dramatist Strindberg, Poe, Melville, and even Proust. But he held Kafka to be the purest literary exemplar and Giorgio de Chirico to be his counterpart in painting, arguing that their "cold and cerebral" style is what distinguished magical realism from the earlier, more romantic flights of fantasy that were based on atmosphere rather than technique (Flores 113). Indeed, with his reference to de Chirico and to "atmosphere" Flores appears to be alluding to, and revising, Bontempelli's *"precisione realistica e atmosfera magica."* In regard to Latin American literature, Flores points to Borges as the initiator of magical realism, followed by the Argentines Bioy Casares, Silvina Ocampo, Mallea, Sábato, and Cortázar; the Uruguayan Onetti; the Chilean María Luisa Bombal' the Mexicans Arreola and Rulfo; and the Cubans Novás Calvo and Labrador Ruiz. Meanwhile, Borges, Bioy Casares, and Ocampo had famously edited their influential collection *Antología de la literatura fantástica* (1940), including a sampling of world literature since ancient times. Significantly, they defined their own work, not as magical realism, but as "fantastic literature."

Luis Leal (1967) credits Flores with producing the first critical study of magical realism in literature, but disagrees with his definition and with his catalogue of magic-realist authors. He also recognizes Roh's first use of the term, but notes that, in Latin America, it is Carpentier who presents a more systematic and coherent view based on his concept of *lo real maravilloso*. Leal concludes that:

> magical realism cannot be identified either with fantastic literature or with psychological literature . . . neither does it distort reality or create imagined worlds. . . . The existence of the marvelous real is what started magical realist literature, which some critics claim is *the* truly American literature. (121–22)

Thus, he sides with Carpentier's thematic approach and not with Borges' formalism. He agrees with some of the authors cited by Flores and adds a few of his own, notably the Venezuelan Rómulo Gallegos and the Cuban Félix Pita Rodríguez. The core difference between Flores and Leal, as well as between Borges and Carpentier, ultimately hinges on their emphasis on form (technique) versus content (the theme of the marvelous real).

A third moment in the development of the term, relevant not only to Latin America, but now also to world literature, arises in 1970, with the publication of Todorov's systematic study, *The Fantastic*. Todorov defined the fantastic as the *tension* between the possibility of a rational explanation and the disquieting acceptance of the supernatural—the unsettling prospect that the "laws of nature" have been violated, thereby compromising the reader's sense of certainty and understanding of the world. To promote this tension, it is best if the narrator has a skeptical, scientific mind, such as that of a detective, who is constantly engaging in deductive reasoning and looking for clues that may lead to a rational explanation. Therefore, the fantastic is structurally related to detective fiction, as can be seen in the works of authors like Borges and Cortázar, whom critic Jaime Alazraki fittingly classified as "neo-fantastic"—as opposed to magic-realist ("¿Qué es . . ." 21–33). As long as this tension or doubt persists, the effect of the fantastic is maintained. On the other hand, if the characters and narrator do not care to look for a rational explanation, but instead accept the events as normal, then the story belongs to the genre of the *merveilleux* (the marvelous), such as in the case of the fairy tale, which requires from the reader a suspension of disbelief. Todorov emphasizes that any poetical or allegorical meaning would serve to naturalize or normalize the story, eliminate the doubt, and, therefore, destroy the tension of the fantastic, which requires a strictly literal reading. Finally, if a rational explanation prevails in the end, then the story is neither fantastic nor marvelous, but simply strange or *uncanny* (*unheimlich*, to use the psychological term developed by Sigmund Freud for that which is taboo or uncomfortably strange).

Todorov's systematic definition of the fantastic was supposed to lead, by elimination, to a more specific definition of magical realism, but that would not turn out to be such a straightforward result. By the mid 1970s, the popularity of the term had grown so much as to lead to numerous studies and almost as many competing definitions. At the landmark 1973 magical realism conference in Michigan, Yale critic Emir Rodríguez Monegal called the debate "a dialog among the deaf" and suggested that the term be discarded altogether (Yates). To begin with, one of the problems with Todorov's theory is that it reduces fiction to only three types of narrated events: the natural, the supernatural, and the strange or preternatural. Following this simplification, Anderson-Imbert suggested that Franz Roh's original dialectics (impressionism + expressionism = magical realism) could be transposed to literature as "a thesis: the category of the veridical, which produces 'realism'; an antithesis: the category of the supernatural, which produces the literature of 'the fantastic'; and a synthesis: the category of the strange, which produces 'magical realism'" (*El realismo mágico* 9). This failed to resolve the problem because the delineation of the fantastic, while helping to narrow down the possibilities, ultimately could not establish what magical realism is, but only what it is *not*.

In *O Realismo Maravilhoso* (*Marvelous Realism*, 1980), Brazilian critic Irlemar Chiampi revisits Todorov's opposition between the "fantastic" (based on doubt and sketicism) and the "marvelous" (where the supernatural is unquestioningly accepted as normal). Following both Leal and Monegal, she discards the term "magical realism" as being too imprecise and problematic and replaces it with "marvelous realism," which she argues is more amenable to definition because of its relation, not only to Todorov's theory, but also to Carpentier's doctrine that the marvelous real is a normal everyday occurrence in Latin America's marginalized cultures. Although Chiampi's study, published in the heyday of structuralism, appears excessively technical and abstract today, it does contribute the view that, in "marvelous realism," the natural and the supernatural appear as non-contradictory and that its core narrative technique is "the de-naturalization of the real and the naturalization of the marvelous" (157–58). That is, the commonplace becomes defamiliarized when seen from a naïve perspective, whereas the miraculous is rendered commonplace from the standpoint of the believer. As Carpentier famously held in his prologue to *The Kingdom of This World*, "the phenomenon of the marvelous presupposes faith" (86).

In a different take on Todorov, Amaryll Chanady proposes, in *Magical Realism and The Fantastic,* three criteria for defining magical realism in contrast to the fantastic. She notes that the fantastic establishes an antinomy between the natural and the supernatural; it affirms the natural as valid, such that the irruption of the supernatural creates an ilogical situation; and it presents a narrator who is reluctant to explain matters and resolve the antinomy. In contrast, magical realism presents as an antinomy two coherent perspectives in conflict, one based on a rational view of reality, and the other one on an acceptance of the supernatural as a normal everyday occurrence. However, according to Chanady, this second, coherent (but non-rational) perspective should not be unnecessarily restricted to that of a marginalized ethnic culture, but could also be that of an individual psyche (dreams, hallucinations, psychopathology, a child's perspective, etc.). The main difference vis-à-vis the fantastic would reside in the *natural attitude* with which the narrator accepts the irrational, thereby "resolving" the antinomy. Nevertheless, it may be objected that the narrator's natural attitude may be recognized as a necessary, but not as a sufficient condition for an accurate definition of magical realism. Accepting both a *collective* (culturally bound) and an *individual* (sui generis) point of view as equally conforming to magical realism, results in grouping together works of very different styles, traditions, and periods under a single, all-inclusive rubric. For instance, García Márquez admired Kafka's penchant for narrating *the absurd* (as opposed to the supernatural) "with a straight face" and even recognized this as a major influence; yet both authors ultimately have very different styles (30, 52). In consequence, despite some important advances, Chanady's definition remains vague in as much as it reduces magical realism to a "mode" or technique that may be employed in very different types of fiction.

Notwithstanding the limited results of such contrastive method, Todorov's delineation of the fantastic did lead most critics to associate modernist authors, like Borges and Cortázar, with the (neo-) fantastic, while more regionalist authors, like Carpentier, Asturias, Rulfo, and García Márquez, became the most often cited as representatives of Latin American magical realism. This ushered a fourth moment in the development of the term, marked by an ethnological approach. From such anthropological perspective, the reader's modern-Western-industrial culture is confronted with the collective worldview of a pre-industrial-ethnic-rural society of believers, for whom the natural and the supernatural coexist within a single, culturally-bound belief system. In his 1960 essay "Alejo Carpentier: realismo mágico," Fernando Alegría was the first critic to point out this contextual dependence of magical realism on the Latin American hinterland, particularly what he called the "Afro-Indian" zone. Along these lines, I contended that, contrary to Carpentier's myth of the marvelous real, subsequent magic-realist authors produced instead a sort of "narrative primitivism," in which Latin American authochthonous culture was technically and, therefore, artificially constructed as a conventionalized pastiche or simulacrum based on classical anthropology's creation of a generic "primitive society"—a composite of early ethnographic depictions of traditional non-Western cultures across the globe, as popularized in twentieth-century ethnology, literature, and film (Camayd-Freixas, "Narrative Primitivism" 112–31). These "primitive" conventions for what constitutes habitual everyday reality (perceived as "magical thinking" by the modern reader) came to replace the rational causality of traditional realism and became a given, an unquestionable *norm* in the magic-realist text. According to this theory, Latin American magical realism is not a "mode," but a historically specific style shared by particular works of contemporary authors who exhibit a definite relation of literary influence, including: Carpentier's *El reino de este mundo* (*The Kingdom of This World*, 1949); Asturias' *Hombres de maíz* (*Men of Maize*,1949); Rulfo's *Pedro Páramo* (*Pedro Paramo*, 1955); García Márquez's *Cien años de soledad* (*One Hundred Years of Solitude*, 1967); Isabel Allende's *La casa de los espíritus* (*The House of the Spirits*, 1982); Laura Esquivel's *Como agua para chocolate* (*Like Water for Chocolate*, 1990); and Vargas Llosa's *El hablador* (*The Storyteller*, 1992). Their style is defined by three common denominators: the adoption of a "primitive" or provincial narrative viewpoint (production); the transculturation of reality norms from modern to archaic (text); and the virtual reader's dual role as believer and skeptic (reception), resulting in an alternate, allegorical interpretation of Latin American history, as opposed to the "official" version of history perpetuated by the structures of power.

In the 1990s, as magical realism declined in Latin American literature after having attained international acclaim, it began to be applied globally to numerous authors in the rest of the world (Moreiras 84). Formerly competing terms, such as "marvelous realism," "the marvelous real," "fantastic realism," and others became eclipsed by magical realism's sheer popularity. But also, as a term of international literature, its earlier Latin American definition became too narrow and had to be complemented by a broader, more inclusive scope. Meanwhile, the fantastic was also experiencing an expansion of scope. Todorov's delineation of the traditional fantastic, applicable mostly to nineteenth-century literature, and even the notion of a neo-fantastic modernist literature in the twentieth century, developed into what Brian McHale defined as a postmodern fantastic. Thus, in the actual practice of contemporary literature, even in Latin America, as Morales and Sardiñas have shown, previously separate elements of the fantastic and of magical realism have begun to coalesce within the same literary works, requiring new and more flexible theoretical formulations of both terms. This has led to a fifth moment in the development of the term: magical realism as a global poetics.

A leading theorist of international magical realism, Wendy Faris, has returned to Chanady's broader concept of magical realism as a literary "mode," and has identified five primary characteristics: an irreducible element of magic; a strong presence of the phenomenal world; some unsettling doubts on the part of the reader in the effort to reconcile two contradictory understandings of events; the narrative's merging of different realms; and the predilection for disturbing received ideas about time, space, and identity (7). Faris observes that "magical realism often originates in the peripheral and colonized regions of the West: Latin America and the Caribbean, India, Eastern Europe, Africa. But the mode is becoming less and less marginal" (29). She then adds, "Magical realism is currently moving out of that primitivist phase" (36). Among the many contemporary authors associated with this tendency are Günter Grass, Wilson Harris, Milan Kundera, Kenzaburō Ōe, Salman Rushdie, D. M. Thomas, Toni Morrison, Thomas Pynchon, José Saramago, Ben Okri, and Tahar Ben Jelloun. "The danger of studying magical realism globally, from a broad, comparative perspective,' warns Faris, "is to colonize diverse cultural traditions by considering them under a general rubric" (40).

In conclusion, there is a tradeoff in theorizing magical realism: the more precise and rigorous the definition, the fewer the works that meet such strict criteria; conversely, the more inclusive the term, the more vague the definition. In order to arrive at a suitable compromise, it is important to note that the single characteristic on which critics agree is that magical realism makes the extraordinary seem commonplace and vice versa. This is dependent on the nonconventional point of view of the ("naïve" or "unreliable") narrator, and on naturalizing devices, such as the extremely detailed and matter-of-fact description and narration of a rationally implausible event. In any case, the narrative point of view is key. In this regard, a further distinction may be drawn as to whether the point of view should be collective and culturally bound (that is, tied to a set of traditional beliefs shared by a particular cultural group) or individual and psychologically bound (that is, relative to an individual as a universal representative of the species, or of the human condition).

Aside from these primary traits, a host of secondary characteristics may be found in some works, but not in others. Epistemologically, therefore, primary characteristics should be considered common denominators, while secondary characteristics would be best conceptualized in terms of Wittgenstein's *family resemblance*—where a wide number of works are linked together as sharing some, though not all, of a set of overlapping traits, much like members of an extended family. By the same token, a group of works within the same national or linguistic tradition may be linked together by strict common denominators, forming a core or nucleus of magical realism, while other works that share a family resemblance may be placed in closer or farther proximity to this relational nucleus. Such is, for example, the general relationship between the Latin American and the international brands of magical realism.

Works Cited

Alazraki, Jaime. "Para una revalidación del concepto realismo mágico en la literatura hispanoamericana." *Homenaje a Andrés Iduarte*. Clear Creek, IN: The American Hispanist, 1976. 9–21.

———. "¿Qué es lo neofantástico? *Mester* 19:2 (Fall 1990): 21–33.

Alegría, Fernando. "Alejo Carpentier: realismo mágico." 1960. *Literatura y Revolución*. Mexico City: Fondo de Cultura Económica, 1971. 92–125.

Alexis, Jacques Stephen. "Du réalisme merveilleux des Haïtiens." *Présence Africaine* 8–10 (1956): 245–71.

Anderson-Imbert, Enrique, ed. *Veinte cuentos hispanoamericanos del siglo XX*. New York: Las Américas Publishing Company, 1956.

———. *El realismo mágico y otros ensayos*. Caracas: Monte Ávila, 1974.

Arnason, H. H. *History of Modern Art*. New York: Harry N. Abrams, 1979.

Asturias, Miguel Ángel. "Magia y política." *Índice* 226 (1977): 38–45.

Bontempelli, Massimo. *L'avventura novecentista*. Florence, Italy: Vallecchi, 1974.

Camayd-Freixas, Erik. "Reflections on Magical Realism: A Return to Legitimacy, The Legitimacy of Return." *Canadian Review of Comparative Literature* 23:2 (1996): 580–89.

———. *Realismo mágico y primitivismo: Relecturas de Carpentier, Asturias, Rulfo y García Márquez*. Lanham, MD: UP of America, 1998.

———. "Narrative Primitivism: Theory and Practice in Latin America." *Primitivism and Identity in Latin America*. Eds. Erik Camayd-Freixas & José Eduardo González. Tucson: U of Arizona P, 2000. 109-34.

———. *Etnografía imaginaria: Historia y parodia en la literatura hispanoamericana*. Guatemala City: F&G Editores, 2012.

Carpentier, Alejo. "On the Marvelous Real in America" and "The Baroque and the Marvelous Real." 1949. *Magical Realism: Theory, History, Community*. Eds. Lois Parkinson Zamora & Wendy B. Faris. Durham, NC: Duke UP, 1995. 75–108.

Chanady, Amaryll B. *Magical Realism and The Fantastic: Resolved Versus Unresolved Antinomy*. New York: Garland, 1985.

Chiampi, Irlemar. *O realismo maravilhoso. Forma e ideologia no romance hispanoamericano*. São Paulo: Editora Perspectiva, 1980.

Faris, Wendy B. *Ordinary Enchantments: Magical Realism and the Remystification of Narrative*. Nashville: Vanderbilt UP, 2004.

Flores, Ángel. "Magic Realism in Spanish American Literature." *Magical Realism: Theory, History, Community*. Eds. Lois Parkinson Zamora & Wendy B. Faris. Durham, NC: Duke UP, 1995. 109–117.

Freud, Sigmund. "Animism, Magic and the Omnipotence of Thoughts." *Totem and Taboo*. 1913. Trans. James Strachey. London: Routledge, 1999. 75–99.

_____. *Civilization and Its Discontents*. 1930. Trans. James Strachey. New York: Norton, 2010.

García Márquez, Gabriel. *El olor de la guayaba: Conversaciones con Plinio Apuleyo Mendoza*. Bogota: Editorial La Oveja Negra, 1982.

González Echevarría, Roberto. "Isla a su vuelo fugitiva: Carpentier y el realismo mágico." *Revista Iberoamericana* 40:86 (1974): 9–64.

Guenther, Irene. "Magic Realism, New Objectivity, and the Arts during the Weimar Republic." *Magical Realism: Theory, History, Community*. Eds. Lois Parkinson Zamora & Wendy B. Faris. Durham, NC: Duke UP, 1995. 33–73.

Husserl, Edmund. *Ideas*. New York: Collier, 1962.

Leal, Luis. "El realismo mágico en la literatura hispanoamericana." *Cuadernos Americanos* 153 (1967): 230–35.

Lins, Alavaro. *O Romance Brasileiro Contemporâneo*. Rio de Janeiro: Tecnoprint Gráfica, 1944.

McHale, Brian. *Postmodernist Fiction*. New York: Methuen, 1987.

Menton, Seymour. *Magic Realism Rediscovered, 1918–1981*. East Brunswick, N.J.: Associated U Presses, 1983.

_____. *Historia verdadera del realismo mágico*. Mexico City: Fondo de Cultura Económica, 1998.

Morales, Ana María, & José Miguel Sardiñas, eds. *Rumbos de lo fantástico: Actualidad e historia*. Palencia, Spain: Cálamo, 2007.

Moreiras, Alberto. "The End of Magical Realism: José María Arguedas' Passionate Signifier (*El zorro de arriba y el zorro de abajo*)." *The Journal of Narrative Technique* 27.1 (Winter, 1997): 84–112.

Portuondo, José Antonio. "La realidad americana y la literatura." *El heroísmo intelectual*. Mexico City: Tezontle, 1955. 125–39.

Roh, Franz. "Magical Realism: Post-Expressionism." Trans. Wendy B. Faris. *Magical Realism: Theory, History, Community*. Eds. Lois Parkinson Zamora & Wendy B. Faris. Durham, NC: Duke UP, 1995. 15–31.

_____. *Nach-Expressionismus. Magischer Realismus. Probleme der neuesten Europäischen Malerei*. Leipzig: Klinkhardt and Biermann, 1925.

Rodríguez Monegal, Emir. "Realismo mágico vs. literatura fantástica: un diálogo de sordos." *Otros mundos, otros fuegos: Fantasía y realismo mágico en Iberoamérica*. Ed. Donald Yates. Pittsburgh: K & S, 1975. 25–37.

Todorov, Tzvetan. *The Fantastic* [1970]. Ithaca, NY: Cornell UP, 1980.

Usigli, Rodolfo. "Realismo Moderno y Realismo Mágico" in *Itinerario del autor dramático*. Mexico City: Fondo de Cultura Económica, 1940. 115–21.

Uslar-Pietri, Arturo. *Letras y hombres de Venezuela*. Mexico City: Fondo de Cultura Económica, 1948.

_____. "Lo criollo en la literatura." *Las nubes*. Santiago de Chile: Editorial Universitaria, 1956. 66–78.

Wittgenstein, Ludwig. *Philosophical Investigations*. Trans. G. E. M. Anscombe. Oxford: Blackwell, 1953.

Yates, Donald, ed., *Otros mundos, otros fuegos: Fantasía y realismo mágico en Iberoamérica*. Pittsburgh: K & S, 1975.

Zamora, Lois Parkinson, & Wendy B. Faris, eds. *Magical Realism: Theory, History, Community*. Durham, NC: Duke UP, 1995.

Magical Realism and Its Discontents
Juan E. De Castro

It is not much of an exaggeration to argue that current Latin American literature is written against magical realism and its best-known example: Gabriel García Márquez's *Cien años de soledad* (*One Hundred Years of Solitude*, 1967). For instance, in a passage from *Historia secreta de Costaguana* (*Secret History of Costaguana*) (2007), by Juan Gabriel Vásquez, perhaps the most successful contemporary Colombian author, one finds a clear reference to some of the best-known events narrated in the earlier masterpiece, including the ascension of Remedios the Beauty and the levitation of Father Nicanor: "this is not one of those books where the dead speak, or where beautiful women ascend to the sky, or priests rise from the ground after drinking a steaming potion" (14).[1] However, more than an homage to García Márquez and his masterwork, Vásquez presents an implicit, but clear critique of magical realism. *Secret History of Costaguana* and, perhaps, Vásquez's writing as a whole, is defined by the rejection of Colombia's and Latin America's most famous novel.[2]

But Vásquez is not alone in distancing himself from magical realism. Eleven years earlier, two groups of novelists and narrators made their name by publicly rejecting the validity of magical realism as a representation of Latin America. The first group, McOndo, led by the Chileans Alberto Fuguet and Sergio Gómez, included such novelists as the Bolivian Edmundo Paz Soldán and the Peruvian Jaime Bayly in its phalanx. They made their criticism clear in the name they adopted, which juxtaposed the Irish/Scottish/(North) American/always capitalist Mc of McDonalds and, with typographical license, of Mac computers, with the mythical locale of García Márquez's novels.

The second group, the Crack, was constituted by Mexican novelists Jorge Volpi, Pedro Ángel Palou, Ricardo Chávez Castañeda, Eloy Urroz, and Ignacio Padilla. Again, the name is indicative of the relationship of these writers with their predecessors of the 1960s. If Boom refers to a moment of expansion, in Spanish, the Anglicism 'Crack' is used to denote contraction, especially, economic. However, rather than a criticism of the Boom, the Crackites expressed a belief that the creative wave represented by García Márquez and his contemporaries had long since crested and that, by the 1990s, had lost any remaining vitality. In his contribution to the foundational and promotional "Crack Manifesto," Padilla writes: "There is . . . a reaction against exhaustion; weariness of having the great Latin American literature and the dubious magic realism converted, for our writing, into tragic magicism" (n. p.).[3] Padilla criticizes Latin American literature as characterized by a desiccated and commercialized magical realism, a position shared by his Crack confrères.

Although the Crack cohort was explicit in its rejection of magical realism, though not of García Márquez's best work, it would be the McOndo gang who would make opposition to this mode of writing into a defining trait.[4] Not only that, Fuguet created what could be described as the founding myth of the Latin American rejection of magical realism: first, in his and Sergio Gómez's introduction to the McOndo anthology and, then, with more personal details in his "I Am Not a Magic Realist." Fuguet, already the author of influential novels and short story collections came to the Iowa International Writer's workshop on a fellowship. His secret goal was to be published in English. To his delighted surprise, he discovered that: "Bookstore shelves were peppered with Latino names and colorful dust-jackets. . . . There seemed to be a Spanish-language wave that I wanted to ride on my South American board. . . . I figured that all I had to do was get someone to translate something I wrote" ("I Am Not a Magic Realist"). However, the translator he contacted informed Fuguet that his work "lacked magical realism" ("I Am Not a Magic Realist"). Despite the absence of "flying abuelitas and the obsessively constructed genealogies", he submitted a story to the *Iowa Review* that, in turn, informed him "that it wasn't what they were looking for. . . . the story. . . . could easily have taken place right here, in America, they said" ("I Am Not a Magic Realist"). Fuguet eloquently concludes his story:

> I went back to the bookstores and took a closer look at all those novels with Hispanic authors. Sure enough, they fit the formula. . . . Each book offered either color-by-numbers magical realism or the cult of the underdeveloped. Sagas of sweaty migrant farm laborers, the plight of misunderstood political refugees or the spicy violence of the barrio. All decent themes, of course, but quite removed from my middle-class, metropolitan Chilean existence. . . . I was Latin American, all right—I just wasn't Latino enough." ("I Am Not a Magic Realist")

The Chilean novelist's surfboard lacked the magical realist accoutrements necessary to ride the US Latino publishing wave. Fuguet comes face to face with US editorial reality. Hispanic writers are expected to provide the world market with specific literary products: politically correct stories of exploited migrants or magical realist narratives that repeat what had once been García Márquez's novelistic innovations. Underlying the editorial expectations Fuguet encountered during his stay in Iowa is the essentialization of Latin Americans into a unified cultural, perhaps even racial group, that he calls "Latino." Given this essentialization, the obvious cultural and ethnic differences that characterize actually existing Latin America, as well as the differences between the inhabitants of the region and their mostly Anglophone and often culturally assimilated descendants is elided. Nevertheless, one can still note an implicit thematic division among the books in Iowa's bookstores. Those dealing with immigrants, a topic one can preliminarily identify as linked to US Latinos, and those written in a magical realist style, which would include books written by both US Latino and Latin American Latino writers. As his statement about flying grandmothers and elaborated genealogies implies, Fuguet's lack of interest in magical realism—as we have seen, shared by most writers who came of age after the 1960s and 1970s heyday of the Boom—was the true objection to his writings on the part of the US book industry and cultural movers and shakers, as represented by his translator and the editors of the prestigious *Iowa Review*.

his privileging of magical realism responded to the search for a proven commercial formula on the part of the US book media. The international sales success of *One Hundred Years of Solitude*, reinforced by the run-away best-seller status of Isabel Allende's re-elaboration of García Márquez's topics in a female clef in *La casa de los espíritus* (*The House of the Spirits*), published the same year the Colombian master received the Nobel Prize (1982), helped establish a commercial formula to which all Latin American, Latino, and other writers of the global south were expected to follow, in order to be published in the United States. The commercial wisdom of the formula is evidenced by the commercial and critical success of such magical realist Latin American epigones as Laura Esquivel; of US Latino and Latina authors, such as Rudolfo Anaya and María Elena Viramontes; of Africa American writers, such as Toni Morrison; Anglo-Indian writers, such as Salman Rushdie; or African narrators, such as Ben Okri.

Despite these postcolonial examples, it was Latin America that became primarily identified with magical realism not only in the mind of New York editors, but also for much of the US opinion, in and out of academia. Thus US Latin Americanists Erik Ching, Christina Buckley, and Angélica Lozano-Alonso write about "one of Latin America's most important literary movements, the Boom. In the 1960s and 1970s, Latin American authors gained worldwide recognition for their innovative narrative form, known commonly as magical realism" (59). While Ching, Buckley, and Lozano-Alonzo raise questions about magical realism "revealing the authentic Latin America" (60), they still present it as the paradigmatic literary expression of the region.

In his programmatic essays, though not in other statements, Fuguet also identifies the Boom with magical realism:

> Writers today who mold themselves after the Latin American "boom" writers of the 1960s (García Márquez, Carlos Fuentes, Mario Vargas Llosa, to name a few) have transformed fiction writing into the fairy-tale business, cranking out shamelessly folkloric novels that cater to the imaginations of politically correct readers—readers who, at

present, aren't even aware of Latino cultural realism. ("I Am Not a Magic Realist" n.p.)

Even if, as is the case with Padilla and the Crack, this description is couched as an attack on their epigones, from reading this passage one cannot but conclude that the Boom as a whole was a magical realist movement.

One of the paradoxes of this identification of magical realism with Latin American literature is that it was never the dominant narrative mode in the region. For instance, of the four core writers of the Boom—in addition to García Márquez, 2010 Nobel Prize winner Peruvian Mario Vargas Llosa, Mexican Carlos Fuentes, and Argentine Julio Cortázar—only the Colombian novelist is identified with magical realism. Vargas Llosa is a realist; Cortázar, a writer of fantastic and experimental narratives; and Fuentes, though more of a maverick, only occasionally flirted with magical realism. Moreover, with the obvious exception of *One Hundred Years of Solitude*, García Márquez has mainly written works that are not magical realist, such as *Crónica de una muerte anunciada* (*Chronicle of a Crime Foretold*, 1982) or *El general en su laberinto* (*The General in his Labyrinth*, 1989). The question is then: why did the association between magic and Latin America become entrenched in the US imagination? Or to put it in Fuguet's terms: why are flying grandmothers Latin American?

One cannot avoid noticing the congruence between US and European views of Latin America as not following "normal" rules of social and economic development and magical realism's representation of the region as outside the usual laws of nature. Ironically, the frequently left-wing magical realists, from García Márquez to the young Rushdie, ended up creating literary worlds that, despite their apparently radical rejection of Western and, therefore, capitalist modernity, were fully compatible with the views not only of the average citizen of Europe and North America, but of Western political, economic, and academic elites. Even if they disagreed in their political solutions to the problems it raised, for both García Márquez, at least in his best-known fiction, and the average Wall Street banker, Latin America seemed to resist Western normalization.

But beyond Fuguet's flying *abuelitas*, which are only to be found in his imagination, even if flying beauties and levitating priests are present in *One Hundred Years of Solitude*, how can one define magical realism? In "Presentación del País McOndo," their introduction to *McOndo*, Fuguet and Gómez quote fellow Chilean poet Óscar Hahn's attempt at a definition: "A type of narrative that transforms prodigies and marvels into everyday events and that places at the same level levitation and tooth brushing, incursions into the after-life and countryside" (16).[5] Some, such as, on occasion, García Márquez himself, have argued that this juxtaposition of the marvelous and everyday is precisely what characterizes Latin American history and/or society. Thus in an interview published in *Playboy Magazine*, García Márquez states: "Clearly the Latin American environment is marvelous. Particularly the Caribbean" (112). García Márquez thus claims that magical realism is actually realism applied to a region, a continent, in which nature, history, and cultural expectations exceed the parameters established in Europe and the United States.

In this and other statements, García Márquez is basically repeating the ideas expressed some thirty years earlier by Alejo Carpentier, another major Latin American writer. In the *Prólogo* (*Prologue*) to *El reino de este mundo* (*The Kingdom of this World*, 1949), unfortunately not included in the English language translation, Carpentier attempts to define the "real marvelous" he discovered while researching and writing this novel set in Haiti. (García Márquez's reference to Latin America as "marvelous" is a clear nod to Carpentier's formula). According to the Cuban author: "due to the virginity of the landscape, due to its formation, due to its ontology, due to the Faustian presence of the Indian and the black, due to the revelation that its recent discovery constituted, due to the fruitful mixtures it propitiated, America is far from having exhausted its mythologies" (Carpentier 7–8).[6] A paragraph later, the Cuban author concludes the *Prólogo* by asking rhetorically: "But what is the history of all of America but a chronicle of the real marvelous?"

(Carpentier 8).⁷ While García Márquez limited the marvelous to Latin America, if not the Caribbean, Carpentier extends its presence to the whole hemisphere, including the United States and Canada. Nevertheless, in his practice—the novel is set in Haiti—Carpentier still limits the marvelous to Latin America, if not the Caribbean.

Carpentier, who had witnessed and participated in the French surrealist and avant-garde movements of the late twenties and early thirties, contrasts the "marvelous reality lived" in Haiti and the Americas "with the exhausting pretension of convoking the marvelous that characterized certain European literatures of the last thirty years" (1).⁸ Thus, for the Cuban author one can establish a difference between the "real marvelous" of the Americas and what could be called the "fake" marvelous of European surrealism and other avant-gardes.

There is an obvious tension in Carpentier's discussion of the real marvelous as both a representation of a reality that exceeds and violates scientific rationality and one in which American difference is rooted in a mythic perception of a reality that is, however, explainable by the scientific laws applicable to European nature and history. After all, "an exaltation of the spirit that leads to a limit state" needs not to correlate with a natural world unexplainable by scientific laws (Carpentier 3).⁹ Or to raise a similar question regarding García Márquez's statements: regardless of the "marvelous" qualities he identifies in Latin America and the Caribbean, he cannot avoid immediately qualifying this earlier statement by noting "in the Caribbean, we are capable of believing anything, because we have the influence of all those different cultures, mixed in with Catholicism and our own local beliefs" (García Márquez 112). Like Carpentier, García Márquez presents a dual vision of the marvelous as rooted in reality—for instance, he mentions a man who magically dewormed cows just by his presence (112)—and as based in the cultural context in which reality is experienced.

The Kingdom of this World purports to represent the Haitian revolution of the late eighteenth and early nineteenth centuries. Carpentier in the "Prólogo," writes about Lautreaumont's *Maldoror*, who, "pursued by all the police in the world . . . escapes . . . adopting the guises of diverse animals" (Carpentier 7).[10] He then adds: "But in America, where nothing like this has been written, there lived a Mackandal granted the same powers by the faith of his contemporaries, and who animated, with this magic, one of the most dramatic and strangest rebellions in history" (Carpentier 7).[11] Thus *The Kingdom of this World* not only paints a fresco of the Haitian revolution of which Mackandal was an early instigator, but does so through the magical mindset that supposedly characterized the risen slaves. The binary opposition between a constructed marvelous associated with Europe and a real marvelous of the Americas is intrinsic to the mode in which the novel is narrated. The real marvelous would, therefore, find its justification outside literature itself: in the historical-anthropological correlation between the marvels depicted and the actual beliefs of the social groups represented. *The Kingdom of this World* is real marvelous precisely because it claims to accurately represent the magical manner in which the former slaves saw the world. While it is not clear in the novel whether Mackandal could actually turn into animals—his execution by the French authorities is narrated in a manner that casts doubt regarding the magical events narrated up to that moment—there is no doubt that this belief in his lycanthropic or zoothropic powers represents the views of the Haitian revolutionaries. Magical realism, or to be more exact, the real marvelous, thus would narrate from the perspective of the world narrated, rather than from that of the (often) Westernized and rational author.

Although few, if any, later magical realists have shared in Carpentier's obsessive archival and historical research,[12] similar claims to represent the perspectives of what we now call the subaltern have been made for later magical realists. As Jesús Benito, Ana María Manzanas, and Begoña Simal argue: "both magical realism and *lo real maravilloso* [real marvelous] can be grouped together in their championing of indigenous and postcolonial cultural perceptions and in their rejection of the playful literary experimentation associated with the West" (106). Magical realism would be a case of what has been ambiguously called, given its association with George Lucas' film, the empire writing back. It seemed to prove that literature could be the means through which alternative social and cultural perspectives to those hegemonic in Europe and the United States could be expressed in literature.

Obviously Fuguet, the other McOndians, the Crackites, Vásquez, Hahn, and many other Latin American writers beg to disagree with García Márquez, Carpentier, and their European and US academic acolytes. For these Latin American writers, the privileging of magical realism implies the elevation of a writing style as artificial as any other into the specifically Latin American literary mode. For them, magical realism is not the representation of Latin American difference, whether real, cultural, or ideological. After all, can one imagine any world, no matter how non-Western, in which brushing one's teeth and levitating were equally commonplace?

Moreover, magical realism in its *García Márquezian* archetype is rooted in rural imagery or, at least, an educated and urban vision of the countryside. Despite clichés about Latin America as a land of sombrero-wearing peasants, it is the most urbanized region of the world.[13] Thus, Fuguet and Gómez argue: "For us to sell a rural continent when, in reality, it is urban is too easy, immoral and an aberration (regardless of the fact that its overpopulated cities are chaotic and do not work)" (16).[14] If, for many (North) American and Europeans, magical realism managed to finally represent Latin American difference, for Fuguet, Gómez, Hahn, the Crackites, and Vásquez, among others, the literary style necessarily implies the misrepresentation of the region's reality. For them, it is as if Southern Gothic or science fiction were seen as providing an accurate representation of the whole of the United States.

If we accept the fact argued by many contemporary Latin American writers and critics that magical realism is not a valid representation of region's difference—whether this be natural, social, or cultural—the question is then raised why there were there so many magical realist texts found in the Iowa bookstore visited by Fuguet. We have already seen that magical realism became a formula by which the United States and, to a lesser degree, Spanish and Latin American presses, attempted to repeat the commercial successes of *One Hundred Years of Solitude* and, later, of Isabel Allende's novels.

(Allende is among the best-selling Spanish–language novelists in and out of the Hispanic world). But the other side of the coin is the willingness of writers to pander to these market requirements, to self-exoticize in order to be published in the United States or elsewhere. Fuguet and Gómez write about "calculated magical realism for export" (16).[15] Unlike these writers, the McOndo, the Crackites, and other contemporary Latin American writers would be writing primarily for a Spanish-language market, whether local or continental. Fuguet thus approvingly quotes David Gallagher's comment that the McOndians and other likeminded writers:

> don't have an international reputation to protect. Nor do they feel the necessity of submerging themselves in the waters of the politically correct. Since they don't have the advantage of living abroad, they wouldn't even know how to write a PC novel . . . they aren't writing for an international audience, and therefore, have no need to maintain the status quo of the stereotypical Latin America that is packaged up for export. ("I Am Not a Magic Realist" n.p.)

The new writers would thus gear their fiction not to international expectations and markets but to local realities and readers.

We have come upon the performative contradiction implicit in McOndo and, to a lesser degree, the Crack. As we have seen, Fuguet's story is ultimately one of (temporary) failure breaking into the US market. However, he was already the author of three well-received novels in his native Chile. The prestigious fellowship at the Iowa workshop was the result of his success as a Chilean writer. If he had been primarily interested in being a Chilean and/or Latin American writer, he could have just shrugged his shoulders and continued writing.

By now, his public and successful campaign against magical realism must be seen as part of the ritual parricide—the predictable demeaning of predecessors—which new generations of writers employ to open space among presses, critics, and readers for their work . The Boom's denigration of *indigenista* writers, such as Ciro Alegría or José María Arguedas, or even early avant-gardists, like Miguel Ángel Asturias or Leopoldo Marechal, is a prime example of this literary parricide.[16] The twist provided by Fuguet, McOndo, the Crack, etc., is to transfer the attacks from the Boom masters, to whom respect is always expressed, even if they are often misrepresented as a coterie of magical realists, to their epigones, against whom no mercy is shown. However, the fact that the intended readers of these attacks are located in the US and European cultural and editorial circles is evidenced by the way Fuguet repeats and attacks stereotypes—such as the primarily magical realist character of the Boom or of Latin America—held mainly outside Latin America. As we have seen, in Latin America, most knew that magical realism was only one of several writing styles used by the Boom masters available for emulation by later novelists. And no one thought toothbrushing was as noteworthy as levitation.

Fuguet's attacks on magical realism are thus rooted in two distinct arguments. First, on the disconnect between the representation of the region implicit in magical realism and Latin American reality: This argument is not without its difficulties. It is not clear whether the criticism is made on the grounds that Latin America was once more or less compatible with magical realism—when it was rural, when indigenous and Afro-American cultures were less impacted by modernity, etc., or on the notion that it was never referentially valid, since there has never been a society in which levitation has ever taken place.

If Latin America cannot be represented any longer by magical realism, it is a consequence of cultural, economic, and social evolution. It is capitalist modernization that has made magical realism untenable. In fact, even if Fuguet does not deny Latin American difference, it is a difference saturated, even defined, by globalization. While the centrality of globalization is implicit in both the "Presentación" and "I Am Not a Magic Realist," his 2010 "Magical Neoliberalism," a retroactive look and defense of McOndo, makes the point much clearer:

> The market reforms all over Latin America had to reform us as well. How could they not? If the point of liberalization was to open the doors, a cultural and social flood had to pour in. And it did. Add to this mix advances in communications (cybercafes in slums, cell

phones on cramped city buses), and you had a clean canvas on which to paint and new stories to tell. Yes, the economy grew (for a while), but creativity did even more so. . . Perhaps that was our strength—to be young, mestizo hybrids speaking and writing in a language like Spanish that has always been open to foreign influences. Our stories went private, introspective, but "our land" went global. (Fuguet, "Magical Neoliberalism" n.p.)

As the title of Fuguet's essay—"Magical Neoliberalism"—makes clear, Latin American difference is rooted not in an absolute difference whether magical or social, but in the juxtaposition of modern technology with a poverty that Fuguet implies does not exist in Europe and the United States: i.e., cybercafés. Moreover, by becoming "private," the region's literature ultimately become closer thematically and stylistically to the literatures of the United States and Europe.

But, as we know, globalization necessarily implies participation in the world market. Thus implicit in Fuguet's McOndean celebration is not only a cosmopolitan opening to foreign influences, but also the desire to participate in world literature not only as buyers, but as sellers. Despite the criticisms of magical realists' slavish following of international editorial clichés about Latin America, McOndo shares in their desire to be found in Iowa's bookstore. Given his aim to participate in global literary networks, what has been called the world republic of letters, Fuguet cannot avoid thinking about exporting his literature.

In his essays on magical realism, Vásquez establishes a contrast between Carpentier's real marvelous and García Márquez's *One Hundred Years of Solitude*. After noting the subjective elements present in the Cuban author's definition of the real marvelous, Vásquez argues: "the real marvelous has nothing to do with *One Hundred Years of Solitude*, novel in which the marvelous, instead of leading anyone to a limit state, rather than exalt anyone's spirit, does not surprise anyone" ("El arte de la distorsión").[17] Vásquez's attempt at differentiating Carpentier's real marvelous from *One Hundred Years of Solitude*'s magical realism is not without difficulty; as we have seen, García Márquez repeated Carpentier's ideas when explaining his novel. Moreover, not only Fuguet interpreted magical realism in Carpentierian terms, even if he believed these were mistaken, but Vásquez's own comments in *The Secret History of Costaguana* imply a similar critique of magical realism as misrepresentation.

Nevertheless, Vásquez's stress on the subjective exaltation central to the real marvelous can serve to establish a point of contact between Carpentier, García Márquez, and the Latin American writer who has most benefitted from literary globalization: Robero Bolaño. Although Fuguet has tried to incorporate Bolaño ex post facto into McOndo,[18] there is one central difference between the two Chilean novelists: the latter's ability to represent exalted psychological states. One only need to think of novels such as *Amuleto* (*Amulet*) (1999) and *Nocturno de Chile* (*By Night in Chile*) (2000). Both are constituted by first-person soliloquies that, without implying magical realities, present desperate interior monologues that incorporate borderline political and social hallucinations. Bolaño's works prove how the marvelous can subsist within contemporary realism and how it may still be a trait necessary for Latin Americans to enter globalized literary markets.

Notes

1. "Éste no es uno de esos libros donde los muertos hablan, ni las mujeres hermosas suben al cielo, ni los curas se levantan del suelo al tomar un brebaje caliente" (Vásquez, *Historia secreta de Costaguana* 24).

2. In his essay "El arte de la distorsión," Vásquez calls *One Hundred Years of Solitude* "the great nemesis of Colombian writers" ("esa gran Némesis de los escritores colombianos" n.p.). However, in the case of Vásquez and other writers mentioned in this essay, the rejection of *One Hundred Years of Solitude* as a model should not be taken as implying a denial of its status as a Colombian and Latin American classic. Vásquez, for instance, has claimed "lo que digo no niega la posición preeminente de *Cien años de soledad*" ("what I say does not deny the preeminent position of *One Hundred Years of Solitude*" ("Malentendidos alrededor de García Márquez" n.p.). In these cases, as in all those of texts in Spanish in the works cited list, the translation is mine.

3. "Hay . . . una reacción contra el agotamiento, cansancio de que la gran literatura latinoamericana y el dudoso realismo mágico se hayan convertido, para nuestras letras, en magiquismo trágico" (Padilla, et al. 5).

4. Responding in 1999 to an interviewer's comment that "your work breaks . . . with magical realism,'" Jorge Volpi, perhaps the most successful of the Crackites, made clear his relationship (or lack of it) with magical realism and *One Hundred Years of Solitude*: "it was the permanent stigma that a Spanish-American narrator has to continue doing magical realism and we discovered that, at least in this generation, almost no one is doing it. Some have a reaction against magical realism, but, in my case and in that of many others, there is not even a negative reaction because we have never written in the style. García Márquez has always been one of our mandatory readings, one of the classics, part of our library, but not a writer close to us. This is why . . . there has not been a violent reaction against magical realism on our part because it has not been a direct influence" ("era como el estigma permanente, que un narrador hispanoamericano tenía que seguir haciendo realismo mágico y descubrimos que, por lo menos en esta generación, no hay nadie casi lo practique. Algunos sí tienen todavía cierta reacción contra el realismo mágico, pero en mi caso y en el de muchos otros pues ni siquiera hay una reacción porque nunca lo hemos practicado. Siempre ha sido García Márquez una de nuestras lecturas obligadas, uno de los clásicos para nosotros, un autor de biblioteca, no alguien que tengamos tan cerca, de tal modo que en la reunión no ha habido una reacción violenta por nuestra parte contra el realismo mágico porque no ha habido una influencia directa") ("Las respuestas absolutas" n.p.).

5. "Ese tipo de relato que transforma los prodigios y maravillas en fenómenos cotidianos y que pone a la misma altura la levitación y el cepillado de dientes, los viajes de ultratumba y las excursiones al campo" (Fuguet and Gómez 16).

6. "Y es que, por la virginidad del paisaje, por la formación, por la ontología, por la presencia fáustica del indio y del negro, por la revelación que constituyó su reciente descubrimiento, por los fecundos mestizajes que propició, América está muy lejos de haber agotado su caudal de mitologías" (Carpentier 7–8).

7. "¿Pero qué es la historia de América toda sino una crónica de lo real-maravilloso?" (Carpentier 8).

8. "La acotante pretensión de suscitar lo maravilloso que caracterizó ciertas literaturas europeas de estos últimos treinta años" (Carpentier 1).
9. "una exaltación del espíritu que lo conduce a un estado límite" (Carpentier 3).
10. "perseguido por toda la policía del mundo . . . escapa . . . adoptando el aspecto de animales diversos" (Carpentier 7).
11. "Pero en América donde no se ha escrito nada semejante, existió un Mackandal dotado de los mismos poderes por la fe de sus contemporáneos, y que alentó, con esa magia, una de las sublevaciones más dramáticas y extrañas de la Historia" (Carpentier 7).
12. In the "Prólogo," Carpentier notes, "the narrative about to be read has been based on extremely rigorous documentation that not only respects the historical truth of the events, the names of characters—even secondary ones—places and even streets, but hides, under its apparent atemporality, a careful evaluation of dates and chronology" ("el relato que va a leerse ha sido establecido sobre una documentación extremadamente rigurosa que no solamente respeta la verdad histórica de los acontecimientos, los nombres de personajes—incluso secundarios—de lugares y hasta de calles, sino que oculta, bajo su aparente intemporalidad, un minucioso cotejo de fechas y de cronologías" 8).
13. Commenting a 2012 United Nations report, Paulo A. Paranagua stated in *The Guardian*: "Latin America is no longer a largely rural region. After 60 years of chaotic but rapid urban development, four-fifths of its population now live in towns or cities, a prey to all the ills of modernity and globalisation. Despite the fact that exports from these countries depend mainly on farming and mining, more than two-thirds of their gross national product comes from cities, home to services and industry. Although Latin America has huge expanses of territory, nowhere else has achieved this level of urbanisation" (n.p.).
14. "Vender un continente rural cuando, la verdad de las cosas, es urbano (más allá que sus sobrepobladas ciudades son un caos y no funcionen) nos parece aberrante, cómodo e inmoral" (Fuguet and Gómez 16).
15. "realismo mágico para la exportación (que tiene mucho de cálculo)" (Fuguet and Gómez 16).
16. Writing about his novelistic predecessors, Vargas Llosa notes: "from a literary point of view, the primitive novel confused creation with

information, art with artifice"; and "the primitive novels are valid geographic testimonials, important documentaries, but their aesthetic significance is nevertheless slight" (7–8).

17. "Lo real maravilloso no tiene absolutamente nada que ver con *Cien años de soledad*, novela en la que lo maravilloso, lejos de llevar a nadie a ningún estado límite, lejos de exaltar de ninguna manera ningún espíritu, no sorprende a nadie" (Vásquez, "El arte de la distorsión" n.p.).

18. According to Fuguet, "Bolaño is without a doubt—although he is much more than this—a writer whose books could have carried the label of McOndo" ("De hecho, me parece que Bolaño es, sin duda (aunque es mucho más que eso), un escritor cuyos libros podrían tener la etiqueta McOndo") ("Entrevista al escritor chileno Alberto Fuguet" n.p.).

Works Cited

Benito, Jesús, Ana María Manzana & Begoña Simal. *Uncertain Mirrors: Magical Realisms in US Ethnic Literatures*. Amsterdam: Rodopi, 2009.

Carpentier, Alejo. "Prólogo." *El reino de este mundo*. San Juan: La Universidad de Puerto Rico, 2006.

Ching, Erick, Christina Buckley, & Ángelica Lozano-Alonso. *Reframing Latin America: A Cultural Theory Reading of the Nineteenth and Twentieth Centuries*. Austin: U of Texas P, 2007.

Fuguet, Alberto. "Entrevista al escritor chileno Alberto Fuguet." Interview by Pedro Medina. *Suburbano Revista Cultural Miami*. 26 Nov 2012. Web. 1 Jan 2014.

—————. "I Am Not a Magic Realist." *Salon*. 11 Jun 1997. Web. 1 Jan 2014.

—————. "Magical Neoliberalism." *Foreign Policy*. 8 Jul 2010. Web. 1 Jan 2014.

Fuguet, Alberto, & Sergio Gómez. "Presentación al País McOndo." *McOndo*. Madrid: Mondadori, 1996, 9–18.

García Márquez, Gabriel. "*Playboy* Interview: Gabriel García Márquez." Interview by Claudia Dreifus. 1993. *Conversations with Gabriel García Márquez*. Ed. Gene Bell-Villada. Jackson: U of Mississippi P, 2006. 93–132.

Padilla, Ignacio, et. al. "Manifiesto Crack." Latin-America Institut 1996. Web. 23 May 2007.

_____. "Pocket Septet." Trans. Celia Bortolin & Scott Miller. *Dalkey Archive Press*. Dalkey Archive. n.d. Web. 1 Jan 2014.

Palou, Pedro Ángel, Eloy Urroz, Ignacio Padilla, Ricardo Chávez Castañeda, & Jorge Volpi. "Crack Manifesto, Context No. 16" Trans. Celia Bortolin & Scott Miller. *Dalkey Archive Press*. Dalkey Archive. n.d. Web. 1 Jan 2014.

Paranagua, Paulo A. "Latin America Struggles to Cope with Record Urban Growth." *The Guardian*. 11 Sep 2012. Web. 1 Jan 2014.

Vargas Llosa, Mario. "The Latin American Novel Today: An Introduction." *Books Abroad* 44.1 (1970): 7–16.

Vásquez, Juan Gabriel. "El arte de la distorsión." *El arte de la distorsión*. Madrid: Alfaguara, 2009. Nook file.

_____. *Historia secreta de Costaguana*. Buenos Aires: Alfaguara, 2007.

_____. "Malentendidos alrededor de García Márquez." *El arte de la distorsión*. Madrid: Alfaguara, 2009. Nook file.

_____. *The Secret History of Costaguana*. Trans. Anne McLean. New York: Riverhead, 2011.

Volpi, Jorge. "Las respuestas absolutas siempre son mentiras." Interview by Joaquín María Aguirre Romero & Yolanda Delgado. *Espéculo: Revista de estudios literarios* 11 (1999). Web. 1 Jan 2014.

Magical Realism and Subaltern Studies

Maggie Ann Bowers

The relationship between Subaltern Studies and magical realism has been oddly underexplored given the close association of both with Postcolonial Studies. There are several critics of magical realism who use of the term "subaltern" or "subalternity" (e.g., Wendy Faris, Amaryll Chanady, Brenda Cooper, and Eva Aldea), but very few who have carried out any wider study relating the two. This chapter aims to provide an overview of the development of subaltern studies and the ways in which they have been applied and are applicable to magical realist novels, revealing how closely related discussions of liminality and marginalization so often found in magical realist criticism are to those of subalternity.

This study follows a chronological coterminous development of the rise of magical realism as an internationally recognized genre and the founding of the subaltern studies groups in both India and the Americas. The analysis of magical realist texts from across the globe helps identify the radical connection between the disruption that magical realist narratives can cause to authoritative discourses and how subaltern studies provide alternative accounts of authoritarian history.

The definition of the subaltern has most famously been proposed by Gayatri Chakrabarty Spivak in her essay "Can the subaltern speak" (first published in 1988) as "A person without lines of social mobility" (28). She associates this with colonial women, who are marginalized due to their race, sex, and class. The subaltern, it is usually understood, is disallowed any voice, agency or authority in society due to their sex and ethnicity (usually associated with their race and colonial oppression). Spivak's essay drew international attention to work that had already been carried out since the 1980s in India by the Subaltern Studies Group. Although influenced by Antonio Gramsci's early twentieth-century Marxist study of the Italian peasantry, their work exposed the appropriation of the history of the Indian nation by bourgeois groups. Therefore, Spivak's definition, though useful, needs to be situated within the wider discussion of the exclusion of the subaltern from authorized versions of history, whether written by the new anti-colonial elite or from an older colonial perspective. South Asian subaltern studies attempts to find ways to articulate the histories of those who do not have the agency to have their role in the development of the Indian nation acknowledged. The specific aim is to make sure that historical accounts recognize "the peasant as an active and conscious subject of history" (Chatterjee 17).

In later years, as a result of the interest in Marxist postcolonial studies in the United States during the 1990s, subaltern studies was adopted as a template for Latin American historiography, that is, the study of how history is constructed. Here, the desire for liberation from right-wing dictatorships had already gone hand-in-hand with examinations of how history was being controlled and contained by those in power. This interest was transformed into fictional texts, such as Isabel Allende's *The House of the Spirits* (1982), which had been in turn influenced by magical realist predecessors, such as Gabriel García Márquez.

As part of this discussion, it is essential to recognize the issue of ventriloquism. Ventriloquism acts as a central idea in both Gayatri Spivak's influential conceptualization of the difficulties of representation for the subaltern, and Wendy Faris' identification of the complex relationship between the cosmopolitan and "primitive" voices of magical realist narratives (Faris 145–54). Ventriloquism is the term used to indicate that, in Western literary fiction and criticism, the author speaks for those who do not have access to the language, literature, or institutions to speak for themselves. For Spivak, it is the very elitist ventriloquizing that silences the subaltern's self-representation, whereas, citing Roberto González Echevarría, Faris claims that the ventriloquism in a magical realist narrative works by creating a postmodern, ironic, "mock anthropology" (146). In other words, ventriloquized subaltern voices in postmodern magical realist novels show the reader the difficulty of articulating their narratives without altering or misrepresenting them.

Despite the risks of ventriloquism, critics have often discussed the radical possibilities of magical realist discourse, focusing upon its capability to express the voices of those who are oppressed or silenced by authority, particularly and often by colonialism. In *Magical Realism in West African Fiction: Seeing with a Third Eye*, Brenda Cooper sees the creation of a third space between the magical and the historical with the creation of a theoretical approach that encapsulates both Marxist and postmodern tendencies (1). This, she claims, has opened spaces in discourse where "the once-colonized have re-written history" (3). In *Ordinary Enchantments*, Faris explains that the "bridging techniques of magical realism subvert the colonial authority of European realism by disengaging it from the empirical basis on which that authority seems to be built" (154). In other words, the breaking down of binary oppositions and master narratives, thence the construction of new definitions that move beyond such divisions, disengages the work from colonial and class structures. It is the creation of a new discursive space in which the magical real can exist unchallenged, and that is also the space in which the subaltern can speak and be heard.

Given the origins of postcolonial subaltern studies in India in the 1980s, it is perhaps not surprising that most of the work examining the subaltern in magical realist fiction has been done considering Salman Rushdie's 1981 text *Midnight's Children*. This chapter explores the connection made by Dipesh Chakrabarty, among others, between the Subaltern Studies Group's examination of Indian history and Rushdie's expansive novel of post-independence Indian historiography. This "historiographic metafiction," to use Linda Hutcheon's phrase (2), self-consciously produces a narrative that represents the methods that are used to create historical accounts. But in Rushdie's case, he does so by presenting us with multiple and fragmented narratives of history, which are narrated by an unreliable narrator. The constant refrain from the narrator throughout the text is the cry to "Please believe . . ." (Rushdie 38). He relies upon his reader believing his magical tales to disrupt the categories of rationalism and truth perpetuated by European colonialism and its post-Enlightenment reason. In doing so, Chakrabarty argues,

"Salman Rushdie's *Midnight's Children* contains a subplot which illustrates how the problem of 'force' or 'coercion' may arise in the conversation between the so-called 'modern' and 'non-modern'" (268), thus illustrating the link between the promotion of modernity and the forcefulness of European dominance.

The fact that Rushdie wrote *Midnight's Children* in 1981, just as interest in the subaltern as a significant figure in Indian history was gaining ground in Indian academia, is no coincidence. It indicates that India had reached a point in its reassessment of itself after its independence. This presented an acknowledgement by many historians that the histories written in postcolonial India about the twentieth century were not satisfactorily comprehensive. Focus was placed most particularly on the construction of historical narratives that reinforced the authority of a particular interested group. As Ranajit Guha notes, "The historiography of Indian nationalism has for a long time been dominated by elitism—colonialist elitism and bourgeois-nationalist elitism" (1).

Rushdie, while sharing this dissatisfaction with modern Indian historical narratives, was being influenced as a novelist by writers of world literature, who were experimenting in the creation of fictions that pushed the boundaries of how far fiction can be believed, which embraced unauthorized, forgotten, or overlooked histories. The two most notable and most influential upon Rushdie's work were, famously, Gabriel García Márquez and Günter Grass. Hence, Rushdie's Anglophone Indian historiographic novel borrowed magical realist techniques from both, creating the expression of historical perspectives that were otherwise difficult to articulate. Gyan Prakash calls these alternative versions of unauthorized histories "mythographies." He sees their role as more far-reaching than simply providing alternative narratives: "Such mythographic accounts revealing the previously hidden histories of the subordinated selves of first and third worlds will also expose the mythic quality of colonial and postcolonial fables of modernity" (Prakash 184).

Ultimately, the aim of subaltern studies, as stated by Ileana Rodríguez (9), is not the study of the subaltern, but the study of historiography and the causes of subaltern exclusion. Charkrabarty is clear that this calls for a different type of historical discourse that examines and critiques the on-going influence of colonial modernity, built upon European post-enlightenment thinking (270). With this in mind, the mythographies discussed by Prakash allow for a different kind of historical discourse that is not built upon histories requiring empiricist reason. Rather, they can call upon myth and even anecdote to embellish their alternative perspectives. The problem that the subaltern historian confronts is that the creation of histories that start from differing ideological positions within the colonial discourse of modernity, can be easily dismissed if they take place in the arena of modern history. Charkrabarty points out that the subaltern can speak in modern historical discourse, but "this dialog takes place within a field of possibilities that is already structured from the beginning in favor of certain outcomes," which are pre-determined against him/her by the post-enlightenment ideological framework in which he/she speaks (273).

However, by examining Rushdie's *Midnight's Children*, Chakrabarty sees a possibility for a subaltern articulation in a discursive space, where post-enlightenment rationalism and "monomania" (275) is not the default position. In other words, Rushdie's magical realist, postmodern, fragmented historiography provides a discursive space where subaltern voices can be articulated and possibly even heard. Chakrabarty moves into a hopeful, speculative position when he asks:

> Can we imagine another moment of subaltern history, where we stay—permanently, not simply as a matter of political tactics—with what is fragmentary and episodic, precisely because [it] does not, cannot, dream of the whole called the state and therefore must be suggestive of knowledge-forms that are not tied to the will that produces the state? (276)

The hope for this shift in "knowledge-forms" is inspired by the inclusion of the voice of Naseem Aziz in the text, as relayed by her grandson Saleem Sinai. Chakrabarty claims that the novel is an "allegory of the *origins* of modernity" (270) and a critique of its necessity. The reader witnesses Adam Aziz's attempts to force his wife, Naseem, into taking up Western habits (to discard her veil and "move" in bed) (Rushdie 34). As a European-trained doctor, he adopts a modern secular view, aligning him with the colonial power that he appropriates to control his wife. She attempts to adhere firmly to her religious and traditional attitudes, thus creating a tension that replicates the process of European cultural colonization.

Ursula Kluwick also notes that Rushdie's magical realism is founded upon a similar opposition; that is, Rushdie's magical realism is created by the tension that exists between opposing forces of the magical and the real, creating the characteristic "ambivalence" of his narratives (22). In Rushdie's narratives, the relationship between the magical and the real remains in a "conflict between two codes" resulting in "an irresolvable paradox" (Kluwick 28). In other words, the conflict that Chakrabarty notes in *Midnight's Children* between modern and non-modern modes of thinking repeats the pattern of conflicting beliefs presented in Rushdie's use of magical realism. Rushdie's work challenges the acceptance of the inevitability of modernity through the constant undermining of the reliability of post-enlightenment rationalism and, most especially, authoritative history.

Far from the colonial class structures that he critiques, Rushdie's fiction is most particularly democratic. The strength of the magical gifts acquired by the midnight's children is determined by the time of birth rather than the class or caste of the character (Rushdie 195). However, their identity as a group of powerful children can only exist if the power of Saleem, a liminal character living between two positions as both elite and subaltern, is brought into play. Saleem's telepathic magic is not the stuff of superstition or ancient belief, but a pastiche of modern telecommunications. Being born at the moment of independence, he is the embodiment of modern India. Still, the embodiment that Rushdie proposes is the illegitimate child of a street performer, fathered by a colonial in the final days of British rule, swapped at birth to live in an elite family. Rushdie's history of India must include "the consumed multitudes" (11) and all its contradictions, meaning that his history must be inclusive of the subaltern, but also of the voice of the elite.

What we do not find in Rushdie's fiction is the liberation of the subaltern by means of magical powers. For instance, while Parvarti can help Saleem escape from her slum house as it is demolished by the authorities, she cannot save herself (Rushdie 419). Padma is the most influential female subaltern voice in *Midnight's Children*. Passing comment upon the narrative as it is produced, she enacts what John Beverley identifies as the role of the subaltern in subaltern studies, that is, "the subject that 'interrupts' the modern narrative of the transition from feudalism to capitalism" (51). However, where Beverley is suspicious of magical realism (associating it with unreflective primitivism), he is also rather too focused upon class struggle, not seeing the wider radical possibility of the subaltern. Padma's role in the text is to challenge the credibility of the narrative, not because she adheres to non-modern views, but because she does not trust Saleem. The final irony of the text, then, is that *Midnight's Children* is a subaltern history of modern India, critiqued by a fictional subaltern character Padma—the creation of Rushdie cosmopolitan's mind. Padma continually interjects into the narrative, but only ever does so via Saleem's report. Saleem, in other words, creates a narrative that challenges and critiques itself. This concurs with Faris' understanding of ventriloquism in postmodern magical realism, inspired by Roberto González Echevarría's identification of Latin American texts that draw upon local myths as "mock anthropology." By "mock anthropology," he means that the workings of anthropology and ethnography are employed in order to be critiqued by these novels (González Echevarría 159), thereby, as Faris states, "undercutting the power of the univocal world view" (147).

However, this does not avoid other accusations of elitist appropriation by Rushdie. Born into an elite family and educated in English in Britain, some question his adequate familiarity with his subaltern subject matter. Timothy Brennan most famously notes Rushdie's cosmopolitanism, not only in terms of upbringing, but, more significantly, in relation to his position in world literature. By openly borrowing influences from Grass and García Márquez (which he discusses in detail in *Imaginary Homelands*), Rushdie places his writing in a global context. Writing Indian literature in English, his readership inevitably spans the English-speaking world (including English speakers in India), but does not address a readership of any one of the indigenous languages of India. As Brennan notes, Rushdie's fiction may well be an attempt to place the diversity of Indian experience into fiction, including the history of the subaltern, "But it is not addressed to them" (58). In this sense, Rushdie's magical realism creates a discourse that allows for the articulation of subaltern history, but it does so at the exclusion of the direct subaltern voice and without a subaltern readership.

His cosmopolitanism leaves Rushdie open to accusations of "ventriloquism" in both Wendy Faris' and Gayatri Chakrabarty Spivak's senses. In other words, Rushdie's fiction does not allow the individual subaltern to speak by failing to avoid "the ventriloquized nature of the representation of the subaltern (spoken for and spoken about, as Spivak points out)" (Rodríguez 3). However, I contend that he does create a history that acknowledges the subaltern as an active agent and, moreover, creates the possibility for subaltern articulation by his magical realist deconstruction of master narratives. I would add that Rushdie is a trailblazer, who creates the possibility of other subaltern fictions and histories to be told in Anglophone Indian writing (and many have been written in the years that follow, not least Arundahti Roy's *The God of Small Things*, which makes direct reference to the influences from Rushdie upon her text).

The relevance of both Indian and Latin American magical realist criticism in relation to Rushdie's work reinforces the cosmopolitan nature of the form. It is this international aspect of theory that led to the formation of the Latin American Subaltern Studies Group in the United States in the 1990s. This coincided with magical realism's height of international popularity, exampled by the production of an English-language film version of Allende's *The House of the Spirits* (1993). Critical work has since applied the ideas of Latin American subaltern studies in retrospect to the seminal texts of Latin American magical realism, such as *The Kingdom of this World* (1949) and *One Hundred Years of Solitude* (1967). These studies identify the representations of female and/or indigenous and enslaved subalterns from specifically Latin American cultural contexts.

What sets the treatment of the subaltern as a subject in Latin American magical realism apart is two-fold: the magical realism in Latin American fiction predominantly takes place in the narratives of the past, thereby allowing the reassessment of subaltern histories; additionally, many of the subaltern characters possess magical powers that can provide them with liberation. The most famous example of this is Mackandal in Alejo Carpentier's *El reino de este mundo*. He is based upon a historical figure, an African slave who turns rebellion leader after he gains alternative knowledge by introduction to Haitian vodou. This concurs with Charkrabarty's and Beverley's views of the radical possibility for change that the subaltern can assert when able to articulate his position from outside the system. In other words, Mackandal is able to see his radical potential when he can see beyond a discourse that posits colonial thinking as the only ideology. By seeing things differently, he is able to "interrupt" the colonial system and become, to use Beverley's term, "ungovernable" (49). This is reinforced by Mackandal's magical powers as a shape-shifter that allows him to escape (even if seemingly only temporarily) from the French landowners intent on killing him. Whether Mackandal survives in any of his forms is irrelevant to the wider story. His ungovernability and magical powers provide the people with another way to imagine their futures. In this way, the "third space" created by the magical real becomes a narrative space of radical possibility for the subaltern.

Thus, Latin American magical realism is personal as well as historiographic. It provides alternative narratives for the individual characters and possibilities for the creation of different historical perspectives for "the people." The most significant example of this in Allende's *The House of the Spirits* is the story of Alba, the main narrator. Although she is the daughter of a senator and, therefore, part of the elite, the treatment that she receives as a woman places her in a subaltern position. In the male-dominated world of Chilean politics and civil war, she loses her agency, is raped repeatedly, and left to die. Alba, however, is able to call upon the magical powers that she shares with her grandmother, in order to leave her physical existence and live inside her imagination until she is released and brought back to health. During this cerebral existence, she is able to construct the very narrative around which the novel is structured. She narrates the past of her family and of her own childhood, linking the mistreatment of the peasantry on the Tres Marías estate to her own destiny. She acknowledges the place of the subaltern in the history of her community and, from there, is able to reconceive a non-violent future that might be possible for them all, hoping to "break the cycle of violence" (368).

However, the liberating ending of the magical reconstruction of the family's narrative does not extend to provide any form of liberation for those who have already suffered. For instance, old Pedro García saves Tres Marías and Esteban Trueba by first diverting ants away from the estate and then setting Esteban's bones after a seemingly fatal injury in an earthquake. Pedro García's magical powers are connected in the novel with his traditional knowledge of plants and medicines, linking his magic not only to his lowly social status, but also to his indigenous knowledge. However, his subaltern position is not altered by his magical abilities or his alternative forms of knowledge. His daughter is still raped by Esteban, and she still dies from disease. Ultimately, his indigenous knowledge and magical powers are not enough to counter the brutality of the ruling classes or of the diseases of poverty.

Moreover, with the exception of Alba's story, although these accounts attempt to create subaltern narratives within the framework of the novel, they are subsumed, ultimately, under the larger narrative of the novel. Pedro García's story is just one in a series of small anecdotes related in Clara's notebooks. Mackandal's story is possibly the only one that is unhindered by a more authoritarian narrative thread. However, even here, the cosmopolitan identity of the author causes unease in accepting these as subaltern histories. Rodríguez makes clear the problem of elitist history, in which "The poor had not been recorded in a history of their own, but rather had been subsumed in a narrative which was not exactly their own" (3). Yet again, despite the space for an alternative articulation of history, despite the inclusion of subaltern characters with their own agency, the stories are ventriloquized both by other non-subaltern characters and by inclusion in the novels of cosmopolitan writers.

According to Rodríguez, this too is the nature of subaltern studies in Latin America. As Latin American Subaltern Studies emanated from a group of academics in the United States, "The convergence of Latin American and South Asian subaltern studies is a case of South-South dialog, but paradoxically it passes through the North" (Rodríguez 5). The same can be said of the influence of Latin American magical realism in contemporary world literature: it passes through translation in Western publishing houses from Latin America to the English-speaking world. It is this that makes Rushdie's postcolonial historiographies possible, but it does so via the necessity of global communication, commercial publishing and international education systems.

Of course, magical realism is neither entirely a mode of the "South," nor only of the postcolonial subject. It has roots in early and mid-twentieth century Europe and emerges in the late-twentieth century and contemporary Western world. The slippage of people into extremes of poverty in the United States and the development of an "underclass" in Britain are also represented in magical realist texts. Angela Carter's English magical realist novels, employing postmodern narrative unreliability and inspired by a Bakhtinian urge for carnivalesque, topsy-turvy disruption, explore the lives of magical characters from the edges of British and European society. Carter's *Nights at the Circus* is populated with subaltern figures from the world of circuses and side-shows. The characters have varying degrees of magic, both empowering and alienating. The character Lizzie even directs the reader towards considering "class analysis" when she can (Carter 53). She notes, "'It is the lot of those who toil and suffer to be dumb" (Carter 60). Fevvers, the focus of the narrative, is the surrogate daughter of Lizzie, an orphan brought up in a brothel, who is both marveled at and marginalized by her unusual physique. She is a giantess who (appears) to have a full set of usable wings. She is both a performer, creating a myth for her own identity, and a magical creature with no place in regular society. That said, she does have influence within the alternative world of circus performers and is the creator of her own unreliable narrative. In this sense, she has a voice and can "speak" within her own realm, but her exclusion from wider society is absolute.

Some of Carter's figures are so exaggeratedly subaltern that one begins to read the excesses of suffering as almost comic irony. Mignon is the absolute epitome of a subaltern: a pathetic orphan, with a murderous father, having been beaten, raped, and left as a beggar and prostitute on the streets. She appears covered in bruises, stinking and with semen dribbling down her leg. Moreover, making her even more akin to the colonial subaltern, Mignon is literally incapable of speech. Her only communication is to sing in a foreign language: "Mignon sang her foreign song without meaning, without feeling, as if the song shone through her, as though she were glass, without the knowledge she was heard; she sang her song, which contained the anguish of a continent" (Carter 134). However, the inclusive warmth of Carter's narrative provokes the reader's sympathy for these characters. When Fevvers relates her story to Walser, she provides relief from oppression by the creation of a world of carnivalesque excess, where their magical gifts can find expression rather than be met with repulsion. Hence, Carter's subalterns are both of our world and beyond it. The characters themselves exist beyond our own reality, but offer an allegorical reminder to us of those excluded and expelled from society.

Like the narratives of Rushdie and Allende, Carter's subaltern fictions communicate the histories of the subalterns existing in the peripheries of societies and nation states. Their magical realism and excessive fictionality break the hold of authoritative versions of history to create fissures that allow even the smallest of liminal spaces to be inhabited. Ultimately, despite the emphasis in South Asian Subaltern Studies upon the racial ethnicity of the colonized subject, these texts of world literature reveal that gender, ethnicity, and social exclusion can all play their part in any location of the world to force people into subaltern positions. Although the issue of ventriloquism will always need to be negotiated, it is the global influence of the magical realist form that provides the radical possibility to articulate the histories and create a new historiography based upon the expression of these multiple voices.

Works Cited

Aldea, Eva. *Magical Realism and Deleuze: The Indiscernibility of Difference in Postcolonial Literature.* New York: Continuum, 2011.

Allende, Isabel. *The House of the Spirits.* Trans. Magda Bogin. London: Black Swan, 1986.

Beverley, John. "The Im/possibility of Politics: Subalternity, Modernity, Hegemony." *The Latin American Studies Reader.* Ed. Ileana Rodríguez. Durham, NC: Duke UP, 2001. 47–63.

Brennan, Timothy. *Salman Rushdie and the Third World: Myths of the Nation.* New York: St. Martin's Press, 1989.

Carpentier, Alejo. *El reino de este mundo.* Barcelona: Biblioteca de Bolsillo, 1984.

Carter, Angela. *Nights at the Circus.* London: Vintage, 1994.

Chakrabarty, Dipesh. "Rama, Ángel." *Mapping Subaltern Studies and the Postcolonial.* Ed. Vinayak Chaturvedi. London: Verso, 2000. 256–80.

Chanady, Amaryll. "Magic realism revisited: the deconstruction of antinomies." *Canadian Review of Comparative Literature* 30.2 (2003): 428–44.

Chatterjee, Partha. "The Nation and Its Peasants." *Mapping Subaltern Studies and the Postcolonial.* Ed. Vinayak Chaturvedi. London: Verso, 2000. 8–23.

García Márquez, Gabriel. *One Hundred Years of Solitude.* Trans. Gregory Rabassa. London: Penguin, 1996.

Cooper, Brenda. *Magical Realism in West African Fiction: Seeing with a Third Eye.* London: Routledge, 1998.

Faris, Wendy. *Ordinary Enchantments: Magical Realism and the Remystification of Narrative.* Nashville: Vanderbilt UP, 2004.

González Echevarría, Roberto. *Myth and Archive: a Theory of Latin American Narrative.* Cambridge, UK: Cambridge UP, 1990.

Guha, Ranajit. "On some aspects of the historiography of colonial India." *Mapping Subaltern Studies and the Postcolonial.* Ed. Vinayak Chaturvedi. London: Verso, 2000.

Hutcheon, Linda. *A Poetics of Postmodernism: History, Theory, Fiction.* London: Routledge: 1988.

Kluwick, Ursula. *Exploring Magic Realism in Salman Rushdie's Fiction.* New York: Routledge, 2011.

Prakash, Nandy. "Writing Post-Orientalist Histories of the Third World: Perspectives from Indian Historiography." *Mapping Subaltern Studies and the Postcolonial.* Ed. Vinayak Chaturvedi. London: Verso, 2000. 163–90.

Rodríguez, Ileana. "Reading Subalterns Across Texts, Disciplines, and Theories: From Representation to Recognition." *The Latin American Studies Reader.* Ed. Ileana Rodríguez. Durham, NC: Duke UP, 2001. 1–32.

Roy, Arundhati. *The God of Small Things.* Hammersmith: Harper Perennial, 1997.

Rushdie, Salman. *Midnight's Children.* London: Jonathon Cape, 1981.

_____. *Imaginary Homelands: Essays and Criticism 1981–1991.* London: Granta, 1991.

Spivak, Gayatri Chakravorty. "Can the Subaltern Speak?" *The Postcolonial Studies Reader.* Eds. Bill Ashcroft, Gareth Griffiths, & Helen Tiffin. London: Routledge, 1995. 28–37.

Magic and Realism in History: Magical Realism vs. the Fantastic Today

Gene H. Bell-Villada

(In memoriam Audrey Dobek-Bell, 1945–2013)

I.

Magic. Unreality. The supernatural. These elements of narrative are as old as recorded narrative itself. Mythical deities play an active role in moving the plot of *Gilgamesh*, as well as in the comparatively more realistic *Iliad* or in the fairy tale-like *Odyssey*. Homer's second epic further includes larger-than-life monsters, like the one-eyed giant Cyclops, the cannibalistic sea creature Scylla, and the enchantress Circe, who transforms men into swine. Virgil's *Aeneid* prominently features gods, goddesses, phantoms, and harpies. Another ancient author, Aesop (assuming he existed), is credited with inaugurating what readers of all ages know as animal fables, an allegorical mode that has held its own throughout history, and was revived at the hands of La Fontaine in the seventeenth century and Orwell in our twentieth.

Moving to medieval times, a dominant narrative form under Christendom was hagiography, tales of Vatican-sanctioned saints who, besides leading exemplary lives, reportedly performed miracles—the Catholic Church's equivalent of deeds deemed magical. Supernatural figures, such as angels and devils, along with divine interventions from an almighty God, a blessed Virgin Mary, or their only son Jesus were common fare in medieval Christian folklore. For secular storytelling in the high Middle Ages, there was oral epic, with its occasional mythological beasts (Grendel in *Beowulf*) and magical objects (the horn Olifant in *Song of Roland*). Later on in lettered narrative, there emerged the now-notorious phenomenon of the chivalric novel, with unreal, impossible beings and doings of its own. These were famously spoofed by Cervantes.

Most literary historians agree that the first strictly realistic narratives in Europe were the French *fabliaux*, earthy, verse accounts of ordinary life and of non-heroic characters (e.g., corrupt clerics) or low-life personages (peasants, beggars, sex workers). The *fabliau* tradition was itself distilled into high art by Chaucer's *Canterbury Tales* and Boccaccio's *Decameron*. The Spanish picaresque arguably qualifies as the beginnings of a full-fledged, realistic prose fiction, and has its latter-day avatars in Defoe's *Moll Flanders* and Lesage's *Gil Blas*. "The first realist novel" is the singular honor usually bestowed on *Don Quixote*, with its depiction of rounded characters moving about in the real world and in society and developing as the plot proceeds ahead. Among *Don Quixote*'s obvious heirs are Fielding's *Joseph Andrews* and *Tom Jones*.

With the nineteenth century and its in-depth consciousness of the workings of society and its secular, scientific outlook, the stage was set for the triumph of realistic fiction. Although the realist template later became subject to some broadening and then-daring experiments in content and form (Joyce, Woolf, Faulkner), the depiction of inner and outer reality as we know them has remained its primary approach and purpose. To this day, realist story-telling remains the default medium for most prose writers with "stories to tell," for commercial publishers with their indispensable "fiction" lists, and for public libraries with local patrons and readerships to serve.

Still, despite the dominance of the realist paradigm, narratives with some version of the supernatural or the uncanny continued to be published: Gothic novels; horror stories (Poe, Bram Stoker, H. P. Lovecraft); seemingly realistic works with ghosts in them (Brontë's *Wuthering Heights*, Dickens' *A Christmas Carol*); or the apparent visit paid by the Devil to Ivan Karamazov in his room. The very master of realist fiction, Balzac, allots a special role to an eponymous magic skin in his *La peau de chagrin*. And Henry James famously tells of phantom apparitions in *The Turn of the Screw* (about which more will be discussed later). Finally, Jules Verne and H. G. Wells invented the genre of science fiction, with unreal events springing into existence via the unlimited marvels of science and technology.

Popularity and sales aside, these were marginal and exotic growths, sprouting at the edges of a broader realist mainstream. (In this regard, it is not for nothing that, even today, libraries and bookstores—such as these exist—tend to place their "Sci-Fi & Fantasy" sections separate from that of "Fiction" or "Literature."). E. M. Forster, in his lecture series *Aspects of the Novel*, has a chapter specifically entitled "Fantasy." The Edwardian novelist at first lends tentative consideration to the topic: "Once in the realm of the fictitious, what difference is there between an apparition and a mortgage?"—yet follows with a caveat immediately thereafter: "I see the soundness of the argument, but my heart refuses to assent" (108). In Forster's view, fantastical narratives, with "the oddness of [their] method or subject matter," are analogous to "sideshows inside the main show"—a reservation he voices twice. Along these lines, theorist Northrop Frye, in his extensive discussion of narrative genres, states explicitly that "the supernatural, or the suggestion of it . . . is difficult to get into a novel" (304).

The foregoing overview, however rapid and summary, serves as a necessary first step in approaching the question of "Magical Realism" and seeking to situate it within a larger continuity. The coinage of the phrase in 1924 by art historian Franz Roh as a means of denoting a particular moment in painting, the diffusion of the term in Weimar Germany and its later implantation in German literary criticism post-1945, and its dissemination in Latin America via a 1927 Spanish translation of Roh's book and then by refugee scholars from the Third Reich—all this is a fascinating set of developments in its own right.[1] What concerns me more at this juncture, though, is that, in the 1950s and 60s, with the gradual rise of makers of non-realistic fiction, such as Borges and Carpentier and, later, Cortázar and García Márquez, critics and scholars in both Americas (notably Ángel Flores and Luis Leal) took to adopting and employing the phrase when denoting these Hispanic artificers and the magical, marvelous, and supernatural things played out in their fictions. And, of course, the astounding, world-wide success of *One Hundred Years of Solitude* made the term common currency in the general press and the academy.

The underlying implication in these speculations was that a newer rubric was needed when dealing with this new kind of writing. The existing terminology, presumably, was deemed insufficient, incomplete. For a symptomatic instance, in what is perhaps the most ambitious and encyclopedic compendium of literature in recent times, Northrop Frye's *Anatomy of Criticism*, there is scant intellectual room for a precise focus on these emerging narratives of the supernatural. Frye's broad, traditional category of *romance*, while genuinely fruitful and inclusive as a retrospective, historical term, paradoxically enough did not jibe with the well-grounded, strongly *realistic* side of magical realism, while his brief, scattered discussions of ghost stories and the Gothic proved too narrow, too confining to embrace the wide gamut of unrealities to be found in Carpentier, Borges, and García Márquez. Significantly, Frye's index entry for "Kafka" in *Anatomy* lists the Czech writer's more manageably "mythic" works, *The Trial* and *The Penal Colony*, yet makes no mention of the far more influential, revolutionary, "magical realist" tale, *The Metamorphosis*. Frye's grand system, however monumental, proved too time-bound and culture-bound when faced with a new brand of literature.

It would be helpful, at this point, to establish just what "magical realism" is and how it works. At the risk of stating the obvious, we should stress the *realism* half of the equation. In what is the locus classicus of the genre, *One Hundred Years of Solitude*, the magical occurrences all take place within the tropical small town of Macondo (based on the author's original hometown of Aracataca) and almost invariably go hand in hand with plausible, often ordinary events—e.g., a priest soliciting funds for a church (he levitates), the burial of the founding patriarch (flowers rain from heaven), and a young woman hanging the laundry (she rises to heaven, waving).

Similarly, the phantom that is Aura in Fuentes' novella by that name inhabits a colonial mansion on La calle de Donceles, a real street in downtown Mexico City (indeed, one of the imperial capital's oldest); and she is depicted doing mundane things, like leading the protagonist Felipe Montero through the house and joining him in dinner. Beloved, the eponymous, adolescent, hat-bedecked ghost in Toni Morrison's novel, rather than a fearsome or awe-inspiring creature, simply takes up residence with her mother Sethe at 124 Bluestone Road in nineteenth-century Cincinnati. And Salman Rushdie's 1,001 Midnight's Children perform their clairvoyance and magic along the length and breadth of twentieth-century India and Pakistan, with chronological markers, place-names, and locations all duly specified.

Returning to the subject of ghosts, in *Pedro Páramo* virtually all of the inhabitants of Comala, an imagined town in author Juan Rulfo's desert region of Jalisco, are phantoms who nonetheless lead everyday existences in broad daylight; and Juan Preciado, the buried protagonist, routinely converses with and tells his story to Dorotea in her adjacent grave. Touches of this spectral realism are found in Cristina García's *Dreaming in Cuban*, where the young art student Pilar communicates telepathically in New York with her grandmother, Celia, in Havana, while Pilar's mother, Lourdes, occasionally chats with the ghost of her own father, Jorge, Celia's deceased husband. In another American instance, the vagabond Francis Phelan of William Kennedy's beautiful *Ironweed*, on a stealthy return visit to his native Albany after a twenty-two-year absence, visits the local cemetery, where his deceased parents respond to him in their graves and where he, in turn, talks with the phantom of the infant son he had accidentally killed. Later, in buses, Phelan addresses the specters of three men he had murdered. Going back to García Márquez's novel, the ghost of Prudencio Aguilar regularly haunts the Buendía couple, and so Úrsula, feeling sorry for the revenant, leaves jugs of water for him, while a guilt-ridden José Arcadio Buendía tells him to "go to hell," as if the apparition were more of a common nuisance.

In such instances, the reader encounters a recognizable reality, of which the supernatural, rather than being an intrusion, is simply a component part. Magical things, as it were, "really happen," are "really there." We are not in an alternate world, and magical realism is, thus, a fusion—not "an oxymoron" as Stephen Slemon argues in an otherwise perceptive article (409). To cite Amaryll Chanady's words, "In magical realism, the supernatural is not presented as problematic" (23) and "does not disconcert the reader," but occurs instead "without any judgment" (24).

Luis Leal already observed, in a pioneering essay from 1967, that magical realism is "more than anything else, *an attitude toward reality*" (121; emphasis added), one that neither employs dreams nor aims to "distort reality or create imagined worlds" (121). Magical realism qualifies not even as a broadly definable movement, but rather, in John Burt Foster's astute insight, as "an international cultural tendency" (267), not restricted to any country nor associated with any epoch. The very term allows us to look back retrospectively and see the "tendency" at work in earlier texts—a bit like Borges' conceit about Kafka *creating* his precursors. Among such precedents one might single out Gogol's story "The Nose," in which Major Platon Kovalev, a rather ordinary government official, finds out one morning that his nose has disappeared; the wayward organ is eventually to be seen in uniform, strolling about St. Petersburg, where city streets and buildings are alluded to by name; it even spends some time as State Councilor. And in Kafka's classic *The Metamorphosis*, Gregor Samsa, a traveling salesman, awakes to find himself transformed into a dung beetle, and the entire subsequent narrative unfolds inside a bourgeois apartment (save for the dénouement, set in a tram in a nameless urban center) and amid the bosom of a typical bourgeois family.

There is yet another antecedent to magical realism, indeed "a powerful precursor to overcome" (Faris, "Scheherazade's Children" 164). That precursor, Wendy Faris remarks, is none other than European realism itself ("Scheherazade's Children" 164). In the case of Latin America, during the region's first one-hundred-fifty years of independence, numerous realist novels were written and published; yet the genre, the approach, never took on a living shape or established themselves with any solidity or legitimacy. Few of those works survive today, and none have gained entry into what Pascale Casanova calls, in her seminal study of the same name, "the world republic of letters." Moreover, classic realism in Hispanic America had often mingled outwardly with social protest and didactic literature, a mode of writing that tends to become quickly dated and loses force as its targets recede into history. It was with magical and fantastical narrative that the literary continent—precisely by breaking away from the model of nineteenth-century, linear realism—slowly, but steadily, found its voice.

In a sense, then, realism is the precondition for *magical* realism, much in the way that the magical, chivalric novel is, conversely, the existing precondition for the realism of *Don Quixote*. And just as Cervantes set out to *dis*enchant the world of knights errant by placing a would-be knight and his squire in everyday reality, García Márquez set out to *re*-enchant everyday reality by showing that what ordinary people believe and feel—via popular beliefs, folklore, home remedies, and even superstitions—is part of that reality. (As he likes to say, "Reality is not restricted to the price of tomatoes.") Significantly, García Márquez, during his years as a cub reporter, spent long hours as an amateur anthropologist, collecting folk tales and inserting them into his newspaper columns.

At this point, some genre distinctions are in order. Magical realism is not akin to horror stories (though it might chance to depict horrors), inasmuch as it moulds the supernatural into something ordinary, quotidian, and not necessarily terrifying. It is not the world of pure fantasy *à la* Tolkien or Walt Disney, nor is it what Frye calls "Menippean satire," fictions such as *Gulliver's Travels* or the *Alice* books, in which unreal characters represent mental attitudes. Neither is it fable, with its animals serving as allegorical figures in a morality play. Nor is it science fiction, which by definition places events in a future transformed or a present reconstituted by science and technology (unlike magical realism and its familiar settings). Finally, it is not fairy tale, a form that, like the previous instances, is "a fictitious world totally removed from our conventional view of reality" (Chanady 2).[2]

Magical realism can nevertheless fuse with those traditional narrative forms of the supernatural. Fuentes' *Aura* closely resembles the fairy-tale account of a captive princess, an old witch, and a prince charming, who comes to the rescue. Similarly, García Márquez's "Innocent Eréndira" is a spoof of the same Cinderella-type genre, featuring an enslaved damsel, a wicked stepmother, and an enamored (though bungling) hero. As in fairy tales, the numbers three (three kidnappings, three murder attempts) and seven (seven chapters) and hard metal objects (diamonds in the oranges, the gilded piano, the gold vest) have a role to play in the novella (Hancock, *passim*; Bell-Villada, *García Márquez* 196–98). The Colombian's "A Very Old Man with Enormous Wings" approximates the tales of folk religion, of apparitions of the Virgin or a saint or an angel, complete with miracles, albeit comical ones. In José Saramago's novel *Essay on Blindness*, a blindness epidemic slowly descends upon a modern city; the town and its localities, however, are generic, as are the characters (known only as, e.g., "the boy," "the doctor," "the doctor's wife," "the girl with sunglasses," etc.), bringing the narrative, which has no proper names, closer to folk-tale idiom.

By contrast, the talking and singing animals in Kafka's stories "The Burrow," "A Report to the Academy," "Investigations of a Dog," and "Josephine the Singer, or the Mouse Folk" all shade into traditional fable without taking on the full allegorical flavor of the Aesopian. In another sort of direction, the 1930s couple in John Cheever's story "The Enormous Radio" purchases a radio console that mysteriously and vividly conveys to them the private conversations of their neighbors in their building in New York, a bit of technology-based magic that hints slightly at science fiction without actually being of that school.

II.

There is yet another genre distinction calling for special attention: that of magical realism vs. the fantastic (the latter also known as fantastic literature). Between the 1950s and 1970s, with the rise of a vital new narrative of unreality from Latin America, critics in the general press, as well as on college and university campuses, began to employ the terms interchangeably and, conversely, to place the writing of Borges, Cortázar, and García Márquez freely in one category or the other. Many of the contributors to the Faris-Parkinson Zamora anthology *Magical Realism* apply the titular term indifferently to the Argentine pair and the Colombian novelist both. Some major contrasts, however, merit a closer look.

The key critical text in this regard is Tzvetan Todorov's *Introduction à la littérature fantastique* (1970). Concentrating primarily on nineteenth-century works, the Franco-Bulgarian Structuralist observes early on in his second chapter, "In a world much like ours . . . an event is produced that cannot be explained by the laws of the same familiar world" (Todorov 29). There are thus "two possible solutions: either we are faced with an illusion of the senses, a product of the imagination, and the laws of the world remain as they are; or the event has truly taken place and is an integral part of reality, but then that reality is ruled by laws unknown to us" (Todorov 29). Todorov thus arrives at his central insight: "*The hesitation of the reader* is the first condition of the fantastic" (36). In so experiencing a narrative, in which the supernatural plays a role, the reader is forced to "hesitate between a natural explanation and a supernatural explanation" of the events depicted in the work (Todorov 37, translations mine).

Todorov's reading helps illuminate many of Borges' fantastical stories. In "The South," the entire final sequence, in which Dahlmann is released from the hospital and then boards a train that takes him into the wilderness, can be interpreted either at face value or as a vivid delusion undergone by the protagonist on his deathbed (Bell-Villada, *Borges and His Fiction* 86–87). Similarly, the "secret miracle" in the tale by that name, in which the universe stops for a year, in order that condemned writer Hladík can finish his masterpiece in his head, may well be an hallucination that extends between the execution squad's gunfire at 9:00 and the victim's reported death at 9:02 (Bell-Villada, *Borges and His Fiction* 90–91). The rapture that, in "The God's Script," seizes Tzinacán could be either a true vision of the vast, cosmic power that he has attained in his sunken jail cell, or an inadvertent theophany that has overcome the Mayan prisoner as a result of his accidentally going through the standard preparatory procedures of mysticism (Bell-Villada, *Borges and His Fiction* 212–19).

Similarly, in Cortázar's "Letter to a Young Lady in Paris," the anonymous narrator may, as he reports, indeed have vomited bunnies; or he may be lying (perhaps he simply brought the rabbits into the Buenos Aires apartment); or he could simply be out of his mind. The sacrificial acts occurring toward the end of "The Idol of the Cyclades" might, in fact, have been prompted by a magical spell, cast over Morand and Somoza by the prehistoric statuette; otherwise, the two men may have both turned psychotic together. The unspecified home invaders in "House Taken Over" could be anything—ghosts, family phantoms, the people in revolt, the military. The cultured, upper-class narrator never specifies, even though he and his sister both know who "they" are—knowledge that is left up to the story's hesitating reader. These are simply a few such instances from the totality of Cortázar's oeuvre.

To take an example familiar enough from the English-language canon, in James' *The Turn of the Screw*, most evidence in the text indicates that the apparitions of the deceased Quint and Miss Jessel are but figments of the unnamed governess' imagination. And yet, she describes each of them as they looked, physically, when they were alive (as confirmed by the housekeeper Mrs. Grose). The reader, therefore, hesitates: Is the nanny deluded? Or are they true revenants from the past that only she can see?

On the other hand, there are stories by Borges and Cortázar that can indeed be considered under the "magical-realist" heading. The unforgettable vision of the Aleph that character "Borges" confronts in the shabby cellar of Carlos Argentino's family home is very much there as an objective presence, even though the wry narrator later undercuts the experience by dismissing it as a "false Aleph;" moreover, everything that precedes and follows the high moment is ridiculous and funny, all of it unfolding in a Buenos Aires with place names and daily rituals specifically spelled out.

By the same token, in Cortázar's "Lejana" ("The Distances"), the telepathy between Alina Reyes in Buenos Aires and the beggar-woman in Budapest and the interchange of selves on the bridge, are a process narrated without any gaps or uncertainties. "Secret Weapons" likewise leaves no ambiguity as to whether Pierre has taken on the personality of the German rapist or gone mad. (The two pieces could be seen as updated, latter-day specimens of the horror-story genre.) Finally, unless the Hispanic narrator of "Axolotl" is demented, we have to accept it on his word that he has metamorphosed into the Mexican amphibian.

By the same token, at times a magical-realist text can elicit some hesitations of its own. In chapter fifteen of *One Hundred Years of Solitude*, an army officer searches the Buendía house, turns on the light in Melquíades' room, and stares directly at the fugitive José Arcadio Segundo—yet declares that there's no one there. The soldier's negative response can be taken in two ways: either the magic of Melquíades' space has rendered the strike leader invisible to the military man's gaze, or the officer has consciously chosen to feign ignorance and claim not to have seen a hiding son of Macondo's leading clan. Similarly, in "A Very Old Man with Enormous Wings," the protagonist is, at one point, identified by a nameless wise old woman as an angel, and he certainly turns out to have miraculous powers of a sort attributable to a divine being. But that is just one woman's opinion. And are the visitor's comic miracles the result of ineptitude or sheer mischief on his part? No one knows. Other than what the title says, the old man's identity remains a mystery at which we can only "hesitate."

Todorov further notes still another kind of "hesitation" that could actually be applied to works looking to be more magical-realist than fantastical. Further down the spectrum from fable, which is purely allegorical, there are those tales that suggest an allegorical reading, yet do not seem to fulfill that function completely. As Todorov puts it, in these cases, the reader "goes so far as to *hesitate* between an allegorical interpretation and a literal reading" (74). Hence the question might arise: is Stevenson's *Strange Case of Dr. Jekyll and Mr. Hyde* simply a story about a scholarly recluse with a split identity? Or is it some sort of allegory about the twoness of Man, about the beast in all of us? Is the eponymous picture of Dorian Gray in Oscar Wilde's novel "merely" a magical artifact or a deeper symbol of the true fact of aging? Is Borges' "Circular Ruins" little more than an ancient-flavored Orientalist tale about a dreamer being dreamt? Or can it "really" be seen as an allegory about identity, about the delusion of believing our selves and our actions to be our own? (To play on a familiar phrase: is a cigar in a fantastic story just a cigar? If it's sometimes more than that, then when?)

Borges himself, commenting over French radio on "The Library of Babel," said that his fantastical tale has "a feeling . . . of the mysterious nature of the universe, of time, and, what is most important, of ourselves" (Bell-Villada, *Borges and His Fiction* 120). Stated otherwise, the Argentine author does suggest here—without using the words—that the story is something of a parable, even a fable about humankind today. Along such lines, Kafka's animal stories can perhaps invite an allegorical interpretation; those creatures may well be seen as stand-ins for us human beings and our follies. Yet the stories do not completely fit the mould; the mice, the dog, the ape, and Gregor the beetle have enough texture and specificity of their own to be accounts of themselves for their own sake. Over the years, I have encountered readings of *The Metamorphosis* that construe Gregor's situation as a religious allegory, as a symbol for the "irreparable estrangement" that is the plight of the artist (Corngold xx), as "a metaphor for an unexpected physical disability that his family members have to cope with" (Quayson 73), and so forth. Such interpretations may make sense, if argued skillfully enough; this reader hesitates to settle on any single one.

In this regard, Todorov, not surprisingly, considers Gogol's "Nose" and weighs in on the possibility of a linguistic, or a psychoanalytical, or a social explanation—and, in the end, finds them all wanting. The gratuitousness of the event itself, in his view, contradicts any allegorical sense (77–78). Significantly, toward the end of Todorov's concluding chapter, the critic takes an extended look at Kafka's *The Metamorphosis* and finds that its procedures go against everything he has been saying about the fantastic. First of all, the story starts out with, rather than leads to, a supernatural situation, one that is described not as shocking, but likely, and that, in time, even turns domestic and quotidian. Moreover, the ending of the novella is "as far removed as it could be from the supernatural" (Todorov 179). Indeed, the unreal element in *Metamorphosis* does not prompt alternative explanations in the reader, the characters, or the text. "As a result, all hesitation becomes useless," Todorov admits (179).

By seeing Kafka as a special case within his own groundbreaking theory of the fantastic, Todorov hints at an insight that lies at the root of this essay: to wit, Kafka is something new in narrative, and what is new is, precisely, his magical realism *avant la lettre*. It is not coincidental that García Márquez has oftentimes described his discovery of *The Metamorphosis* as an epiphany, a revelation that opened his novice eyes to an alternative means of telling a story and changed his approach to writing (Bell-Villada, *García Márquez* 72). Kafka's kind of everyday *un*realism led eventually to García Márquez's brand thereof, which, in time, became the prime instance of what we now term "magical realism."

In the eons-long history of the supernatural in literature, then, magical realism, *le mot et la chose*, is a special and recent phenomenon. Being both realistic and magical, it breaks with former modes of unreality as well as with traditional realism itself. From scattered precursors, it has assumed shape as another way of fashioning fictions about ordinary human beings. Moreover, as several critics have pointed out, there is in magical realism a strong "post-colonial" aspect that has helped liberate the imagination of writers heralding from formerly "peripheral" cultural zones—Latin America, South Asia, Africa, and US African Americans.[3] Perhaps not accidentally, Gogol and Kafka were on the periphery of the Europe of their time, the former in Russia, the latter in Prague as part of a German–speaking Jewish minority at the margins of the late Austrian empire.

With *One Hundred Years of Solitude*, there arose a grand, dramatic, yet accessible touchstone for the representation of unreality in literature (if I may revise the subtitle of Erich Auerbach's *Mimesis*). In conclusion, magical realism, and what it stands for, are here to stay.

Notes

1. For more on this, see Irene Guenther's essay "Magic Realism in the Weimar Republic."

2. The formulaic phrases of fairy tale immediately place it in another, distant realm: "Once upon a time . . . ;" French, "Il était une fois . . . ;" Spanish, "Había una vez . . . " (In Spanish, moreover, there is a set phrase for oral legend that similarly sets things apart: "Cuenta la leyenda que . . . "). The English word "tale" further connotes a dimension "other" than that implied in "novel" or "story."
3. See, for instance, Slemon, 422 ff.

Works Cited

Auerbach, Erich. *Mimesis: The Representation of Reality in Western Literature*. Trans. Willard Trask. Princeton, NJ: Princeton UP, 1953.

Bell-Villada, Gene H. *Borges and His Fiction: A Guide to His Mind and Art*. 1981. Austin: U of Texas P, 2000.

_____. *García Márquez: The Man and His Work*. 1990. Chapel Hill: U of North Carolina P, 2010.

Borges, Jorge Luis. *Collected Fictions*. Trans. Andrew Hurley. New York: Viking, 1998.

Casanova, Pascale. *The World Republic of Letters*. Trans. M. B. DeBevoise. Cambridge, UK: Harvard UP, 2004.

Chanady, Amaryll Beatrice. *Magical Realism and the Fantastic*. New York: Garland, 1985.

Cheever, John. "The Enormous Radio." 1947. *Collected Stories and Other Writings*. New York: The Library of America, 2009. 41–51.

Corngold, Stanley. "Introduction." *The Metamorphosis*. By Franz Kafka. New York: Bantam Books, 1972. xi–xxii.

Cortázar, Julio. *End of the Game and Other Stories*. Trans. Paul Blackburn. New York: Pantheon Books, 1968.

Faris, Wendy B. "Scheherazade's Children: Magical Realism and Postmodern Fiction." *Magical Realism: Theory, History, Community*. Eds. Lois Parkinson Zamora & Wendy B. Faris. Durham, NC: Duke UP, 1995. 163–190.

_____ & Zamora, Lois Parkinson. Introduction by the editors. *Magical Realism: Theory, History, Community*. Eds. Lois Parkinson Zamora & Wendy B. Faris. Durham, NC: Duke UP, 1995. 1–14.

Forster, E. M. *Aspects of the Novel*. 1927. New York: Harcourt, Brace, 1954.

Foster Jr., John Burt. "Magical Realism, Compensatory Vision, and Felt History: Classical Realism Transformed in *The White Hotel*." *Magical Realism: Theory, History, Community*. Eds. Lois Parkinson Zamora & Wendy B. Faris. Durham, NC: Duke UP, 1995. 267–283.

Frye, Northrop. *Anatomy of Criticism*: *Four Essays*. 1957. New York: Atheneum, 1965.

Fuentes, Carlos. *Aura*. Trans. Lysander Kemp. New York: Farrar, Straus & Giroux 1965.

García, Cristina. *Dreaming in Cuban*. New York: Knopf, 1992.

García Márquez, Gabriel. *Collected Stories*. New York: Harper & Row, 1999.

_____. *Innocent Eréndira and Other Stories*. Trans. Gregory Rabassa. New York: Harper & Row, 1978.

_____. *One Hundred Years of Solitude*. 1970. Trans. Gregory Rabassa. New York: Avon, 1971.

Gogol, Nikolai. "The Nose." Trans. Richard Pevear & Larissa Volokhonsky. *The Collected Tales*. New York: Knopf, 1998. 294–318.

Guenther, Irene. "Magical Realism in the Weimar Republic." *Magical Realism: Theory, History, Community*. Eds. Lois Parkinson Zamora & Wendy B. Faris. Durham, NC: Duke UP, 1995. 33–73.

Hancock, Joel. "Gabriel García Márquez's 'Eréndira' and the Brothers Grimm." *Studies in Twentieth Century Literature* 1 (1978): 43–52.

James, Henry. *The Turn of the Screw*. 1908. Ed. David Bromwich. New York: Penguin, 2011.

Kafka, Franz. *Selected Stories*. Trans. Willa & Edwin Muir. New York: Random House, 1952.

Kennedy, William. *Ironweed*. New York: Viking, 1979.

Leal, Luis. "Magical Realism in Spanish-American Literature." Trans. Wendy B. Faris. *Magical Realism: Theory, History, Community*. Eds. Lois Parkinson Zamora & Wendy B. Faris. Durham, NC: Duke UP, 1995. 119–24.

Morrison, Toni. *Beloved*. New York: Knopf, 1987.

Quayson, Ato. "Fecundities of the Unexpected: Magical Realism, Narrative, and History." *The Novel: Vol. 1: History, Geography, and Culture*. Ed. Franco Moretti. Princeton: Princeton UP, 2006. 726–56.

Rulfo, Juan. *Pedro Páramo*. Trans. Margaret Sayers Peden. New York: Grove, 1990.

Rushdie, Salman. *Midnight's Children*. New York: Knopf, 1981.

Saramago, José. *Ensayo sobre la ceguera*. Trans. Basilio Losada. Madrid: Alfaguara, 1998.

Slemon, Stephen. "Magical Realism as Post-Colonial Discourse." *Magical Realism: Theory, History, Community*. Eds. Lois Parkinson Zamora & Wendy B. Faris. Durham, NC: Duke UP, 1995. 407–26.

Todorov, Tzvetan. *Introduction à la littérature fantastique*. Paris: Editions du Seuil, 1970.

CRITICAL READINGS

When Magical Realism Loses Its Spell: Revisiting Gabriel García Márquez's *Of Love and Other Demons*

Rudyard J. Alcocer

Not all magical realist texts are equally effective. What factors account for the differences? In the pages that follow, this essay argues that a fresh perspective on magical realism can be obtained through a critical discussion of a lesser-studied novel by that great exponent of Latin American magical realism, Gabriel García Márquez. The novel in question is *Of Love and Other Demons* (*Del amor y otros demonios,* 1994). Like all of García Márquez's novels, it is a provocative and well-crafted tale of pertinence to the most important issues facing Latin America, both in the present era as well as in the colonial times in which it is set. There have been, however, issues that have dogged the novel not only in terms of its critical reception as a discrete work, but also in comparison with its author's more heralded novels. To state the matter in coarse terms, the novel is flawed. Its flaws, however, are quite interesting and illuminating. In explaining this judgment on the novel, the essay will survey relevant discussions on magical realism as well as on *Of Love and Other Demons* itself. The argument here about the novel, ultimately, pertains to its problematic attempts to incorporate magical realist techniques in what is, on the whole, a different sort of novel. In exposing the novel's flaws, this essay seeks to shed useful light not only on the novel itself, but also on magical realism as a literary style.

We can begin with magical realism as a literary style. Since numerous studies have already traced the genealogy of the style (which predates García Márquez's literary production by several decades), the following historical survey will be brief, but nonetheless important in that, through it, it is possible to contextualize *Of Love and Other Demons*. These studies on magical realism have, for instance, linked the style to the art critic Franz Roh's comments, during the 1920s, on a new wave of German painting that, in his view, moved beyond the then-prevailing expressionist style. Roh, in fact, coined the term "magic realism." Although Roh's conceptualization of magic realism, in its insistence on the magical qualities evinced in otherwise realist paintings, differs somewhat from later permutations or understandings of the style, critics have, since the time of Roh, extended or expanded the concept to encompass, in general terms, artistic production that somehow blends realism with the patently unreal. With this expansion of the concept, critics have been able to identify magical realist qualities in literary works as geographically and temporally disparate as those by Franz Kafka, Toni Morrison, John Updike, Salman Rushdie, and—of course—several Latin American writers.

In a Latin American literary-historical context, the principal milestone in the conceptual evolution of the magical realist style lies in an essay by the Cuban novelist Alejo Carpentier, "De lo real maravilloso americano" (The marvelous real in the Americas), which served as the prologue to his 1949 novel, *The Kingdom of this World*. As Amaryll Chanady explains, it was Carpentier's essay that first territorialized or demarcated the notion of a marvelous reality as being proper to and synonymous with Latin America: Carpentier ascribed the marvelous real, which he considered:

> the appropriate style of the contemporary Latin American novelist, to the existence of a uniquely New World marvelous reality, characterized by an impressive geography, cultural and racial miscegenenation, early chronicles fictionalizing the continent, and a turbulent political situation. The existence of a marvelous reality legitimated and territorialized a literary marvelous, which Carpentier opposed to the literary artifice of European writers of fantastic and surrealist literature. (133)

In the essay, Carpentier writes upon his return home from numerous foreign lands (including a lengthy sojourn in France, where he became familiar with surrealism and other artistic movements then in vogue) that "the Latin American returns to what is his and begins to understand a lot of things"(127).[1] More to the point, he writes that:

> many forget, by readily dressing as magicians, that the marvelous begins being as such unequivocally when it rises from an unexpected alteration of reality (the miracle), by a privileged revelation of reality, of an illumination uncommonly or singularly favored by the unexpected richness of reality, by an amplification of the scales and categories of reality, perceived with particular intensity by virtue of an exaltation of the spiritual that leads it in a way to a "liminal state." To begin, the sensation of the marvelous presupposes a faith (131–32)[2]

Following Carpentier's essay, as well as landmark critical interventions by Ángel Flores and Luis Leal in 1955 and 1967 respectively, magical realism began to assume its current conceptualization: one that significantly departed from Carpentier's initial vision of a matter dependent on a sort of religious faith or purchase. As Leal clarifies in a 2000 autobiographical interview, the mechanisms of religion and *deus ex machina* are absent from the vision he articulates of magical realism: "You can't explain the way things happen. They just do. If you can explain it, then it's not magical realism. But this has nothing to do with God as divine intervention" (García 128).

What is, then, magical realism? Is it, in fact, subject to explanation? Definitions and explications abound. We can start with those offered by Lois Parkinson Zamora and Wendy B. Faris in their edited volume on the subject. In ways that echo Leal's comments, they assert that:

> In the magical realist texts under discussion in these essays, the supernatural is not a simple or obvious matter, but it *is* an ordinary matter, an everyday occurrence—admitted, accepted, and integrated into the rationality and materiality of literary realism. Magic is no longer quixotic madness, but normative and normalizing. It is a simple matter of the most complicated sort. (3)

As such, the magic or supernatural that occurs in fictional narratives—whether they be from Latin America or elsewhere, occupies an ontological status no different from other events or realities in those narratives. From the perspective of the fictional characters in the narratives in question, it seems just as natural and real for any given character to float away supernaturally as it would have been for the same character to sit down to drink a cup of coffee. Similarly, there is no change in terms of the author's language generally speaking or the tone he/she uses in describing such magical realist events. The events, as Leal explains, just seem to happen and, as such, have been held in contradistinction to fantastic literature or science fiction: these tend to underscore more explicitly the strangeness of supernatural events and/or to offer a plausible rational or scientific explanation for them.

Within a Latin American (and occasionally a postcolonial) historical and political context, instances of magical realism in fictional narrative have been identified as carrying a broader sociopolitical or culturally symbolic weight. As Zamora and Faris explain with regard to the essays in their edited volume, they:

> generally agree that magical realism is a mode suited to exploring—and transgressing—boundaries, whether the boundaries are ontological, political, geographical, or generic. Magical realism often facilitates the fusion, or coexistence, of possible worlds, spaces, systems that would be irreconcilable in other modes of fiction. (5–6)

An example of such transgressions might be found in what is often considered the magical realist novel *par excellence,* García Márquez's *One Hundred Years of Solitude* (1967). This novel conflates Latin American temporal periods, as is seen, for instance, through the unexplained appearance of the ruins of a Spanish galleon in the middle of the jungle. Such temporal conflations have led many critics to see this novel as emblematic of the whole of Latin American history. Although he makes it with reference to Carpentier's essay commented above, David Mikics' observation about temporal and cultural conflations and combinations is equally valid in the case of the Spanish galleon in *One Hundred Years of Solitude,* despite the different degrees to which the writings of Carpentier and García Márquez fall within the category of magical realism. According to Mikics, the work of Carpentier juxtaposes "the relics of European conquest with the practices of Amerindian and African cultures. We might infer that the uniqueness of the New World and its aesthetics derives from the dynamism of such cultural combinations" (373). In terms similar to the uniqueness (and, perhaps, coherence) that Mikics envisions for the New World, Shannin Schroeder identifies, specifically within the magical realist movement, a comparable framework for positing the commonality of the region: "As a tradition with roots in both [American] continents, magical realism supplies a vital link in our discussions of the literature of the Americas" (xiv).

Of Love and Other Demons is, of course, a Latin American novel deeply rooted in the region's history and culture. Furthermore, its author is often linked—sometimes inextricably so—with the magical realist style he helped popularize. That stated, the novel is not only, in broad terms, a Latin American novel, it is also very much a novel about the Caribbean region in particular: a region that, more than any other, has been associated with pronounced cultural flux, combination, and conflict since its earliest colonial days. Writers from the Caribbean (and García Márquez, given his upbringing in the coastal lowlands of Colombia, fits this description) have also employed magical realist techniques. One of the principal precursors to magical realism, Carpentier, after all, was Cuban, and his famous essay on marvelous realism appeared as prologue to a novel about Haiti. Other Caribbean writers, including Wilson Harris, Daína Chaviano, Nalo Hopkinson, and Kevin Baldeosingh, are often grouped together with the magical realists. The reasons for this recall the transgressive and culturally meaningful qualities often found in magical realism. As Mikics explains, "The lucid fantasia that the magical realist mode offers is not an aesthete's intoxicant: magical realism appeals to Caribbean writers because it addresses the weight of historical memory that survives in the day-to-day life of the West Indies" (373). Interestingly, then, magical realism is not only a literary style, but also what could be described as a cultural or symbolic movement that purports to challenge and disrupt established boundaries of many varieties. Although it is a literary style with a traceable history and an identifiable peak moment of popularity and artistic accomplishment (i.e., *One Hundred Years of Solitude*), it has nevertheless been seen as capable of conflating and transcending historical epochs in general. It has also been seen as an effective literary tool for articulating social issues within a region, giving that region coherence (cultural, historical, etc.) in the process. In its finest examples, there is no doubt that magical realist texts have carried out these tasks effectively. However, what of other examples of the style? We can now turn directly to *Of Love and Other Demons*.

Given the copious commentaries and descriptions of the novel, only a brief description the storyline is needed.[3] In eighteenth-century Colombia (then called La Nueva Granada), in the important Caribbean port city of Cartagena de Indias, a girl from an aristocratic family in decline is bitten in the ankle by a rabid dog. The girl, Sierva María, has largely been ignored by her loveless parents during her short life; consequently, she has sought (and found) refuge and community among the Black slaves who inhabit the family compound. She has learned African languages and cultural practices; has given herself a new, Africanized name ("María Mandinga"); and is, at most, a specter as far as her parents are concerned. When the father, the second Marquis de Casualdero, Don Ygnacio de Alfaro y Dueñas, learns of the dog bite, he takes it upon himself to cure his daughter, finding in the process a new mission in life. His quest takes him to Abrenuncio, a skilled doctor and man of letters who fled Europe on account of his Judaic heritage and who is held in suspicion by the powerful religious authorities in Cartagena. Despite Abrenuncio's prescription of rest and joy to combat Sierva María's dog bite (he makes it clear to the marquis that the girl may, after all, not have contracted rabies), the marquis is summoned by the bishop. The latter has heard tales of his dog-bitten and highly eccentric daughter, and feels that the Church's intervention is in order. The remainder of the story is a downward spiral, detailing the Church's effort to exorcise Sierva María's "demons." This effort involves a thirty-six-year-old Jesuit, Cayetano Delaura, who has been appointed by the bishop to save the girl's soul, even if—in their estimation, at least—her physical health is beyond salvation. Delaura's relationship with the girl, to a significant extent, constitutes the "love" portion of the novel, particularly in its later segments: Delaura becomes romantically attracted to the girl and she, eventually, to him. In the end, and despite no signs of rabies in Sierva María, she succumbs mortally to the Church's exorcistic methods, while Delaura is banished to a leper colony. In the novel's preface, we had already learned that Sierva María's hair had grown, *post mortem,* to an astonishing length (twenty-two meters), even though the girl's famously long hair had been shaved off just prior to her death.

While *Of Love and Other Demons* is plainly a text about the Caribbean colonial period and, more broadly, about the Spanish American colonial period, the question remains as to whether or not (or to what extent) it is a magical realist text. One scholar, Fernando Reati, argues that the novel, in fact, distances itself from its author's previous magical realist tendencies:

> In his most recent novel . . . García Márquez undertakes a critical revision of the magical realist vision of Latin America that characterizes his work in earlier years. Aware that the magical realism of the sixties and seventies has become a caricature of the continent, and that some of its more recent manifestations—certain novels by Isabel Allende and Laura Esquivel, for example—contribute to the fossilization of a stereotyped image and *for export* of the continent, the author labors now to dismantle what Adriana Bergero terms the "holiday or tourist aesthetic of Latin America" practiced by some proponents of magical realism. (91)[4]

For Reati, the novel's emphasis on hybrid states, whether these involve ethnic and religious mixture, or the line between mental sanity and insanity, form part of "a multicultural vision on the part of the author, in large measure different from the continental, modernist project of the *Boom,* and certainly running counter to the exotic representations of the *Boom* for export in the wake of García Márquez."[5] Ilan Stavans, in his assessment of magical realism (although without specific reference to *Of Love and Other Demons*), concurs with Reati's by identifying in the literary style "an artistic vision that exoticized the Americas . . ." ("On García Márquez" 3).

There has not been, however, a scholarly consensus as to whether or not *Of Love and Other Demons* is indeed a magical realist novel. While Reati finds, in the novel, a distancing on the part of García Márquez from the literary style he made famous worldwide, other scholars argue that the novel does contain magical realist elements. With reference, for example, to the great length of hair on Sierva María's corpse, the renowned García Márquez scholar, Gene H. Bell-Villada, observes that "the very notion of a human corpse growing gorgeous hair to a length of sixty-six feet seems the stuff of legend and even fairy tale rather than objective chronicle. (One physician informed [him] that it is 'medically impossible')" (254). Certainly, there have been no documented instances of such a phenomenon; as such, even a casual observer might conclude that the novel contains at least some elements that transgress, or at least challenge, the norms of everyday reality. For Bell-Villada, there is no question that the novel is, albeit perhaps not to the extent of some of García Márquez's earlier novels, a work of magical realism: "A supernatural atmosphere permeates much of *Of Love and Other Demons*. To a limited degree, the book is a return to the García Márquez who made 'magic realism' a celebrated byword" (256). Similarly, shortly after the novel was published, a *New York Times* reviewer asserted that "García Márquez's luminous novel demonstrates that one of the masters of the form is still working at the height of his powers" (Katukani C1+). Roy Arthur Swanson, meanwhile, lauds the reception given to *Of Love and Other Demons*, and points to a different critic's implied magical realist assessment of the novel: "Critics and reviewers continued their praise of [García Márquez's] talent and creative imagination upon the appearance of his short novel *Of Love and Other Demons* . . . The novel, as R. Z. Sheppard notes, extends the gallery of Maconderos and maintains 'the daring and irresistible coupling of history and imagination'" (9). By linking *Of Love and Other Demons* to the inhabitants of the fictional town of Macondo in the earlier *One Hundred Years of Solitude,* not to mention the asserted commonality in the two novels' treatment of history and imagination, the magical realist bond between the novels would seem to be solidified, a bond that runs counter to Reati's reading. The question remains: is *Of Love and Other Demons* a magical realist novel? This tension regarding the magical realism of the novel could speak to the novel's complexity and its interpretive richness. It could also, however, suggest a problem.

Symptoms of this problem can be located in the novel's uneven critical reception. For his part, Bell-Villada provides a view of *Of Love and Other Demons* in which he balances his admiration for the novel with theories of why it has not been as successful as other García Márquez novels. He writes, for example, that the novel pushes "the customary boundaries of romantic experience, plumbing hitherto unknown emotional depths and coming up with some strange surprises along the way" (237). Bell-Villada does not stop there in his praise of the novel: he adds that the novel is "populated by a wide array of vivid, fully drawn, memorable characters who stand out as much as do the two lovers" (239), and that Delaura's "ardent and unconsummated passion stands among literature's great depictions of genuine, obsessive, all-giving yet tragically illicit love" (244). I agree with much of this assessment. Abrenuncio, for instance, is without question a compelling character who, arguably, may stand out *more* than the two lovers: he is a witty erudite, capable of intervening in Sierva María's life without falling under the clutches of the Church, which—throughout the novel—has him in its crosshairs.

This reader would hesitate, however, to elevate *Of Love and Other Demons* anywhere near the rank of a world literature masterpiece. Indeed, it may not even rate highly within García Márquez's own oeuvre. Bell-Villada, to his credit, does not hesitate to highlight some of the tepid critical and popular response given to the novel:

> Unlike most of García Márquez's previous major works, *Of Love and Other Demons* drew relatively little fanfare when it first appeared. While the initial printing of 100,000 copies sold out within weeks and the reviews were, as expected, glowing, there was precious little of

the excitement that had accompanied *The Autumn of the Patriarch* or *Love in the Time of Cholera*. One possible reason was simple public fatigue. His Nobel Prize was in the past; and the attentions lavished on the author and on his various literary and political activities had played themselves out. (237–38)

There is undoubtedly some truth in the reasons Bell-Villada adduces for the lackluster response to *Of Love and Other Demons*: times change, societies change, and even the best artists (García Márquez being an example) run the risk of over-exposure to the public. Meanwhile, in his examination of thematic matters *internal* to the novel, Bell-Villada adds that the novel's interests in Black slavery, Africa-derived religious practices, and the Catholic Church during the colonial period are "recondite" topics and do not constitute "matters that most book critics—foreign, non-Hispanic ones in particular—might feel able to discuss comfortably or authoritatively" (238). Once again, although this reader (and most certainly Bell-Villada) find the novel's thematic elements markedly engrossing and timely to the degree that *Of Love and Other Demons* could be considered a very useful introduction to several crucial issues underpinning Spanish American society, there may very well be truth in Bell-Villada's theory.

Other critics have been less diplomatic in their evaluation of García Márquez's novel. Writing soon after the novel appeared, Lon Pearson issued what is, on the whole, a favorable review, albeit with some caveats: contrary to Bell-Villada, for instance, he opines that the novel "is lacking in depth of character development" (180) and later laments that "some may feel that the genius who produced his previous masterpieces is just not present in this volume" (181). With likely reference to García Márquez's later works (which include *Of Love and Other Demons*), Stavans signals other critics who "suggest that [García Márquez's] literary output is repetitive, his dialog stiff, and the spontaneity in his characters nonexistent" ("On Gabriel García Márquez" 5-6). Elsewhere, and with explicit reference to *Of Love and Other Demons,* Stavans argues that "while García Márquez's story is engaging and well-crafted, it ultimately becomes a showcase of his recent excesses: an overly compressed style that creates a sense of suffocation in the reader, a plot that seems flat, and a lack of spontaneity in the prose that ends up undermining any kind of suspense" ("The Master of Aracataca" 61).

Quite some words. In this reader's view, all the aforementioned assessments of the novel, whether favorable or unfavorable, contain kernels of truth. On the one hand, *Of Love and Other Demons* is a masterful and philosophically nuanced denunciation of class distinctions, race relations, and the excesses of the Church and its Inquisition during the colonial period (among other topics), all handled with its author's customary sharpness of vision and gift for dialog. On the other hand, for a variety of possible reasons, this novel has not achieved the status of García Márquez's other works, despite seemingly possessing all the necessary ingredients. Why is this so?

In some crucial respects, the novel has a problematic and unclear relationship with the magical realist style. A symptom of this relationship is the confusion outlined above as regards whether or not the novel is in fact a magical realist work. If we recall Leal's remarks about how magical realism is intuited in texts of the genre as opposed to being a matter that can be explained rationally or precisely, then we can better understand the flaw in *Of Love and Other Demons*: perhaps narratives need to be or not be magical realist; in other words, perhaps there should be no intuition involved in making that first, preliminary determination about a novel's style. The problem with *Of Love and Other Demons* is that it teeters along that distinction: some critics trace a clear stylistic continuity between the novel and its antecedents by the same author. Meanwhile, for other scholars (Reati, for instance), the novel is not only *not* magical realist, it instead distances itself from the style in foregrounding very *real* issues of cultural mixture, diversity, and marginalization in Latin America in general and the Caribbean region in particular, as opposed to an exoticizing and homogenizing view of these regions. Furthermore, in his discussion of the magical realist elements in the novel, Bell-Villada offers pointed—and, in this reader's opinion, accurate—qualifications. The narrative moment in question is a scene toward the end involving a confrontation between Delaura and Sierva María in which the former entreats the girl to go see her father. She refuses and a physical struggle ensues. At this point, "Delaura witnessed the fearful spectacle of one truly possessed. Sierva María's hair coiled with a life of its own, like the serpents of Medusa, and green spittle and a string of obscenities in idolatrous languages poured from her mouth" (118).[6] While "idolatrous languages" probably refers to Sierva María's facility with multiple African tongues, the behavior of her hair seems nothing short of supernatural (as does, one might add, its spectacular growth beginning at the moment of her death). Bell-Villada astutely issues a non-magical realist explanation for the phenomenon: "Even here, however, the occurrence is qualified by its reportedly being seen through the eyes of Cayetano [Delaura]" (256). In addition to this example, there are others in the novel that suggest (and usually only *suggest*) supernatural forces, namely Abrenuncio's hundred-year-old horse (perhaps there is no coincidence with this number), as well as—generally speaking—the physical strength and demonic powers attributed to Sierva María by the nuns in the convents, an attribution readily explained by the Manichean religious filter through which the nuns experience the world.

However, not all of the unusual events in the novel merely suggest the possibility of the supernatural. A particularly striking example of an inexplicable, magical realist occurrence in the novel involves the marquis' first wife, who was killed by a lightning bolt in an otherwise calm, cloudless day. As if this were not a strange enough event, on his return home from the funeral, the marquis notices small bits of paper falling from a tree. Choosing one at random, he opens it and reads: "That lightning bolt was mine" (38).[7] There is no rational, realist explanation for this event, and I do not see how one could argue that it is colored by the marquis' perspective; it is, and unquestionably so, an example of magical realism: one of the very few in the novel.

Before making final observations on the novel, it is worth considering some critical remarks leveled against recent magical realist works by the novelist and scholar Tabish Khair. Without specific reference to any novel or novelist, he writes that magical realism runs "the risk of positing an implicit or explicit sameness" (134). This assertion, in many ways, recalls Reati's criticism of magical realism as having become a holiday or tourist literary style designed for export, that is, one that advances a vision of Latin America characterized by a false and naïve homogeneity or sameness. Khair adds that, recently, magical realism's more general, homogenizing tendencies reflect poorly on the style as concerns its artistic integrity: "Without being too polemical, one can argue that some of what is considered magical realism today distils a whiff of laziness" (134). This leads us to what may be, for present purposes, the most relevant portion of Khair's observations:

> It is easy to defend . . . examples of authoritative laziness by thumping the drums of anti-realism, non-European perspectives and the "fantastic." But the fact remains that the best of magical realism (such as Marquez [sic] or, for that matter, Rushdie in *Midnight's Children*) used to create a world that—as is the case with realistic narratives—established, and operated according to, its own internal coherence. (134)

Although Khair does not discuss García Márquez in the detail necessary to distinguish between novels by the writer that, in his view, belong or do not belong to the category, "the best of magical realism," his notion of a world with its own internal coherence is a useful one.

While ascertaining the degree to which a narrative successfully develops a world with its own internal coherence is necessarily a highly subjective process, it can still be argued that the ambiguities surrounding the magical realist status of *Of Love and Other Demons* renders it a world without an "internal coherence." On the one hand, by advancing a more nuanced vision of Caribbean socio-cultural diversity, the novel may indeed break with the conventional, homogenizing tendencies of the magical realist style its author helped popularize. On the other hand, the novel contains some examples of what most critics would consider magical realist events. Ultimately, *Of Love and Other Demons* suggests an author attempting—but perhaps not fully committed—to moving past his previous literary production; an author, moreover, attempting to appeal to two kinds of audience. To express the matter in terms of Khair's remarks, the internally coherent "world" of the novel is one that effectively exposes the many contradictions or oppositions of Spanish American colonial society; the novel's magical realist moments, in contrast, seem out of place and unnecessary. The reader knows, for example, that Sierva María is neither crazy nor possessed (nor, for that matter, infected with rabies): she is a regular girl (i.e., not a superhuman) who—on account of an unusual upbringing—has been exposed to ideas and cultural practices at odds with the Church's authority. This general theme is a compelling one, but, unfortunately, one that is distorted by the narrative's misplaced magical realist episodes. The conclusion that can be drawn from the interesting tensions surrounding the magical realism of García Márquez's novel is that, for a narrative of this genre to be successful (in terms of Khair's internal coherence but also, perhaps, in terms of critical reception and sales), it has to be fully committed to the genre, that is, to the development of an internally coherent magical realist world. Similarly, an effective magical realist text probably needs a critical mass of magical realist occurrences for the illusion of internal coherence to be attained. The case of *Of Love and Other Demons* may suggest that even in a shorter novel, more than just a couple of magical realist events are necessary to keep these events from seeming random and unnecessary.

Notes

1. "Vuelve el latinoamericano a lo suyo y empieza a entender muchas cosas" (127). Citation taken from *Tientos y diferencias*. Translations are my own unless otherwise indicated.

2. "Pero es que muchos se olvidan, con disfrazarse de magos a poco costo, que lo real maravilloso comienza a serlo de manera inequívoca cuando surge de una inesperada alteración de la realidad, de una iluminación inhabitual o singularmente favorecedora de las inadvertidas riquezas de la realidad, de una ampliación de las escalas y categorías de la realidad, percibidas con particular intensidad en virtud de una exaltación del espíritu que lo conduce a un modo

de 'estado limite.' Para empezar, la sensación de lo maravilloso presupone una fe" (*Tientos y diferencias,* 131–32).

3. For readers desiring a more detailed overview of the novel, I refer them to Gene H. Bell-Villada's very useful description and commentaries in the second edition of his *García Márquez: The Man and His Work* (2010). The first edition predates the publication of *Of Love and Other Demons.*

4. "En su más reciente novela, *Del amor y otros demonios* (1994), Gabriel García Márquez lleva a cabo una revisión crítica de la visión realista mágica de América Latina que lo caracterizara en textos de años anteriores. Consciente al parecer de que el realismo mágico de los años 60 y 70 ha terminado por convertirse en una caricatura del continente, y de que algunos de sus productores más recientes—ciertas novelas de Isabel Allende y de Laura Esquivel, por ejemplo—contribuyen a fosilizar una imagen estereotípica y *for export* del continente, el autor colabora ahora en desmontar lo que Adriana Bergero denomina la 'estética vacacional o turística de América Latina' que practican algunos cultores del realismo mágico" (Reati's reference is to an unpublished essay by Bergero presented at the 1995 LASA convention).

5. "la *contaminación* de lo europeo por lo africano (y, en menor medida, por otras formas de marginación como el judaísmo y la locura) forma parte de una visión multicultural y de una afirmación de la identidad costeña por parte del autor, en gran medida diferentes al proyecto modernista continental del *Boom,* y ciertamente contrarias a las representaciones exóticas del *Boom* de exportación post-García Márquez" (94).

6. "Entonces Delaura asistió al espectáculo pavoroso de una verdadera energúmena. La cabellera de Sierva María se encrespó con vida propia como las serpientes de la Medusa, y de la boca salió una baba verde y un sartal de improperios en lenguas de idólatras" (136).

7. "Ese rayo era mío" (49).

Works Cited

Bell-Villada, Gene. *García Márquez: The Man and His Work.* 2nd edition. Chapel Hill: of North Carolina P, 2010.

Carpentier, Alejo. *Tientos y diferencias: ensayos.* Mexico City: UNAM, 1964.

Chanady, Amaryll. "The Territorialization of the Imaginary in Latin America: Self-Affirmation and Resistance to Metropolitan

Paradigms." *Magical Realism: Theory, History, Community.* Eds. Lois Parkinson Zamora & Wendy B. Faris. Durham, NC: Duke UP, 1995. 125–44.

García, Mario T. *Luis Leal: An Auto/Biography.* Austin: U of Texas P, 2000.

García Márquez, Gabriel. *Del amor y otros demonios.* Barcelona: Random House Mondadori, 2006.

_____. *Of Love and Other Demons.* Trans. Edith Grossman. New York: Alfred A. Knopf, 1995.

Katukani, Michiko. "Magical Realism from 2 Cultures." *New York Times.* 2 Jun. 1995, natl. ed: C1+.

Khair, Tabish. *Gothic, Postcolonialism and Otherness: Ghosts from Elsewhere.* New York: Palgrave Macmillan 2009.

Mikics, David. "Derek Walcott and Alejo Carpentier: Nature, History, and the Caribbean Writer." *Magical Realism: Theory, History, Community.* Eds. Lois Parkinson Zamora & Wendy B. Faris. Durham, NC: Duke UP, 1995. 370–404.

Pearson, Lon. "*Del amor y otros demonios* by Gabriel García Márquez: Review." *Chasqui* 23.2 (Nov. 1994): 180–82.

Reati, Fernando. "Andes españoles, costa africana: Multiculturalismo e identidad en *Del amor y otros demonios* de García Márquez." *Proceedings of 1998 Jornadas Andinas de Literatura Latinoamericana (JALLA).* Quito, Ecuador: Universidad Andina Simón Bolívar, 1998. 91–96.

Schroeder, Shannin. *Rediscovering Magical Realism in the Americas.* Westport, CT: Praeger, 2004.

Stavans, Ilan. "On Gabriel García Márquez." *Critical Insights: Gabriel García Márquez.* Ed. Ilan Stavans. Hackensack, NJ: Salem Press, 2010. 3–6.

_____. "The Master of Aracataca." In *Critical Insights: Gabriel García Márquez.* Ed. Ilan Stavans. Hackensack, NJ: Salem Press, 2010. 34–63.

Swanson, Roy Arthur. "Biography of Gabriel García Márquez." *Critical Insights: Gabriel García Márquez.* Ed. Ilan Stavans. Hackensack, NJ: Salem Press, 2010. 7–11.

Zamora, Lois Parkinson, & Wendy B. Faris. "Introduction: Daiquiri Birds and Flaubertian Parrot(ie)s." *Magical Realism: Theory, History,*

Community. Eds. Lois Parkinson Zamora & Wendy B. Faris. Durham, NC: Duke UP, 1995. 1–14.

The Plague of Modernity: Macondo, Inc. and the Branding of "Magical" Latin America

Martín Camps

"Colombia, realismo mágico" (Colombia, Magical Realism) is the new slogan of a Colombian campaign to attract tourists. It has replaced the old slogan "Colombia: El riesgo es que te quieras quedar" ("Colombia: The Risk Is That You May Want To Stay"), in effect from 2006 to 2012, which played with the idea of "risk" as a result of the violence created by terrorist groups and drug trafficking. It is safe to assume that this is the first time that a narrative style or definition of a literary movement has been used as a slogan for a tourism campaign. Magical realism has become a sort of registered trademark, defining the countries south of the Rio Grande. It brands them as places of magic and harsh realities, of beautiful landscapes and beaches, and cheap prices. The Colombian slogan even had the endorsement of Gabriel García Márquez. This article examines how magical realism has become an easy currency to describe and brand Latin America in what has also been known as *macondismo*. The essay will also study *One Hundred Years of Solitude*, the masterpiece of this style, from the perspective of the "pest of modernization." The novel provides a road map of the desire for modernization in Latin America, a desire to find a route to connect to and receive the "wonders" from the outside world, which ultimately brought despair and destruction to Macondo. The essay will explore how magical realism is used to package an *ad intra* stereotype, or product, to be sold to foreigners.

By drawing from research conducted by geographer Harm de Blij, it is possible to understand global tourism in the context of the division of the world into different realms. De Blij refers to the "global core" as a place protected by the "great wall" of the Western world: "Undoubtedly the most portentous manifestation of this effort is the demarcation of the border between Mexico and the United States" (16). Following de Blij's nomenclature, the global core protects "locals" (rurals) and "globals" (urbans), which are the citizens benefiting from global economical disparities from the "mobals." Outside of the barricades, the "mobals," or "undocumented aliens," try to sneak in to find a way to improve their lives. The mobals are a major force of twelve million, concentrated in the United States. De Blij recognizes that current demographics show the demand for cheap labor in industrialized countries. Using de Blij's terminology, tourism is generally performed by the "globals" because "mobals" transfer for economic reasons, leaving their own countries, which in turn become "destinations" for others. Hence, contemporary travel responds to a global design of haves and have-nots.

Sandro Mezzadra and Brett Neilson, in their book *Border as Method or the Multiplication of Labor*, study the broad picture of world borders not as objects, but from an epistemological angle, offering productive perspectives of inclusion and exclusion that transform into systems of domination and exploitation. For Mezzadra and Neilson, "Borders play a key role in the production of the heterogeneous time and space of contemporary global and postcolonial capitalism" (10). Borders are central to the production of time and space, and they help to configure the world and global capitalism. Crossing borders is the purpose of travel, which allows for movement outside the barricades of the global core and permits rich, industrialized citizens of the world to travel to the pauperized countries that play the exotic game. Reading magical realism as a tourism strategy sheds light on the process of identity commercialization on the world stage, and here, macondismo comes into play as an "ideology through which to inscribe local soundscapes (and García Márquez's writings) into cosmopolitan imaginations" (Ochoa 209). Or in the definition by Brunner, "it means interpreting Latin America through literature or, more exactly, as a product of the narratives that we tell to ourselves, in order to mark out our identity" (14). Brunner warns about confusing those narratives with our national realities and also about perpetuating the discussion of the power of Nature.

The ideology of macondismo is the oversimplification of identity conveyed by magical realism; a place of perpetual rain showers, of strange beliefs that thwart the arrival of progress. Since Humboldt, "a narrative of Latin America was created in which the subcontinent is primarily nature while Europe is culture" (Von Der Walde 225). Macondismo explains the geopolitical divisions and becomes a "seal of approval," a "catchword" for the foreigner's gaze. Magical realism has launched the careers of writers, such as the Chilean Isabel Allende and the Mexican Laura Esquivel, whose literature may continue to brand Latin America as a magical place. Even movements that tried to distance themselves from magical realism, such as the McOndo group (led by the Chilean Alberto Fuguet and the Bolivian Edmundo Paz Soldán) with the "McDonaldization of Latin America" implied in the title of their anthology, understood the "tactical realism" of stamping Latin America as a place of fantastical absurdities. However, from a distance, it seems that they were also claiming the relevance of their own group aesthetics, and, as sons of their times, they accepted neoliberalism and chanted the influence of television, MTV, and popular culture (mostly American). A similar group strategy is seen by the members of the "Crack generation" in Mexico (Jorge Volpi, Ignacio Padilla, and others), which began as a market scheme by Sandro Cohen. Recently, the success of Roberto Bolaño, who, in this reader's view, was ultimately the only author able to distance himself irreversibly from "magical realism" and the Boom, has been criticized for being a "market strategy" and a bloated literary fashion. In an essay appearing in the journal *Comparative Literature*, Sarah Pollack argues that Bolaño "foments a (pre) conception of alterity that satisfies the fantasies and collective imagination of U.S. cultural consumers" (347). Magical realism has proliferated in the world as a literary genre and has expanded to other literary realms (Hart 2003). A quick reading of the almost four hundred articles titles appearing in the Modern Languages Bibliography in English shows the presence of the style in African, French, and English Literatures (Salman Rushdie, Toni Morrison). Magical realism is now a global phenomenon, a genre with identifiable devices that are easily replicated in different contexts to translate what is foreign to

American or European audiences. It has become a vector to translate strangeness or complex contradictory identities.

Magical Realism as Orality of a Medieval Mindset

In defining magical realism in *One Hundred Years of Solitude*, Stephen Hart identifies a difference in the acceptance of the supernatural in economic terms between First and Third World: "A leitmotif of the novel is the sense in which occurrences seen as supernatural in the First World . . . are presented as natural from a Third World perspective" (116). Perhaps this division in economic terms provides a distinction in point of views of the magical in the novel, but also perpetuates a picture of stereotypical underdevelopment in Latin America, where the First World discards the supernatural as sorcery or superstition and the Third World sees technological advancements as paranormal. This reinforces the idea of the "magical" as an ancient practice that influences the world with the help of rituals and ceremonies that favor the occult or preternatural.

In tracing a definition of magical realism, we can say that hyperbole is a simple way to define it in the classroom. This device can also be found in a medieval mindset that believed in fabulous fairy tales. Thus, historian Barbara W. Tuchman writes: "The average layman acquired knowledge mainly by ear, through public sermons, mystery plays, and recital of narrative poems, ballads, and tales" (58). In her study, Tuchman examines Ingelram de Coucy, the French nobleman who plays a pivotal role in the fourteenth century. Tuchman sheds light on the importance of orality in this epoch. Walter Ong'g *Orality and Literacy* (1982) has also explained the mechanisms of oral tradition, such as repetition as a technique for the speaker to keep the audience's attention. Indeed, medieval laymen depended on oral, face-to-face conversation, as reading was a scholastic practice, rare among the masses in those centuries. In this context, García Márquez has stated that his stories came from the tales his grandmother would tell him, which is noticeable in *One Hundred Years*. We can see an oral technology taking shape in the story, an exaggeration that is specific to stories told out loud, to embellish an anecdote (a sort of science fiction of the underprivileged). The listener accepts this overstatement as a mechanism of face-to-face conversation where there is not a need to corroborate or formalize a fact with the act of writing. Magical realism is a device for communities relying on oral tradition, a stratagem that vanished when stories began to be transferred to paper.

Franz Roh is often credited with being the first to describe "magical realism" in 1925. He was referring to post-expressionist painting in an article that was translated into Spanish in 1927 and published in the influential *Revista de Occidente*. Roh writes that expressionism had an exaggerated preference for the fantastic, the exotic: "If a painter wanted to sing the exuberance of southern provinces in a landscape, he came up with the tropics of an extraterrestrial world where men of our race burned like piles of paper under dry flames of color" (Zamora & Faris 17). He opposes the imitation of nineteenth-century painting (trampled by the imitative marvels of film and photography) as "not like copies of nature but like another creation" (Zamora & Faris 23). Other critics trace the term "magischer Realist" to Novalis (Friederich Freiherr von Hardenberg) and German idealism, but Novalis never developed the idea and described instead the term "magical idealism" (Warnes 487). In distinguishing "magic" from "mystic," Roh states: "the mystery does not descend to the represented world, but rather hides and palpitates behind it" (Zamora & Faris 16). That idea is almost paraphrased in the first page of *One Hundred Years*, when Melquíades explains the properties of the magnet: "Things have a life of their own . . . it's simply a matter of waking up their souls" (García Márquez 2). Indeed, as Erik Camayd-Freixas has pointed out, Magical Realism "is rooted, both historically and aesthetically, in the primitivism of contemporary art that has pervaded since the avant-garde certain tendencies in modern painting" (415). But, as it will become evident in the next section, the opposition of civilization and barbarism is a permanent struggle on the continent. In fact, one of the main themes of *One Hundred Years* is to modernize the primitivism of Macondo, or in a broader sense, Latin America.

The Pest of Modernization After a Century of Solitude

One Hundred Years is a fable about a desire to dominate the immeasurable landscape of Latin America by five generations of the same family over the span of a century. García Márquez accomplishes the regionalist novel's objective, appeasing nature (although its characters are often devoured by it), and achieves this with the "magical" recreation of the original myth of creation. In this reading, José Arcadio Buendía's desire for modernity is evident and his imagination moves him beyond the miracles and magic to use a magnet, in order to find treasures, and a magnifying glass as a weapon. Buendía's desire is to connect the god-forsaken town of Macondo with the world, to cross the swamps and rivers, in order to find a route to establish modes of communication with the world. Even sending a letter was a big risk to undertake in such a rough terrain.

The gypsies, with the use of magic tricks and alchemy, bring "civilization" and entice José Arcadio with the marvels of the world. José Arcadio, knowing that wonderful things are happening out there in the world, tells his wife: "Right there across the river there are all kinds of magical instruments while we keep on living like donkeys" (García Márquez 7). This addresses how far Macondo was from modernization. Melquíades becomes the agent of modernization who alters the bucolic life of Macondo. Macondo's destiny is changed once José Arcadio decides "to open a way that would put Macondo in contact with the great inventions" (García Márquez 8) and to put an end to their isolation, to their destiny of being eaten by the infinite swamps and sierras. But his effort is thwarted when the vegetation grows back again, almost in front of their eyes. José Arcadio is convinced that the possibility of uniting Macondo with the world is impossible because it is surrounded by water. The only option is to travel to escape the reality of their isolation: "We're going to rot our lives away here without receiving the benefits of science" (García Márquez 10). But Úrsula convinces him to stay and take care of his children.

One Hundred Years is a fable of the struggles of Latin America to gain access to the banquet of civilization. José Arcadio dreams one night of a noisy city made of mirrors; this place was Macondo. In what could be seen as a futuristic prophecy of contemporary climate change, José Arcadio states: "Macondo would no longer be a burning place, where the hinges and door knockers twisted with the heat, but would be changed into a wintry city" (García Márquez 19). After Melquíades' death, the new gypsies "had shown very quickly that they were not heralds of progress but purveyors of amusement" (García Márquez 23). And it is Úrsula who finds the route that her husband could not find when she goes in pursuit of her son José Arcadio, who ran away following a girl "where there were towns that received mail every month" (García Márquez 28). Úrsula, the main female character, is the one that finally brings modernization to Macondo. She is the voice of reason and reality and keeps her feet on the ground in the world of illusions of her husband. If José Arcadio is the magic, she is the realism in this dichotomy. She is the matriarch and dispenser of realities, the holder of house logic. Úrsula also brings new people to Macondo, who are attracted by the high quality of its soil. This leads to the first stage of Macondo's modernization, with the eventual arrival of new inventions, such as the daguerreotype. Melquíades also predicts that Macondo will be a luminous city with big houses made of crystal, but with no trace "of the race of the Buendía" (40). But along with inventions, Macondo also receives politicians, such as Don Apolinar Moscote. Macondo is now in the radar of intense Colombian politics. Another arrival is Pietro Crespi, who takes the place of Melquíades in bringing new inventions to the town, but without the same esoteric nature.

After the second death of Melquíades, new mechanical toys begin to arrive: "Mechanical ballerinas, music boxes, . . . the rich and startling mechanical fauna" (García Márquez 56). José Arcadio speculates that time is also a mechanism, but a broken machinery because every day is the same. José Arcadio, attacked by the "pest of time," breaks all the alchemist machines, the daguerreotype cabinet, and the workshop. He is left tied to a tree, spitting foam. After this, the priest, Nicanor Reyna, arrives as a representative of the Church. He is seen with distrust, as another pest. The priest also shows an affinity for the supernatural by levitating after drinking a cup of chocolate.

The war between the liberals and conservatives momentarily halts Macondo's process of modernization. Progress had irremediably brought politics and a corrupt democracy that releases the war of a thousand days. War is a setback for transformation, but also for the consolidation of powers and the conservative project. Another benchmark in the process of Macondo's renewal is the arrival of the telegraph, which would also bring miscommunications: the fame of Aureliano Buendía grows because of the tardiness of a telegram, one that erroneously announces his death; another one mentions the growth of his rebellion, thus starting his ubiquitous legend.

But the height of Macondo's progress would come with Aureliano Segundo, when "His mares would bear triplets, his hens laid twice a day, and his hogs fattened with such speed that no one could explain such disorderly fecundity except through the use of black magic" (García Márquez 140). This fecundity was attributed to the influence of Petra Cotes who had the virtue of "exasperating nature" (García Márquez 140). This proliferation of wealth is as intense as the other pests that consumed Macondo. The extravagance reaches excessive proportions when Aureliano Segundo uses money as tapestry in his house. This juncture could be read as a moment of decadence in Macondo, a parable of the overexploitation of nature. The original Macondo disappears and constructions of brick and cement floors take its place. His twin brother, José Arcadio Segundo, in another irrational attempt of their bloodline, works "breaking stones, digging canals, clearing away rapids, and even harnessing waterfalls" (García Márquez 143).

Undoubtedly, a key moment in the Macondian modernity enterprise is the arrival of Aureliano Triste, who brings an industry to make ice and decides to bring the train: "not only for the modernization of his business but to link the town with the rest of the world" (García Márquez 162). This is the first and only time that the word "modernization" is mentioned in the novel. The arrival of the train signifies the beginning of the era of transportation and the possibility of rapid travel. It is significant that the novel does not talk about Macondians going abroad or bringing back discoveries by themselves; instead, it is always others who bring civilization. The arrival of the train, for example, worries the people in town, who hear something "like a kitchen dragging a village behind it" (García Márquez 163). At the same time, the invention carries with it the freight cars that are full of problems and will be related to the biggest tragedy in Macondo: "The innocent yellow train that was to bring so many ambiguities and certainties, so many pleasant and unpleasant moments" (García Márquez 164).

The railroad is the threshold of Macondo's industrialization process. It finally speeds the process of bringing the inventions that revolutionize the twentieth century: light bulbs, gramophones, telephone, car, and cinema—the iron horse revolution that shaped the landscape of Latin America.

The new inventions are seen as artifices that will put to test their capacity to marvel because they cannot distinguish the limits of reality. Henceforth, the illogical pests of insomnia do not surprise Macondians, but they are puzzled by the mechanism of the gramophone. These inventions are premonitions of the arrival of Mr. Herbert, as a sort of Mr. Danger from the telluric novel *Doña Bárbara* (1929), by the Venezuelan Rómulo Gallegos.

Mr. Herbert is an American who, after comparing the local banana to a diamond, brings a regiment of engineers, agronomists, hydrologists, and topographers to start the cultivation of banana trees. This was the start of the exploitation of the tropical gold, or the "banana pest." This exploitation modifies nature itself: "they changed the pattern of the rams, accelerated the cycle of harvest" (García Márquez 167). The "gringos" build an alternate city to Macondo, which is encircled by wire. Even though the modernization of Macondo is in full throttle, its citizens still believe in the supernatural; for example, when Amaranta announces that she will die after she is done sewing her shroud, villagers bring her letters to be taken to the other side. Nature will also send messages of the tragedies to come, such as the arrival of yellow butterflies announcing the apparitions of Mauricio Babilonia.

Excess will be the decay of Macondo as seen when Aureliano Segundo competes against Camila Sagastume, better known as "The Elephant," in an eating contest that illustrates the immoderation of the times in Macondo: "on awakening each one had the juice of forty oranges, eight quarts of coffee, and thirty raw eggs" (García Márquez 188). Aureliano Segundo is the most pantagruelic of the Buendías. Two events would mark the decline, but also the mortal blow to Macondo: the strike in the Banana Company that shows the real intentions of the newcomers and the killing of three thousand workers. The "plague of the banana tree" is the only affliction that actually takes lives. Just like the train had brought new inventions to Macondo, the train also carries the bodies of repressed workers from the factory: "and those who had put them in the car had had time to pile them up in the same way in which they transported bunches of bananas" (García Márquez 223). The government denies that there were any killings and the company decides to restart operations once the rain stops. This brings the "plague of rain," a deluge that will expel the company from Macondo and modify the weather conditions that let the banana tree grow. The torrential rain lasts four years, eleven months and two days, allying nature with the old Macondo. This results in the closure of the company that leaves without paying its workers: "Macondo had been a prosperous place and well on its way until it was disordered and corrupted and suppressed by the banana company" (García Márquez 253).

The plague of rain becomes a symbol that can be interpreted as the triumph of nature over technological advancements. If Mr. Herbert and his engineers modified climate, now nature takes over. Rain destroys everything: "the driest of machines would have flowers popping out among their gears" (García Márquez 230). Rain also announces the death of the matriarch who had followed the progression of the novel as the principal star of the planetary system of the Buendía. She says, "I'm only waiting for the rain to stop in order to die" (García Márquez 233). Rain extinguishes love and food, cleanses the town, and almost ruins the house ("The House" was going to be the original title of the novel). After the rainstorm, the town returns to its natural state at the beginning of the novel, the prehistoric era of the foundation of Macondo.

The death of Úrsula instigates a bewilderment of nature: "Santa Sofía de la Piedad . . . noticed during those days a certain confusion in nature: the roses smelled like goosefoot" (García Márquez 249). Úrsula was the axis of the novel, which is why after her death, nature seems confused: Birds crash into the house, and an apocalyptic beast (half man, half animal) appears at the end of the novel to stress the end of times and the extinction of the dynasty. In the last pages of the novel, nature takes over the house. Santa Sofía de la Piedad tries to take care of it, but the animals and the vegetation are faster.

Amaranta Úrsula returns from Europe and also continues the restoration of the house, fighting this time against the ants. Women's return is seen as the only possibility to restore order in the household. Amaranta Úrsula returns with a modernizing spirit and with her husband Gastón, who wants to bring aviation to Macondo, in order to start the airmail. The end of the lineage arrives with the union between Aureliano and Amaranta Úrsula (she is the only one in the novel referred to as a "modern spirit" or "modern woman") and the ensuing torrid romance distracts them from dominating nature. They fight the prehistoric hunger of the ants, but they also produce major destruction with their sexual encounters. Moreover, they become part of nature by conceding to their incestuous desires, and they are defeated by nature; vegetation and ants devour the boy with the tail of a pig, whom prophecy announced would be punishment for their incest. Just like in regionalist novels, where nature devours the main characters, in the same way nature eats the last link of their lineage: "It was a dry and bloated bag of skin that all the ants in the world were dragging toward their holes along the stone path in the garden" (García Márquez 301). The house succumbs to dust and wind whirls and, in the moment of deciphering the old papers, their history also ends their lineage, like a serpent that eats its own tail.

In this reading, García Márquez uses magical realism as a strategy to confront Latin American isolation from science and progress, the impossibility of dominating the torrid landscapes and imposing instead an imaginary technology. We can read magical realism as a brand to explain the contradictory realities of Latin America to foreigners. In García Márquez's masterpiece, he exemplifies and exhausts this style—we see the effort to reach modernity. Latin America is still a place of contradictions on a surreal level, and the countries south of the Rio Grande are still being seen from the colonial gaze as places of magic mixed with harsh realities. In globalization mode, these countries perform their stereotypes, embracing macondismo as nationalism to establish difference and also to attract tourism and travelers. As stated, this is evident in the current tourist campaign in Colombia, which has adopted magical realism as its slogan.

The fructiferous magical occurrences in Macondo are present even in a recent update of the "Departure of the Last Buendía from Aracataca" in the newspaper *El Tiempo* (Benjumea Brito). The Dutch Tim Aan't Goor (who changed his last name to Buendía) created the "Gypsy Residence" very close to the García Márquez Museum, in order to recreate the tourist experience for international readers of García Márquez's novels. The first tourist promoter of the Nobel Prize writer's native place and a "catequerian" resident, the Dutch entrepreneur tried to convince the government of Magdalena to create the "Macondo Route," an ongoing project that proposes to transport tourists from Santa Marta to Aracataca in a yellow train. Like a distant relative of Pietro Crespi, Tim Buendía brings the last of the plagues to the poetic site that gave life to Macondo: "the plague of tourism."

Works Cited

Benjumea Brito, Paola. "El último de los Buendía se va de Aracataca." *El Tiempo*. [Colombia] 16 Feb. 2014. Web. 22 Jul. 2014.

Brunner, José Joaquín. "Traditionalism and Modernity in Latin American Culture." *Latin America Writes Back: Postmodernity in the Periphery*. Ed. Emil Volek. New York: Routledge, 2002. 3–31.

Camayd-Freixas, Erik. "Magical Realism as Primitivism: An Alternate Verisimilitude." *Romance Languages Annual* 9. 9 (1998): 414–23.

De Blij, Harm. *The Power of Place: Geography, Destiny, and Globalization's Rough Landscape*. London: Oxford UP, 2009.

Fuguet, Alberto. *McOndo*. Barcelona: Grijalbo Mondadori, 1996.

García Márquez, Gabriel. *One Hundred Years of Solitude*. 1967. California Lutheran U. n.d. Web. 14 Feb. 2014.

Hart, Stephen M. "Magical Realism in the Americas: Politicised Ghosts in *One Hundred Years of Solitude*, *The House of the Spirits*, and *Beloved*." *Journal of Iberian and Latin American Studies* 9.2 (2003): 115–23.

_____. "From Realism to Neo-realism to Magical Realism: The Algebra of Memory." *Romance Studies* 30.3–4 (2012): 251–67.

Mezzadra, Sandro, & Brett Neilson. *Border as Method or the Multiplication of Labor*. Durham, NC: Duke UP, 2013.

Ochoa, Ana María. "García Márquez, macondismo, and the soundscapes of vallenato." *Popular Music* 24.2 (2005): 207–22.

Ong, Walter. *Orality and Literacy: The Technologization of the Word*. London & New York: Methuen, 1982.

Pollack, Sarah. "Latin America Translated (Again): Roberto Bolaño's *The Savage Detectives* in the United States." *Comparative Literature* 61.3 (2009): 346–65.

Tuchman, Barbara. *A Distant Mirror: The Calamitous Fourteenth Century*. New York: Knopf, 1978.

Von Der Walde, Erna. "El macondismo como latinoamericanismo." *Cuadernos Americanos* 12.1 (1998): 223–37.

Warnes, Christopher. "Magical Realism and the Legacy of German Idealism." *Modern Language Review* 101 (2006): 488–98.

Zamora, Lois Parkinson, & Wendy B. Faris, eds. *Magical Realism: Theory, History, Community*. Durham/London: Duke UP, 1995.

History, Ethnography, and Magical Realism in Marcio Veloz Maggiolo's *The Diffuse Biography of Sombra Castañeda*

Fernando Valerio-Holguín [Translated by María Fernanda Valerio Capellá]

Myth and Magical Realism

In his novel *El hombre del acordeón* (*The Man of the Accordion*, 2003), Marcio Veloz Maggiolo introduces a metanarrative instance to provide his own impression of magical realism. This metacommentary is also a deictic addressed to the reader: "According to what some of the few survivors had told me, it is not that La Salada is a part of a strange, *magic* and unpredictable world, it is just that when things have the possibility of expressing themselves, they do so, because 'everything has its own soul and personality'" (Veloz Maggiolo, *El hombre del acordeón* 12; my emphasis).[1] If in the animistic universe of syncretic religions, like Voodoo, things have a soul and they "express themselves," the reader is, then, not more than a mere recipient and interpreter of the discourse of things. In this writing strategy, Veloz Maggiolo feels the necessity to distance himself from the possible imputations of the influence of magical realism received from canonical Latin American writers. The narrator continues with other metacomments that are worth citing: "It could be bothersome to the reader if he who narrates could never convince himself of anything. . . the only clear line to reconstruct facts where *the magical can surpass reality* was the political influence that prevailed among the inhabitants of the border (Veloz Maggiolo, *El hombre del acordeón* 13; my emphasis).[2] The phrase in italics resonates in another one by Philippe Doubois' in the sense that "fiction reaches and even surpasses reality" (37). Finally, the narrator proposes the mytho-poetic aspects of Voodoo as the source of magic: "Ma Misién wore a red shawl and, in her hands, an image of San Santiago, known among the *magical sources* of Voodoo as Ogún Balendyó" (Veloz Maggiolo, *El hombre del acordeón* 55),[3] and the words (discourse), as a means of expression of that parasympathetic substance that magic is: "Nacha would have lent Remigia those *magic words*" (Veloz Maggiolo, *El hombre del acordeón* 57).[4]

Twenty-four years after the publication of the novel *La biografía difusa de Sombra Castañeda* (*The Diffuse Biography of Sombra Castañeda*, 1980), Veloz Maggiolo continues with a writing program that imbricates history, ethnography, and magical realism.[5] The purpose of this essay is to analyze the relationship between these three aspects in *The Diffuse Biography of Sombra Castañeda*. I also propose to explore what distinguishes Veloz Maggiolo's novel from other magical realist novels: the study of the simultaneous and trans-epochal presence of the white, black, and indigenous races, as well as that of the European, African, and Indigenous cultures in the Dominican Republic as a search for a cultural identity.[6]

Myth, Otherness, and Magical Realism in the "New Historical Novel"

According to Seymour Menton, "although Carpentier's 1949 El Reino de este mundo has been identified as the first New Historical Novel (NHN), the number of historical novels in general published in the past thirteen years (1979–1992) was one-hundred-ninety-four, which outstrips the one-hundred-seventy-three historical novels published in the preceding twenty-nine years (1949–1978)" (26).[7] Among the factors that contributed to this boom during the 1980s and 1990s of the past century, the main one was the proximity of the celebration of the "Discovery" of America (27–28). Santo Domingo played an important role in these celebrations as the first European city and the seat of the first Spanish viceroyalty in the New World.[8]

In *The Diffuse Biography*, Veloz Maggiolo proposes the total reconstruction of the history of the Dominican Republic, from the starting point of the myths of the Taíno and Afro-Dominican cultures, as well as of the ethnographic discourses about these myths and the representation of the Other-Within. One of the functions of myths is to find the origins of the community and to insert them in a universal context. According to Erik Camayd-Freixas, "Carpentier finds in myth the solution to one of the problems of American expression ... 'finding the universal in the core of the local'—according to Unamuno's saying" (96).[9] For this reason, regarding myth, Carpentier states:

> One day, a happy chance makes me fly (in the year 1947) to the Gran Sabana ... an ethnologist that was doing field work in that region ... told me ... about a war that had taken place between two tribes, caused by the kidnapping of a beautiful woman. I said to myself, "Well, but this, in essence, responds to universal myths. This is the Trojan War." And from that moment on, I started seeing everything from the American point of view: history, myths, old cultures that had come to us from Europe. And thinking that there is a legend about Amalivaca, the Noah of the Orinoco, that Humboldt notes and that shocked him, I started to... *bring Europe over here and to see it from here to there.* (Camayd-Freixas 96–97; emphasis in the original)[10]

In this quotation, one can clearly notice how Carpentier relates the ethnographer's work with the study of myths and how, in these myths, universality is associated with Europe. The question then is: Are those myths universal because we first heard them from Europe and then we related them to the myths of diverse "primitive" groups that somehow represent the "infancy" of Europe, as Sigmund Freud proposed? Although Camayd-Freixas interprets the phrase "bring Europe over here and see it from here to there" (which he emphasizes) as a keen inversion of the European gaze on Carpentier's behalf, he is aware that this approach has been interpreted by others as a view of America with Europe as a frame of reference and not as a view of the European gaze with America as a frame of reference (97). The European colonizer's gaze, from the other shore, may be the one that some Caribbean writers have borrowed in their surrealist, magical realist, ethnographic view of Caribbean reality.

In Latin America and the Caribbean, magical realism has been the literary form adopted by history and myth. As Camayd-Freixas notes, "The rise of anthropology, by delving into the study of myth and its functional aspects, made it possible for authors such as Asturias, Carpentier, Rulfo, and García Márquez to use it as a tool for social, political, and historical analysis, interpreting Latin

American reality with it" (8–9). Myth, in these Latin American authors' works, is not just an "analytical tool," but also a worldview, and as cosmogony, it is also an ideology and an art form that has to do with the development of certain epochal discourses. In his famous essay *"Cien años de soledad*: The Novel as Myth and Archive" (*"One Hundred Years of Solitude*: The Novel as Myth and Archive"), Roberto González Echevarría argues that there is an obsession with history and myth in the Latin American novel (358): "It is my hypothesis that the novel, having no fixed form of its own, assumes that of a given document endowed with truth-bearing power by society at specific moments in history" (360). The document mentioned by González Echevarría is the treatise of anthropology. Myth, associated with the origin and the founding of the community, is one of anthropology's objects of study (363–64). Magical realism and surrealism are both expressions of the mythopoetic nature of animism (Camayd-Freixas 100). Carpentier—who formulated, in his introduction to *El reino de este mundo* (*The Kingdom of This World*), his postulates regarding the marvelous real—became interested in surrealism early on. In that sense, he states, "Surrealism taught me to see textures . . .I understood that behind that nativism there was something else, which I call contexts: the telluric context and the epic-political context: he who finds the relationship between both of them will write the American novel" (Camayd-Freixas 36–37).[11] James Clifford, who has studied the relationship between surrealism and ethnography in his parallel development during the 1920s and 1930s, refers to surrealism as "an aesthetic that values fragments, curious collections, unexpected juxtapositions—that works to provoke the manifestations of extraordinary realities drawn from the domain of the erotic, the exotic and the unconscious" (118). And although Clifford does not say it at once, he refers implicitly to the Other-Exotic, considering André Breton and other surrealists' fascination with Mexico. Around the same time, Miguel Ángel Asturias and Alejo Carpentier decide to opt for American reality in their novels *Hombres de maíz* (*Men of Maize*, 1949) and *¡Ecue-Yamba-O!* (1933), respectively.

Mary Louise Pratt refers to the metropolis' obsessive necessity to "present and re-present its peripheries and its others continually to itself" (6). In the same way, that obsessive necessity to represent (or speak for) the indigenous or black Other-Within could be the result of the assimilation of the (view) attitude of the European ethnologist. Accordingly, Camayd-Freixas elaborates on the relationship between the magical realism of some Latin American writers of the Boom with the primitivism and the rise of ethnography in Latin America as a product of the development of European ethnography in the first half of the twentieth century. In turn, Marianna Torgovnick has defined primitivism as a group of diverse and contradictory tropes that conform a grammar and a vocabulary referring to the Other (8). These tropes, which consist of recurring images and ideas, were crucial to the formation of the Europeans' cultural identity. Through them, the Europeans constructed a view of the Other as a way of dealing with cultural differences and also as a justification of colonization in Asia, Africa, and America.

With respect to ethnographic work and its relationship with power, we can observe two contrasting positions that appear represented in the texts of Rigoberta Menchú and Jorge Luis Borges. The first one is that of Menchú and her concern for the danger that the revelation of secrets entails for her community: "I still conceal what I believe no one knows, not even an anthropologist, nor an intellectual, with as many books as they may have, know how to distinguish all our secrets" (271).[12] The second one is that of a character in the story-essay "El etnógrafo" ("The Ethnographer") by Jorge Luis Borges. In it, Fred Murdock, a doctoral student of anthropology, stays a period of time with a group of Native Americans in the west of the United States and is successful at getting a shaman to reveal the secret: "—That's not the problem, sir. Now that I possess the secret, I could enunciate it in one hundred different ways, and it would still be contradictory. I do not know very well how to tell you that the secret is precious and that now science, our science, seems to me a mere frivolity" (Borges 58).[13] In contrast with Menchú, this shaman reveals the secret to a stranger, and in contrast with Elisabeth Burgos, Fred Murdock decides not to write the book and make a living in a different way instead. Both quotations are the two sides of the same coin and reflect two positions in the asymmetry of power between the ethnographer and his informant.

According to Clifford, "To see culture and its norms—beauty, truth, reality— as artificial arrangements susceptible to detached analysis and comparison with other possible dispositions, is crucial to an ethnographic attitude" (119). Veloz Maggiolo textualizes ethnography and retakes from Carpentier the telluric and epic-political contexts in his historical novels. Having the Other as object of study in ethnographic writing always runs the risk of installing an asymmetry of power, in which the marginalized Other; the colonized Other; the primitive, indigenous, or black Other; the Other-Within is represented and spoken for by the upper class, white ethnographer, in what Geertz denominates as "ethnographic ventriloquy" (Sklodowska 83). *The Diffuse Biography* does not escape from the influence of the aesthetic traits of magical realism, nor does it escape from the discourse that was its model: ethnography. For this reason, the aforementioned asymmetric relations of power between the ethnographer and his informants are found in the margins of this novel. On the one hand, it is evident that Veloz Maggiolo, as an anthropologist, archaeologist, and ethnographer, who has written extensively about Dominican culture, is aware of the complicated scheme of ethnographic relationships. On the other hand, it is possible that Veloz Maggiolo felt encouraged by the success of Carpentier's 1949 historical ethno-novel, aside from Dominican writers proneness to writing essay-novels. In this type of new historical ethno-novel, Veloz Maggiolo articulates certain anxieties of Dominican cultural identity through history, myth, and ethnographic discourse.[14] The mytho-poetic discourse offers greater lyrical possibilities and, concomitantly, the opportunity to place local, particular Dominican history within the context of western, European "universality."

The Diffuse Biography of Sombra Castañeda: Magical Ethno-Novel

In *The Diffuse Biography*, winner of the 1981 National Novel Award, Dominican history is fragmented, mixed with Taíno and Afro-

Dominican myths, as well as with fantastic, surrealist, and magical elements interspersed with historical documents. Albeit fragmented, there is a global view of the Dominican history that goes from the pre-Columbian period of the Taínos to the so-called Era of Trujillo (1930–1961). Among the historical references are the colonial period, the 1822 Haitian invasion, and the 1916 US invasion, the country's independence in 1844, and the dictatorships of Pedro Santana, Ulises "Lilís" Heureaux, and Rafael Leónidas Trujillo. In the novel, there are also references to historical individuals, such as the anti-imperialist Gregorio Luperón, the messiah Liborio Mateo, or allusions to more contemporary, politicians, such as the eternal Joaquín Balaguer, whose panegyric to the dictator Trujillo is cited in eleven interspersed fragments.[15] Aside from these fragments, there are sections about Esculapio Ramírez, a figure that unfolds in two temporalities: as Esculapio Ramírez during the Era of Trujillo and as his alter ego Serapio Rendón, during the indefinite time period of Sombra Castañeda, the imaginary dictator that is the protagonist of the novel. These sections introduce a realistic and historical perspective in the novel, which serves as a balance between historical reality and myth; they also introduce two time periods: the Profane Time of history that serves to contextualize the novel and the Sacred Time of Myth.

The Biography takes place in a town called Barrero. Like Macondo, the town is an enclosed mythical space populated by magical-imaginary beings from Taíno and Afro-Dominican mythologies, such as *ciguapas*, *bacás*, *galipotes*, *lugarús*, *opias*, and *biembienes*, Taíno gods like Boinayel, and Afro-Caribbean gods, like Ogún Balenyó: "Barrero was the typical enclosed land. Nothing came in. Nothing came out. Still pristine. Fenced by white walls erected by sea salt and the talc of the roads" (Veloz Maggiolo, *La biografía* 101).[16] The white, walled enclosure, which connotes the circle as a symbol of perfection, repetition, and circularity of mythical time, separate the town (a magical world where everything is possible) from profane space. Within the circle that is Barrero, there are no precise or established borders; the different realms of nature interact among them. The origin of its inhabitants is incestuous: four cousins. The consequences of this incest in some members of the family, like the pig's tail in *Cien años de soledad* (*One Hundred Years of Solitude*), are that "they have degenerated into cross-eyed beings with backwards feet, hooked noses, and in many cases, double hands" (37).

In Veloz Maggiolo's novel, there is an imbrication of the European, African, and Indigenous cultures. The purpose of the presence of these races and their consequent miscegenation is the search for the Dominican identity. The three emblematic characters go through Dominican history: Sombra Castañeda, a descendant of Spaniards; Miguel the Indian (Guacamoel) of Taíno origin, is associated with the waters and escorted by "a female dog with droopy teats and a wild boar;" Curibamgó (don Pedro), descendant of Africans; a "bembú" black man (man with "big lips"), who speaks a language that is a mixture of "old indigenous roots and African languages" (18); and Mimilo, a hermaphrodite witchdoctor, who serves as a "horse"[18] to Curibamgó and is capable of sleeping with one-hundred-thirteen women in a single night. We also have the characters of Antonio the Bacá and the Cernícalo Alfredo, and there is an intersubjective communication among Sombra Castañeda, Miguel el Indio, Mimilo, and Curibamgó. In one instance, all Mimilo had to do is think of a naked woman before Curibamgó sent her to him the next day (32). In another instance, Curibamgó raped some fourteen-year-old girls and donated "the convulsions of their orgasm to Sombra Castañeda" (85).[19] In a way, there is a trans-subjectivity among the three characters.

As an omniscient dictator, Sombra Castañeda is associated with natural elements and phenomena, such as plants, forests, birds, dew, and rain: "My thing was to defeat nature, organize the crickets, give precise orders to the wind and the rain, terrorize the lizards, decorate all the nightingales and assimilate the herons to the clouds of the region" (Veloz Maggiolo, *La biografía* 17–18). The intertextual relationship between Sombra Castañeda and Ti Noel,[20] the protagonist of *El reino de este mundo* (*The Kingdom of This World*), is obvious: both are characterized by innocence, the trans-epochal testimony, and the gaze open to the magical numinous.

Geographical determinism in magical realist novels goes back to Oswald Spengler's emphasis on the nature/culture divide, which influenced Carpentier (Camay-Freixas 7). Sombra Castañeda exercises the absolute power indistinctly over men, animals, and things. Nature is feminized and eroticized as a response to his patriarchal power:

> It was nighttime, and the light of the bright stars slid, stridently, over the tops of the gray mountain range. The yellow brightness leaked from the nipple to the skirt (slope) of the mountain, later going into the streams of the altitude, which then came down converted to a liquid gold that stained of maturity the nocturnal rocks. (Veloz Maggiolo, *La biografía* 26)[21]

Veloz Maggiolo's implicit proposal in this ethno-novel is the presentation of Dominican culture as the historical result of five centuries of hybridity among the Taíno, African, and Spanish cultures. The Dominican author uses his vast knowledge of these cultures to "textualize" his experiences with respect to non-European cultures in a realist-magical account. In the translation of Otherness through the "writing of the voice," one could find the key to heterologous discourses (Sklodowska 82). How does Veloz Maggiolo solve that which ethnographic writing proposes, the asymmetry of power regarding the Other? First, the opinion of Elzbieta Sklodowska:

> In making the consubstantial problems surface in the narrativization of the experience of the otherness—the notion of power in front of the Other and the danger of damaging his/her identity— the new edge ethnography (Geertz, Clifford, Marcus, Cushman and others) seems to inscribe itself in a self-conscious way within the line of discourses that De Certau calls "heterologous." (82)[22]

Historically, although Veloz Maggiolo has not been in the "back then" of history, he has been in the "there" of those Others-Within, of blacks and indigenous people. This author's way of being in writing is sometimes that of the archaeologist, sometimes an anthropologist and ethnographer, and always, a litterateur.

In *The Biography*, there is a heteroglossia through which multiple voices, perspectives, and conflicts coincide among the official and non-official discourses in the context of a national language, while simultaneously two forces struggle with each other: one is centripetal and the other, centrifugal. There also exist tensions between the present and the past and between myth and history (Morris 248–49).

If what distinguishes *The Biography* from other magical-realist novels is the omni-co-presence of the three cultures, Veloz Maggiolo paradoxically resorts to magical realism to solve the previously noted tensions. The three main characters, Sombra, Curibamgó, and Miguel the Indian, are magic and timeless. The hyperbole, so common in this type of novel, is used to accept such extraordinary beings as "natural." There is a trans-subjectivity among these three characters, as well as a fluidity between the animal and vegetable kingdoms. To translate the racial and cultural complexity of Dominican society, the author textualizes the ethnographic and historical document through magical realism.

In the novel, there is a dialogue among the different cultures, which are represented by different narrators and points of view. The historical, mythical, literary, and ethnographic discourses are woven together, forming a complex and elaborate text. There are also two time periods that appear in the novel: a Mythical Time and a Profane Historical Time, which juxtapose themselves and somehow define the perspective of the characters. Like Sombra Castañeda, Veloz Maggiolo understands that there is a close relationship between power and discourse: "New words for new contents; flowery war against the dictionary, tired of all types of dictatorship, where epithets, adjectives, have been worn out by so many unequal eulogies, of unused titles, of appellatives cuntpainted by the fearful and even imprecise exaggeration" (Veloz Maggiolo, *La biografía* 186). For this reason, then, Veloz Maggiolo challenges the monoglossia of the official discourse on Dominican culture through the voices of the black and indigenous Other (Zakrzewski Brown 251).

Conclusion

The Diffuse Biography summarizes the postulates of the new historical novel and of the ethnological novel, as well as those of magical realism. Winner of important awards, this novel has inaugurated and determined a new way of writing novels in the Dominican novelistic canon. Veloz Maggiolo has carried out what, according to Geertz, good ethnographers do: "go to the sites, come back with information about the people that live there" (Sklodowska 83). What distinguishes him from other writers, with respect to an assimilated European ethnological view of the Other-Within, is the heteroglossia of the different voices with which the Dominican culture dialogues, as a response to the monoglossia of the official culture. Although his white, European ethnic background may situate him in a fragile position as an ethnographer, when textualizing his experiences, Veloz Maggiolo is assuming, as a response, heteroglossia through magical realism. He is not what Van Maanen calls a "conference room anthropologist" (Sklodowska 83). The Dominican anthropologist was present "there," which allows him to "textualize" his experiences with the Other-Within.

As a historical novel, *The Diffuse Biography* considers totalizing reconstructions of Dominican history since the conquest, going through colonization, the republican period, and ending with a dictator, an obvious allusion to Trujillo. History is presented as interwoven with myths and other elements belonging to the magical realism of the Taíno and Afro-Dominican cultures. There is a marked intertextuality in these novels, since they constantly allude to other fictional, historical, chronic, and political texts. As in Alejo Carpentier's *El reino de este mundo* (*The Kingdom of This World*), historical subjects are often named, but then moved to the background. Veloz Maggiolo secures the canon of the historical-magical-ethnological novel in the Dominican Republic and somehow translates the culture of the black and indigenous Other-Within for young, urban, globalized, and postmodern readers because blacks do not live in the Learned City; blacks live in Los Mina, Villa Mella, and Mandinga.[23]

Notes

1. "Según me narraran algunos de los pocos sobrevivientes, no es que La salada fuera parte de un mundo raro, *mágico* e impredecible, sino que cuando las cosas tienen la posibilidad de expresarse por sí mismas, se expresan, porque 'todo tiene su propia alma y personalidad'" (Veloz Maggiolo, *El hombre del acordeón* 12, my emphasis).

2. "Molestia para el lector podría ser el que jamás llegase quien narra a convencerse de nada . . . la única línea clara para reconstruir hechos donde *lo mágico puede superar a la realidad* fue la influencia política que predominó entre los habitantes de la frontera (Veloz Maggiolo, *El hombre del acordeón* 13; el énfasis es mío).

3. "Ma Misién llevaba un pañolón rojo y entre sus manos una imagen de San Santiago, conocido entre las *fuentes mágicas* del vudú como Ogún Balendyó" (Veloz Maggiolo, *El hombre del acordeón* 55).

4. "Nacha le habría prestado a Remigia las *palabras mágicas*" (Veloz Maggiolo, *El hombre del acordeón* 57).

5. For an analysis of the relationship between myth and magical realism, see Erik Camayd-Freixas' excellent book *Realismo mágico y primitivismo* (*Magical Realism and Primitivism*, 1998). Also see Carlos Esteban Deive's study *Vodú y magia en Santo Domingo* (Voodoo and Magic in Santo Domingo, 1979).

6. Veloz Maggiolo is the author of numerous treatises on anthropology and archaeology. One of his first books is titled *Sobre cultura dominicana y otras culturas* (*Of Dominican Culture and Other Cultures*, 1977).

7. The new historical novel, in which the past not lived by the author is very important, is characterized by the following postulates: the subordination of history to a philosophical principle, the distortion of history, the use of important historical figures as characters, metafiction, intertextuality, and the Bakhtinian concepts of dialogism, carnivalization, parody, and heteroglossia (Menton 22–24).

8. La Hispaniola was "discovered" and colonized by Christopher Columbus, who disembarked on the northern coast on December 5, 1492. On his second trip, he founded La Isabela, the first European city in the New World. In the city of Santo Domingo de Guzmán—founded on August 4, 1496 by the Admiral's brother, Bartolomé Colón—the Alcázar, seat of the first viceroy, Diego Colón; the first hospital, San Nicolás de Bari; and the first cathedral, Santa María

la Menor, were constructed. The first university, Santo Tomás de Aquino (today the Universidad Autónoma de Santo Domingo), was founded in 1538, while the first Royal Audience was founded in 1511. The historical novel *Enriquillo* by Manuel de Jesús Galván describes colonial life during the sixteenth century.

9. "Carpentier halla en el mito la solución a uno de los problemas de la expresión americana . . . 'hallar lo universal en las entrañas de lo local'—según el decir deUnamuno" (96).

10. "Un día, una casualidad feliz me hace volar (en el año 1947) a la Gran Sabana . . . un etnólogo que se encontraba haciendo trabajos de investigación en aquella región. . . me contó. . . de una guerra habida entre dos tribus causada por el rapto de una hermosa mujer. Me dije: 'Bueno, pero esto, en el fondo, responde a los mitos universales. Esto es la guerra de Troya.' Y a partir de ese momento empecé a verlo todo en función americana: la historia, los mitos, las viejas culturas que nos habían llegado de Europa. Y pensando que hay una leyenda de Amalivaca, el Noé del Orinoco, que lo señala Humboldt y que lo dejó asombrado, empecé . . . *a traer a Europa hacia acá y a verla de aquí hacia allá*" (Énfasis en el original. Citado en Camayd-Freixas 96–97).

11. "El surrealismo me enseñó a ver texturas . . . Comprendí que detrás de ese nativismo había algo más, lo que llamo los contextos: contexto telúrico y contexto épico-político: el que halle la relación entre ambos escribirá la novela americana" (Camayd-Freixas 36–37).

12. "Sigo ocultando lo que yo considero que nadie sabe, ni siquiera un antropólogo, ni un intelectual, por más que tengan muchos libros, no saben distinguir todos nuestros secretos" (271).

13. "—Nada de eso, señor. Ahora que poseo el secreto, podría enunciarlo de cien modos distintos y aun contradictorios. No sé muy bien cómo decirle que el secreto es precioso y que ahora la ciencia, nuestra ciencia, me parece una mera frivolidad" (58).

14. I coined the term ethno-novel to refer to those narratives where the colonized, marginalized, and annihilated Other occupies a preponderant place and poses an ethnographic textualization. The ethno-novels that we know have *El reino de este mundo* as a model. For this reason, I have called them the new historical ethno-novel.

15. Rafael Leónidas Trujillo (1891–1961) joined the Guardia Nacional Dominicana (Dominican National Guard) in 1919 during the US

invasion to the Dominican Republic (1916–1924). After the troops abandoned the country, Trujillo remained as Comandante en Jefe del Ejército nacional (*Chief Commandant of the National Army*). In 1930, General Trujillo reached the presidency of the Republic through electoral fraud. He ruled the country ruthlessly during thirty-one years of terror and crimes. In 1961, he was murdered by a group of enemies, supported by the CIA. Joaquín Balaguer wrote and read the panegyric that appears interspersed in Veloz Maggiolo's novel. Balaguer held various public positions under Trujillo's dictatorship. From 1957 to 1960, he was the vice-president of the Republic. After the resignation of President Héctor B. Trujillo in 1960, Balaguer took over the presidency as Trujillo's figurehead when Trujillo was murdered on May 30, 1961. Balaguer then took over the presidency until popular pressure forced him to resign; he found political asylum in the Nunciatura Apostólica (Apostolic Nunciature) in January 1962. He governed the country dictatorially during three consecutive periods (1966–1978) and then during two more periods (1986–94). The fraud of the 1994 elections was so flagrant that Balaguer could not resist the pressure of the national and international sectors and had to resign to give way to the celebration of new elections in 1996.

16. "Barrero era la típica tierra cerrada. Nada entraba. Nada salía. Prístina aún. Cercada de muros blancos levantados por la sal marina, y el talco de los caminos" (Veloz Maggiolo, *La biografía* 101).

17. "[T]hey have degenerated into cross-eyed beings with backwards feet, hooked noses, and in many cases, double hands" (37).

18. "Horse" is the person who the being or spirit "mounts" or possesses, which is to say, the person who enters into a trance.

19. "[L]as convulsiones de su orgasmo a Sombra Castañeda" (85).

20. Ti Noel in *El reino de este mundo*, just like Sombra Castañeda, "dictated orders to the wind" (134).

21. "Era de noche, y la luz de los luceros resbalaba, chillona, sobre el crestero de la cordillera gris. Los resplandores amarillos chorreaban desde el pezón hasta la falda de la montaña, metiéndose luego en los arroyos de la altura, los que, a su vez, bajaban convertidos en un oro líquido que manchaba de madurez las rocas nocturnas" (26).

22. "Al hacer aflorar los problemas consustanciales a la narrativización de la experiencia de la otredad—la noción del poder frente al otro y el peligro de lesionar la identidad del mismo—la etnografía de nuevo

corte (Geertz, Clifford, Marcus, Cushman y otros) parece inscribirse de forma autoconsciente dentro de la línea de discursos que De Certeau llama 'heterólogos'" (82).

23. Los Mina, a neighborhood located to the east of the city of Santo Domingo, was founded in the eighteenth century by slaves escaped from the French colony of Saint Domingue. They came from a region in Africa with the same name. Founded by African slaves of the Mandé family (Imperio Malí) in the seventeenth century, Mandinga is a town in the outskirts of Santo Domingo. Most of the population in Villa Mella, a town located to the north of Santo Domingo, is black.

Works Cited

Borges, Jorge Luis. "El etnógrafo." *Aproximaciones al estudio de la literatura hispánica*. Eds. Carmelo Virgilio, L. Teresa Valdivieso, & Edward H. Friedman. Boston: McGraw-Hill, 1999. 57–58.

Burgos, Elisabeth. *Me llamo Rigoberta Menchú*. Guatemala City: Arcoiris, 1983.

Camayd-Freixas, Erik. *Realismo mágico y primitivismo*. Lanham, New York & London: UP of America, 1998.

Carpentier, Alejo. *El reino de este mundo*. Buenos Aires: Librería del Colegio, 1975.

Clifford, James. *The Predicament of Culture. Twentieth-Century Ethnography, Literature, and Art*. Cambridge, MA: Harvard UP, 1988.

⎯⎯⎯⎯⎯. "Introduction: Partial Truth." *Writing Culture. The Poetics and Politics of Ethnography*. Eds. James Clifford & George E. Marcus. Berkeley: U of California P, 1986.

Deive, Carlos Esteban. *Vodú y magia en Santo Domingo*. Santo Domingo: Museo del Hombre Dominicano, 1979.

Doubois, Philippe. *El acto fotográfico: De la representación a la recepción*. Barcelona: Paidós Ibérica, 1986.

Geertz, Clifford. *Works and Lives. The Anthropologist as Autor*. Stanford, CA: Stanford UP, 1988.

González Echevarría, Roberto. "*Cien años de soledad*: The Novel as Myth and Archive." *MLN* 99 (1984): 358–80.

Menton, Seymor. *Latin America's New Historical Novel*. Austin: U of Texas P, 1993.

Morris, Pam, ed. *The Bakhtin Reader. Selected Writing of Bakhtin, Medvedev, Voloshinov*. London: Edward Arnold, 1994.

Pratt, Mary Louise. *Imperial Eyes. Travel Writing and Transculturation*. London & New York: Routledge, 1992.

Sklodowska, Elzbieta. "Testimonio mediatizado: ¿Ventriloquía o heteroglosia? (Barnet/Montejo; Burgos/Menchú)." *Revista de Crítica Literaria Latinoamericana* 38 (1993): 81–90.

Torgovnick, Marianna. *Gone Primitive*. Chicago and London: U of Chicago P, 1990.

Valerio Holguín, Fernando. "Primitive Borders: Cultural Identity and Ethnic Cleansing in the Dominican Republic." *Returning Gaze: Primitivism and Identity in Latin America*. Eds. Erik Camayd-Freixas & José Eduardo González. Tucson, Arizona: U of Arizona P, 2000. 75–88.

_____. "Mito y otredad en la Nueva Novela Histórica dominicana." *Murales, figuras, fronteras. Narrativa e historia en el Caribe y Centroamérica*. Eds. Rita de Maeseneer & Patrick Collard. Madrid: Iberoamericana/Vervuert, 2003. 93–108.

_____. "El orden de la música popular en la literatura dominicana." *Revista Céfiro* 8.1 (2009): 101–18.

_____. *Arqueología de las sombras: La narrativa de Marcio Veloz Maggiolo*. Santo Domingo: Editora Amigo del Hogar, 2000.

Veloz Maggiolo, Marcio. *La biografía difusa de Sombra Castañeda*. 1980. Santo Domingo: Taller, 1984.

_____. *El hombre del acordeón*. Madrid: Ediciones Siruela, 2003.

_____. *Sobre cultura dominicana y otras culturas*. Santo Domingo: Alfa y Omega, 1977.

Zakrzewski Brown, Isabel. "El proceso de transculturación en *La biografía difusa de Sombra Castañeda*." *Arqueología de las sombras: La narrativa de Marcio Veloz Maggiolo*. Ed. Fernando Valerio Holguín. Santo Domingo: Editora Amigo del Hogar, 2000. 247–62.

The Construction of the Magic and the Role of Popular Religion in the Caribbean Context

Ángel L. Estévez

> The World is created by magic. The first magician is God who created people with his own hands from the dust of the Earth. People originated by magic in all countries of the world. No one lives of the flesh. Everyone lives of the spirit.
> (André Pierre, *A World Created by Magic*)

That which man has not been able to explain or understand rationally has received numerous labels. At different time periods, events that escape our empirical knowledge of reality, thus challenging our understanding of our conventional worldview, have been described as miraculous, supernatural, fantastic, magic, marvelous, and uncanny, among other labels. Some of these terms have been successfully accepted as the only way to explain a given phenomenon; others have proved to be deficient. While some communities find satisfactory answers through spiritual faith, others have discovered that, what they once believed to be supernatural or unknown, is now explainable by means of scientific, anthropological, or cultural research. One can assume, then, that time and space, along with the ongoing evolution of certain societies, play an important role in what is conceived to exist within the boundaries of the known and what lies beyond them. In the works analyzed here, Alejo Carpentier's *The Kingdom of This World*, Mayra Montero's *The Red of His Shadow*, and Marcio Veloz Maggiolo's *El hombre del acordeón*[1] (*The Man of the Accordion*), there is a close relationship between Vodou[2] and magic. Each author attempts his/her own (re)interpretation of specific social and historical events, integrating mythical figures of the African pantheon as well as religious practices that have been linked to the common history of Hispaniola. Argued here is that these authors adopt the magic of Vodou in order to construct a discursive modality that allows readers to see the Caribbean from within while, at the same time, delving into the "magical realities" of the Other.

A thoughtful assessment of the historiography of Hispanic Caribbean literatures and cultures will confirm that the works of Cuban-born Alejo Carpentier have played a significant role in our understanding of the history and culture of this geographical area. Ironically, although Carpentier was born and lived in Cuba until he was twenty-four years old, it was in France where he deepened his knowledge of Latin America. González Echevarría states that, after spending eleven years in Paris (1928–1939), "Carpentier did not become French but, on the contrary, he fought with all his might to remain Cuban. Carpentier became Spanish American in Paris" (23). In fact, as he himself predicts, after dedicating nearly a decade to reading early Spanish American historical documents, from Columbus through the eighteenth century, "America appeared before me like an enormous haze that I struggled to understand, because I had a remote intuition that my work was going to be produced here, that it was going to be profoundly American"[3] (Müller-Bergh 29). And in fact, most of Carpentier's works deal, in one way or another, with the history and culture of Latin America, with a particular interest in the Caribbean area.

The eleven years Carpentier lived in Paris notably marked his intellectual life, especially the way he *observed* the world. These foundational years are significant not only because it is in Paris where he comes into contact with other artists (some French and some Latin American, like Miguel Ángel Asturias), but also because he also came into contact with the concept of magical realism there. It is well known that Carpentier joined the surrealist group, led by André Breton, and learned the surrealist precepts, most importantly the manipulation of tricks with which surrealism launched a series of artifacts "based on unpredictability, magic, primitivism and surprise that in fiction became loosely called magical realism" (Wilson 67). However, Carpentier's participation in the group was short-lived; constant disagreements and the despotic-like control by Breton, led members to withdraw from the movement, among them Carpentier. From the surrealist doctrine, Carpentier is going to borrow the term *le merveillieux*, "a code word for the thrill of the chance encounter where a frisson or epiphany is sparked by the clash between subjectivity and the objective world of things and other people" (Wilson 70). This "marvelous" way of *observing* the surroundings turns to be *lo maravilloso,* which will form part of Carpentier's own theory on magical realism. In other words, upon Carpentier's disillusionment with surrealism and its artificial magic, he detaches himself from the group, as he came to the realization that, for him, surrealism had nothing else to offer. This is a turning point for Carpentier and his belated eagerness to view and present to others what he called "the uniqueness of the Latin American experience": *lo real maravilloso americano* ("American marvelous realism"). And so begins Carpentier's notion of the marvelous real, or magic.

It was in the early years of the 1940s when Carpentier first experienced, now first-hand, the reality of the Latin America he had read so much about through the lens of history. Although he was, to some extent, familiar with Caribbean culture, it was during his trip to Haiti in 1943 when Carpentier actually *observed*, experienced, and became aware of a reality that had always been there, but whose *raison d'être* he had never bothered to understand to the core. It is during that trip to Haiti that Carpentier comes to the realization of the importance of the Caribbean area, not only the Hispanic Caribbean, but the entire geographic area of the Greater and Lesser Antilles.

The early historical records of the first encounters of Europeans with Native Americans, including legal documents, letters, and chronicles of the time, describe the Caribbean region as a strategic ground for the colonization and conquest of nearby islands, which later extended to the rest of Central and South America. Hispaniola, as the most important harbor of Columbus' trips, became one of the richest and most economically desirable islands to exploit, as it had lots of gold and silver, which represented, for many conquerors, a secure financial future back in Spain. However, the abusive working conditions imposed on natives by the conquerors caused many deaths, including losses brought on by mass suicides, contagious diseases, and food shortages. As a result, the indigenous workforce was drastically reduced. For the Spanish Crown, this required the immediate replenishment of the laborers and eventually, as it turned out, a total and long-lasting substitution of the labor force. The answer was in Africa. Historical records indicate that the first African slaves were brought to Hispaniola as early as 1503. As the extraction of precious metals increased, so did the number of African slaves transplanted to the island. By the mid-eighteenth century, the majority of the population in Hispaniola was of African descent. The first two centuries of colonization were fundamental for the formation of what today constitutes the African legacy in the Caribbean.

As we know today, not all slaves were brought from the same African region. Many did not even speak the same language or have the same religious beliefs. But, in spite of this cultural heterogeneity, these social groups did not remain in a bubble or stationary in the new habitat. This new social redistribution favored cultural exchange among them, and this interaction led to a process of appropriation, coexistence, convergence, and reintegration of the members of the new society. This social intermingling kept producing a never-ending, fertile *mestizaje*, which was both biological and cultural, and gave birth to a new-Other islander: a Creole. As the process of colonization kept its course, so did the development of a *criollo* idiosyncrasy. Carpentier used the term "baroque" to describe this ever-changing amalgamation of cultural complexities. The Caribbean and, by extension, Central and South America, have been experiencing a process of unstoppable cultural hybridization and synthesis that has not slowed down ever since. This is the Latin America Carpentier saw and talked about in the 1940s:

> And why is Latin America the chosen territory of the baroque? Because all symbiosis, all *mestizaje*, engenders the baroque. The American baroque develops along with the *criollo* culture, with the meaning of *criollo*, with the self-awareness of the American man; the awareness of being Other, of being new, of being symbiotic, of being a *criollo*. (Carpentier, "On the Marvelous Real" 100)

Vodou has played (and still does) a significant role in Haitian history and culture. This is not surprising because, although blacks were brought stripped of all material belongings, their religious beliefs and practices remained part of their ceremonies. As indicated previously, adjustments needed to be made as the new Afro-American societies kept forging and integrating new elements imposed by the *conquistadores* and their Catholic beliefs and, to a lesser extent, taken from indigenous people: "Blacks are the living link between the ordinary world of the island and the fabulous THERE, the Guinea that lives in their memory" (Maturo 75). However, the standard practice of the Spanish Crown was to prohibit and eventually eradicate any worshipping of African deities, as Catholicism had become the new doctrine to be adopted. Full indoctrination was never accomplished as many blacks refused conversion, while others adopted the new dogma, but never gave up their beliefs and worshipping practices, therefore merging the two religious systems. This juxtaposition favored the emergence of religious syncretism among the slaves and their descendants. Vodou, then, was regarded as a "subversive" religion, a religion that did not fit the new colonial society and was, therefore, not going to be tolerated. Roland Pierre explains that,

> In the Antilles, the policy of the masters was to force their slaves to give up their culture (language, work methods, religion) and to assimilate a new one; the only possible reaction was to reject or to reinterpret the culture forced on them. This is what gives voodoo its aspect of a *religion of deportees* which, therefore, could only be *a religion of protest and social redemption.* (29, italics in the original)

In order to understand the magic episodes that populate the narratives examined in this essay, it is necessary to likewise study the source from which all three authors have extracted their ideas of the magic. Not by accident, all three have situated their novels in Hispaniola. There are significant historical reasons for them to revisit the past on this island, which is shared by the two nations.

As societies evolve, the role of history becomes an important window to the past. All three authors have made use of specific historical moments in the creation of their works. But why have they decided to re-create history in order to write a novel which, by its nature, is predominantly fictional? Isn't history supposed to be truthful, objective, stripped of any distortion? Who writes history, anyway? It seems safe to assume that either there is a contradiction here or the novels were written with a special *intention*.

In 1949, Carpentier publishes "the first real New Historical Novel," *The Kingdom of This World* (Menton 20). This novel, Carpentier's second, takes place in Haiti. It narrates the insurrection of black slaves and how they were able to defeat Napoleon's army and become the first Latin American country to obtain independence. The role of magic and ancestral African religious practices (Vodou) have permeated the social and political lives of the Haitian people. This essay's scope only allows for the selection from the novel of two incidents, in which magic plays a major role.

Mackandal, perhaps the most important character in the novel, assumes the role of a houngan, a vodou priest destined to lead the rebels. As a runaway slave in the forest, he is initiated by Maman Loi, an old lady *mambo* or priestess, who trains him in all the skills necessary to carry out the insurrection and eventually liberate the Negroes. In order for Mackandal to succeed in this huge insurrection, which eventually will result in the independence of Haiti, he needs the protection of the Higher Beings, which he already has. He also needs the participation and loyalty of all his fellow African slaves. The way to achieve this is by establishing a pact, the historically well-known Pact of Bois Caiman, on August 14, 1791: "The spirit of the Pact of Bois Caiman, which marks the moment of the uprising of the blacks, is both religious and political at the same time. The Pact confirms the historical sense of liberation that Vodou has achieved by the cohesion of the Negroes in the island"[4] (Maturo 78). This time, the central character in the Pact is Boukman, the Jamaican, a Negro with a "mighty voice." In the midst of a heavy rain and thunders, Boukman addressed a multitude of trusted Negroes explaining that "a pact had been sealed between the initiated on this side of the water and the great *Loas* of Africa to begin the war when the auspices were favorable" (Carpentier, *The Kingdom of This World* 60). Having the total attention of his audience, Boukman continued building upon the religious justification for this war: "The white men's God orders the crime. Our gods demand vengeance from us. They will guide our arms and give us help. Destroy the image of the white men's God who thirsts for our tears; let us listen to the cry of freedom within ourselves" (Carpentier, *The Kingdom of This World* 61).

As a connoisseur of plants, medicinal herbs, and fungi, Mackandal became an expert at preparing poisonous potions with which he killed lots of animals and French white men. No one knew how the venom was reaching its victims, and this is one of the magical aspects in the novel: "In response to some *mysterious order* she [Maman Loi] ran to the kitchen, sinking her arms in a pot full of boiling oil," (Carpentier, *The Kingdom of This World* 19) showing no sign of blister or burn. Mackandal, holding supernatural powers, is able to metamorphose himself into just about any animal or insect he wants. This lycanthropic skill works efficiently because, camouflaged, he can deliver the poison and contaminate whomever and whatever he wants. The narrator describes the nature of this phenomenon as follows:

> The poison crawled across the Plaine du Nord, invading pastures and stables. Nobody knew how it found its way into the grass and alfalfa, got mixed in with the bales of hay, climbed into the mangers. The fact was that cows, oxen, steers, horses, and sheep were dying by the hundreds . . . the poison had got into the houses . . . and down the roads, green poison, yellow poison, or poison that had no color went creeping along, coming down the kitchen chimneys, slipping through the cracks of locked doors, like some irrepressible creeper seeking the shade to turn bodies to shades. (Carpentier, *The Kingdom of This World* 27–29)

If one examines closely the way the poison gets to all these places, one may think that it moves like a snake. And, in fact, the "mysterious order" to which Maman Loi responds might very well be to the call of Damballah, one of the most important deities in Dahomey, which is represented by a serpent. The reader of *The Kingdom of This World* does not see the magic in the making, but only the result of Vodou rituals taking effect. The force of a Vodou "work" is like an undercurrent coming from ancestral Africa and committed to the liberation of Haitian slaves.

An event equally amazing as the ones described above is that of the capture of Mackandal, the "lord of the poison." Mackandal is sentenced to be burned alive at the stake. However, making use of his lycanthropic skills, he escapes while turned into a mosquito. For the French, Mackandal is doomed; for Negroes, this outcome is a sheer manifestation of religious magic. Moreover, as a mosquito, "Mackandal had kept his word, remaining in the Kingdom of This World. Once more the whites had been outwitted by the Mighty Powers of the Other Shore" (Carpentier, *The Kingdom of This World* 46). Towards the end of the novel, Ti-Noel, a fellow slave to whom Mackandal has passed on his magical skills, can also metamorphose into different animals, including birds. This is another way of conveying that Mackandal still lives among the Haitians and struggles for their cause.

Mayra Montero's *The Red of His Shadow* (1992) is also a narrative involving mythical African deities. She is a Cuban-born journalist living in Puerto Rico who writes about Haitian, Dominicans, and their African cultural and religious heritages. The novel includes an "Author's Note" where Montero writes:

> This novel narrates real events that occurred a few years ago in La Romana. It is a story of love, hatred, and death involving a *houngan*, or Voudon priest, and a *mambo*, or Voudon priestess . . . Behind a case closed by the Dominican police as a simple 'crime of passion' pulse the magic spells of a war that is still being waged. (xiv)

The narrative ends with a "Glossary," where the author offers a list of terms pertaining to the Vodou pantheon and its rituals. The main text of the novel, then, is sandwiched between two extra-textual interventions of the real author. A guided reading? Underestimating the reader? Montero's novel allows for several interpretations. It may be read as a novel of social and political protest.

The Red of His Shadow narrates the story of Zulé, a Haitian girl who, like other "tens of thousands of Haitians, cross into the

Dominican Republic to work as cane cutters" (Montero xiii). It is important to keep in mind that many of these Haitian immigrants trespass the border undocumented. When the cutting season ends, many return to Haiti but some remain illegally. It is not a secret that Dominican-owned sugar cane plantations, more often than not, have taken advantage of the undocumented status of Haitians on Dominican soil, and many of them have become victims of exploitation, maltreatment, verbal and physical abuse, and, in a literal sense, have been marginalized. Similar to their ancestors, who were brought by force as slaves from Western Africa to the Caribbean, Haitians (willingly and sometimes unwillingly) journey into the Dominican Republic to experience "a life of untold privation and misery in working conditions patterned after the cruelest slave regimes" (Montero xiii). Besides denouncing the infrahuman conditions under which sugar cane cutters barely survive, Montero also delves into the "other reality" that exists in the world of the *bateyes*.

The Red of His Shadow explores the magic, mythical (and tragic!) experience of Zulé as a *dueña*, or Queen of a *Gagá*. It is the account of a young woman who holds a position of power in a highly misunderstood and marginalized spiritual *societé*. *Gagá* is the term used to designate a "degraded" form of Haitian Vodou practiced in the Dominican Republic, especially, but not exclusively, near the border. Margarite Fernández Olmos describes *Gagá* as "a specific religious society with roots in *rará*, the Haitian traveling groups who dance, play music, and display their rituals and traditions in neighboring villages during the Christian Holy Week before Easter Sunday" (273). The flow of cultural exchange between the two nations reach deeply into each other's peoples. Furthermore, over time, rituals and religious beliefs become hybrid and, therefore, more complex as they integrate new elements. Fernández Olmos notices, however, that "*Gagá* is therefore an interesting example of nontraditional Caribbean syncretism: instead of a hybridity between the European and the colonized, *Gagá* exemplifies a secondary type of syncretism, one between (ex)colonized peoples" (273). What Montero suggests in her novel is the fact that, even when both nations are no longer colonies, there still exists the notion of power (politically and economically) and the notion of Otherness between the two. Magical realism seems to be well-suited to represent such reality:

> The critics of magical realism often express their understanding of the concept in terms of cultural conflict between the dominant ruling classes and those who have been denied power. The vocabulary of "otherness" is frequently employed to refer to those who have been denied power. In colonial terms it is understood that it is the political power to govern oneself but also the power to define the world around you that has been denied the "others" . . . The dominant culture remained dominant by denying others the power to govern and the power to challenge the truths that they proposed. (Bowers 68–69)

Gagá, Haitian Vodou, and other forms of popular, socio-religious practices have always existed at the margins of dominant cultures and, sometimes, they have even been persecuted. One only needs to take a closer look at the characters in *The Red of His Shadow*, including Queen Zulé, to find out their precarious social conditions, their chances to come out of that lifestyle and their apparent indifference in realizing how the dominant culture regards them as the Other. What Dominican police ruled as a "crime of passion" in "Author's Note" quoted above, is an example of how poorly understood these popular religious practices are, at least in the Dominican Republic. This is, in part, the surface reality in Montero's novel.

In *The Red of His Shadow*, there is another reality, a mythical one, which, at times, interacts with the everyday life of the characters. The novel describes the spiritual evolution of Zulé, from her arrival at the *batey* to her crowning as Queen of her own *Gagá*. Zulé is characterized as possessing supernatural powers, as being a physically beautiful young woman, and showing an unconventional sexual behavior. Her sexual drive and lust lead her to engage in heterosexual and homosexual encounters, along with other transgressive conduct, considered "unusual" in a woman. This behavior is also attributed to the African deity Erzulie-Freda. Here is where we find the magical link between Zulé's African ancestors and her position as Queen of her own *Gagá*.

The climax in the novel is reached towards the end, when Zulé (Erzulie-Freda) has been "mounted" (possessed) by Belié Belcan, who has agreed to fight and kill Similá Bolosse, an ex-*Tonton Macoute* and *bokor*, or sorcerer, who has, in turn, been possessed by Toro Belecou. Jérémie Candé—in love with Zulé, but unwanted by her—is also mounted by Papá Carfú. These three pairs of entities, represented in the three flesh-and-bone characters in the novel (Zulé-Similá-Jérémie), engage in a fight where Jérémie, rather jealous, strikes Zulé with a machete and kills her. This scene is what Dominican authorities ruled as a "crime of passion." But what dominant culture is unable to understand is that it was Papá Carfú, in the body of Jérémie, who actually killed Zulé. The complexity of this scene in the novel must be studied carefully. Lidia Verson has a brief study that summarizes Zulé's tragic death, pointing out the "dual" reality of the duel. Verson explains:

> Therefore, the metaphor Zulé/Erzulie is constructed as a pure incarnation of the poetic, like a source of light and, at the same time, of impotence. Meanwhile, that [the metaphor] of Similá/Toro Belecou is her opposite: the representation of the mundane, the dark side of the unlawful and the force of treason. (4)

Perhaps the most interesting aspect of the outcome of the novel is how Montero has been able to juxtapose one reality upon the other, while fusing them into one. This is magical realism at its best:

> When we consider magical realism from the position of the 'other' and consider that it brings into view non-logical and non-scientific explanations for things, we can see that the transgressive power of magical realism provides a means to attack the assumptions of the dominant culture and particularly the notion of scientifically and logically determined truth. (Bowers 69)

El hombre del acordeón (*The Man of the Accordion*, 2003) by Dominican ethnologist and anthropologist Marcio Veloz Maggiolo is another novel whose argument, built around a true, historical era, is filled with extraordinary and magical events. As in Carpentier's and Montero's works, the reader needs to be familiar with the Caribbean cultural heritage and history in order to fully comprehend the scope of all three novels. Most of the action in *The Man of the Accordion* takes place in the decade of 1930 in the northwestern region of the Dominican Republic, not far from the frontier with Haiti. In that area, an accordionist, and his two other musicians, have become extremely popular. Honorio Lora is a skillful *merenguero*, womanizer and charismatic, mature man, whose talent playing the accordion is simply "not from this world." Honorio composes his own lyrics and is well known in the country, even by the President.

It is also well known that, in 1930, Rafael Leónidas Trujillo initiates one of the cruelest and bloodiest dictatorships in Latin America, which extended until 1961. Trujillo's regime, right from the first years, was known for its ruthless initiatives and obsessive nationalism. His extremist and xenophobic ruling led the dictator to launch an anti-Haitian campaign to whiten the Dominican border. In 1937, Trujillo went too far: under his orders and through the orchestration of his army, nearly twenty thousand[5] Haitians were killed. Based on this incident, Honorio Lora composed a piece with lyrics blaming the government, and as a result, he was poisoned. Nobody knew who did it, but he died after sipping from a cup of rum that "somebody" passed to him. His poisoning and sudden death caused great indignation among locals, including Ignacia and Remigia, two of Honorio's lovers. Both women are *hounsi* or spirit wives, Vodou servitors who, in the novel, become assistants to a Haitian *mambo*. Extraordinary events start to take place in the area after *hounsi* Ignacia and Remigia take Honorio's body to Haiti and request the practice of a *déssunin* in the hands of Polysona Françoise, a Haitian priestess. Alfred Métraux explains that in certain regions of Haiti,

> The déssunin rite is observed not only for the adepts of Voodoo but also for anyone who excels in his profession. Thus musicians, photographers and experienced sailors are all "dismissed." The talent, or simply the ability which such people have shown during

their lifetime, is taken to be supernatural, therefore the work of a loa, who must of course be withdrawn from the body. (246)

The practice of the *déssunin* rite unchains a series of supernatural, inexplicable events. All those who had anything to do with Honorio's death, received a punishment or were killed in one way or another. As mentioned before, Vodou's magic is like an undercurrent, unseen but effective, which travels freely through time and space. For the devotees of Vodou, the socially neglected, marginalized, and perhaps forgotten "Other" of the dominant culture, magic effects might be the only way through which justice can be served.

Perhaps the most interesting magic moment in the novel takes place when Acedonio Fernández, one of the many children fathered by Honorio, starts acquiring the traits and mannerisms of his father. "The war of the accordions," in which Acedonio plays Honorio's accordion in a competition with a female accordionist, represents a climatic turning point in the "vengeance" that invisibly has been taking place. As Acedonio smoked just the way his father did, "In the midst of a cloud of smoke Acedonio Lora felt some hand within his hands, some fingers that guided his fingers and a deep breathing down his shoulders that was a breathing of a loved one whom he never met"[6] (Veloz Maggiolo 143). As in *The Red of His Shadow*, Acedonio has been used as a *horse* so that Honorio, through Acedonio, could finish avenging his own death. It is important to know that neither the *déssunin* rite nor any other spell is described in the narrative. Therefore, there must be an active participation of the reader in tying the loose ends. It is up to the mastery of the author to construct such an atmosphere without causing disbelief in the reader or the characters: "In contrast to the fantastic, the supernatural in magical realism does not disconcert the reader, and this is the fundamental difference between the two modes. The same phenomena that are portrayed as problematical by the author of fantastic narrative are presented in a matter-of-fact manner by the magic realist" (Chanady 24). For the *rayanos,* or the inhabitants along the Dominican side of the border, incidents like this are as real as their ordinary lives. As neglected and marginalized as they may be, this is their "other" reality. Vodou devotees may travel in and out of that reality. Magical realism offers an avenue to explore that Otherness and allows readers to understand the Caribbean region a little better: "The characteristic of magical realism which makes it such a frequently adopted narrative mode is its inherent transgressive and subversive qualities. It is this feature that has led many postcolonial, feminist and cross cultural writers to embrace it as a means of expressing their ideas" (Bowers 66–67).

Towards the end of the novel, when everything has gone back to normal, the narrator informs that Honorio, after his third burial, has become Barón Samedí: "Thus he was transformed into the San Elías of the Catholic pantheon, according to the beliefs of "the misteries." Remigia says that Honorio's third burial got him out of the *Ginen* and out of the subsequent bottle, turning him into a being half Christian and half Vodou"[7] (Veloz Maggiolo 145). This idea of the intertwining of Christianity and Vodouism is cleverly expressed by the Haitian painter André Pierre, when he states: "The Vodou religion is purely Catholic, apostolic, but not Roman" (xx).

The three novels commented on in this work have many aspects in common. Their three authors have departed from factual, historical events that can be confirmed in official historical accounts. But the fact that they have recreated and fictionalized them is enough reason for readers to assume a more active role as consumers of historical fiction. Each of the novels is an invitation to revisit the "official" version of history and explore the facts not as they happened, but as they might have happened. Carpentier, Montero, and Veloz Maggiolo are thus extending an invitation to question history.

Distancing themselves from traditional Eurocentric expressive modes, these Caribbean authors adopt a more suitable practice to express the reality of the Caribbean region. They have chosen to explore a long-neglected sector of their own society, concentrating on the "Otherness" that generates from religious belief systems and practices linked to their African ancestors. As we have seen, magical realism allows these writers to express the realities of the Other, the neglected and marginalized, and the powerless. Whether taken as social or political protest, these novels and the intention of their authors also signal the acknowledgment of a social class that deserves and needs to be better understood. And perhaps, one valuable way to do so is by understanding its syncretic religious belief system. There is still much work to be done: "America is far from using up its wealth of mythologies. After all, what is the entire history of America if not a chronicle of the marvelous real?" (Carpentier, "On the Marvelous Real" 88). Each novel contains many more marvelous real moments, which this essay has omitted, due to its scope and to space-related considerations.

Notes

1. This novel, to my knowledge, has not yet been translated into English.
2. This term is found in a variety of spellings: Voodoo, Vadou, Vodoun, Vodou, vudú.
3. "América se me presentaba como una enorme nebulosa que yo trataba de entender, porque tenía la oscura intuición de que mi obra se iba a desarrollar aquí, que iba a ser profundamente americana" (Müller-Bergh 29).
4. "El carácter del juramento de Bois Caima, que marca el momento de la insurrección de los negros, es religioso y político a la vez, confirmando el sentido histórico de la liberación que ha alcanzado el vudú al cohesionar a los negros de la isla" (Maturo 78).
5. The number of Haitians killed varies according to the sources. Sources indicate that Trujillo, to wash his hands, did not allow a count to be kept because he wanted to make it seem as if it were a conflict amongst peasants. Juan Francisco Martínez Almánzar, in *Manual de historia crítica dominicana* records "from twelve to fifteen thousand" (464); Franklin Franco Pichardo, in *Historia del pueblo dominicano*, mentions "more than seventeen thousand" (520); and Frank Moya Pons, in *Manual de historia dominicana*, writes: "Trujillo had persecuted and given orders to assassinate Haitians wherever they were, killing some 18,000 of them" (519).
6. "En la nublazón de humo Acedonio Lora sintió unas manos entre sus manos, unos dedos que dirigían sus dedos y un respiro profundo sobre sus hombros, que era el respiro de un ser querido al que nunca conoció en vida" (Veloz Maggiolo 143).

7. "Remigia dice que el tercer enterramiento de Honorio lo sacó del Ginén y de la botella posterior, convirtiéndolo en ser mitad cristiano y mitad vudú" (Veloz Maggiolo 145).

Works Cited

Bowers, Maggie Ann. *Magic(al) Realism*. London: Routledge, 2004.

Cosentino, Donald J., ed. *Sacred Arts of Haitian Vodou*. Los Angeles: UCLA Fowler Museum of Cultural History, 1995.

Carpentier, Alejo. *The Kingdom of This World*. 1949. New York: Farrar, Straus and Giroux, 2006.

_____. "On the Marvelous Real in America." 1949. *Magical Realism. Theory, History, Community.* Eds. Lois Parkinson Zamora & Wendy B. Faris. Durham, NC: Duke UP, 1995. 75–88.

_____. "The Baroque and the Marvelous Real." 1975. *Magical Realism. Theory, History, Community.* Eds. Lois Parkinson Zamora & Wendy B. Faris. Durham, NC: Duke UP, 1995. 89–108.

Chanady, Amaryll Beatrice. *Magical Realism and the Fantastic: Resolved Versus Unresolved Antinomy*. New York: Garland, 1985.

Deive, Carlos. *Vodú y magia en Santo Domingo*. Santo Domingo: Taller, 1975.

De Heusch, Luc. "Kongo in Haiti: A New Approach to Religious Syncretism." *Man* 24.2 (1999): 290–303. Web. 2 Dec. 2013.

Dubois, Laurent. "Vodou and History." *Studies in Society and History* 43.1 (2001): 92–100. Web. 2 Dec. 2013.

Duncan, Cynthia. *Unraveling the Real. The Fantastic in Spanish-American "Ficciones."* Philadelphia: Temple UP, 2010.

Fernández Olmos, Margarite. "Trans-Caribbean Identity and the Fictional World of Mayra Montero." *Sacred Possessions. Voudou, Santeria, Obeah, and the Caribbean.* Eds. Margarite Fernández Olmos & Lizbeth Paravisini-Gebert. New Brunswick, NJ: Rutgers UP, 1997. 267–82.

Franco Pichardo, Franklin. *Historia del pueblo dominicano*. Santo Domingo: Taller, 1993.

González Echevarría, Roberto. *Alejo Carpentier. The Pilgrim at Home*. Ithaca, NY: Cornell UP, 1977.

Gosser Esquilín, Mary Ann. "*Del rojo de su sombra* de Mayra Montero: cruzando fronteras." *Letras Hispanas: Revista de Literatura y Cultura* 7 (2010): n.p.

⸻. "El consumo del cuerpo travesti en *Sirena Selena vestida de pena* de Mayra Santos-Febres." *PALARA:Publication of the Afro-Latin / American Research Association* 14 (2010): 42–53.

Martínez Almánzar, Juan Francisco. *Manual de historia crítica dominicana.* 9th Ed. Santo Domingo: Editora, 2003.

Menton, Seymour. *Latin America's New Historical Novel.* Austin: U of Texas P, 1993.

Métraux, Alfred. *Voodoo in Haiti.* New York: Schocken Books, 1972.

Montero, Mayra. *The Red of His Shadow.* Trans. Edith Grossman. New York: Harper Collins Publishers, 2002.

Moya Pons, Frank. *Manual de historia dominicana.* Santo Domingo: Caribbean Publishers, 2002.

Müller-Bergh, Klaus. *Carpentier. Estudio crítico-biográfico.* New York: Las Américas Publishings, 1972.

Murrell, Nathaniel Samuel. *Afro-Caribbean Religions. An Introduction to Their Historical, Cultural, and Sacred Traditions.* Philadelphia: Temple UP, 2010.

Palmié, Stephan, & Francisco A. Scarano, eds. *The Caribbean. A History of the Region and Its Peoples.* Chicago: U of Chicago P, 2011.

Pierre, André. "A World Created by Magic." *Sacred Arts of Haitian Vodou.* Ed. Donald J. Cosentino. Los Angeles: UCLA Fowler Museum of Cultural History, 1995. xx–xxii.

Pierre, Roland. "Caribbean Religion: The Voodoo Case." *Sociological Analysis* 38.1 (1977): 25–36. Web. 2 Dec. 2013.

Rengifo, Alejandra. "Beyond Magical Realism in *The Red of His Shadow* by Mayra Montero." *A Companion to Magican Realism.* Eds. Stephen M. Hart & Wen-Chin Ouyang. Woodbridge: Tamesis Books, 2010. 123–30.

Rivera Villegas, Carmen M. "Nuevas rutas hacia Haití en la cartografía de Mayra Montero." *Revista Hispánica Moderna* 54.1 (2001): 154–65. Web. 18 Nov. 2013.

Schroeder, Shannin, ed. *Rediscovering Magical Realism in the Americas.* Westport: Preager, 2004.

Uslar Pietri, Arturo. *La invención de América mestiza*. Mexico City: FCE, 1996.

Veloz Maggiolo, Marcio. *El hombre del acordeón*. Madrid: Siruela, 2003.

Verson, Lidia. "Zulé o Erzulie Freda en *Del rojo de su sombra* de Mayra Montero." *InterCambio* 2/2 (2003): 1–6. Web. 2 Dec. 2013.

Wilson, Jason. "Alejo Carpentier's Re-invention of América Latina as Real and Marvelous." *A Companion to Magican Realism*. Eds. Stephen M. Hart & Wen-Chin Ouyang. Woodbridge: Tamesis Books, 2010. 67–78.

Zamora, Lois Parkinson, & Wendy B. Faris, eds. *Magical Realism. Theory, History, Community*. Durham, NC: Duke UP, 1995.

The Unbearable Weight of Being in Daniel Galera and Rafael Coutinho's *Cachalote*

David William Foster

In the evolution of contemporary graphic narrative, there is virtually a prevailing consensus to the effect that the graphic component (which means also the verbal one, since they are so inextricably combined) will lead the reader away from a satisfactory fulfillment of the desire for whatever might be called the realistic or conventional depiction of the texture of human society. Much as creative photography and experimental film wish to defy the illusion of their power to depict lived human experience in a comfortably transparent fashion, graphic art (which, indeed, has a longer history as figural—in the sense of tropological—rather than figurative), as an intertwined component of narrative aspires to a form of abstraction that promotes ambiguity and enhances a sense of mystery and wonderment.

This essay does not argue that this sort of augmented realism—one interpretation of which is the so-called magical realism that is the topic of this volume—is an inherently constitutive part of contemporary graphic narrative. But it does tend to prevail, clearly manifesting the roots of these sustained narratives in the tradition of the weird, fantastic, edgy, and punk tradition of less structurally defined comic book products, where there emerged a tradition of "violating" original criteria of non-contestational realism in favor of the outlandish, whether in the circumstantiality of phenomena, like Rubber Man; the grotesqueries of Marvel Comics; or the speculative universes of comic book art's rich vein of science fiction.

It has been well established that one fundamental difference between comic book art (with its rather ad hoc graphic exuberance and an accompanying thinness of narrative profundity) and graphic narrative, as it has established itself as a contemporary cultural genre, has been a set of underlying principles of narrative coherence that promote reader introspection and the sustained contemplation of a complex and ambiguous aesthetic object.[1] Over-the-top

WHAM! BANG! KERPOW!, often tied to fanciful action images of raw physical experience, yield to the often highly nuanced and multiple ambiguous sequencing of lived human events, often with no conclusive sense of THE END.

Cachalote (2010), written by Daniel Galera and drawn by Rafael Coutinho,[2] Brazilian artists with extensive artistic credentials, may be seen as an iconic representation of the frequently elliptical nature of Latin American graphic narrative. Five different narrative threads are developed in the three parts of this black-and-white novel, and it is important to underscore that they never intersect, although all are essentially anchored in contemporary São Paulo (one moves to Paris and other European locales), a city, as clichés would have it, highly propitious for the anomie of non-intersecting lives. The five threads are the following: 1) An over-the-hill Chinese action actor in São Paulo to promote his latest film, during which time a young man, who is a member of the cast and apparently at least his aspirational lover, dies violently, the victim—maybe or maybe not—of foul play; 2) a bitter sculptor who is obliged to face the emptiness of his life; 3) a spoiled playboy who is exiled to Paris by his fed-up guardian uncle; 4) a hardware store clerk whose sexual fantasies lead him to a woman whose erotic will is stronger than his; 5) an apparently psychotic writer, who has a richer emotional relationship with his ex-wife than they had when they were married. Although the five threads are distributed in a non-proportional manner throughout the three parts of the novel and although they never intersect, not even to the point of the most happenstance presence of characters from one thread in another, they all come together under the aegis of the unbearable weight of human existence, as we see all five main characters (all five are men, evincing once again the androcentrism of the Latin American graphic narrative) struggling to survive existentially. Their existential struggle ranges from the grossness of the decadent Chinese actor to the excruciating Japanese erotic fantasies of the hardware store clerk and from the loucheness of the playboy and the boorishness of the sculptor to the psychotropic drug-induced evanescence of the writer and his ex-wife, with whom he shares his medications.

However, there is a *cornice*, an enveloping narrative frame, for the five threads. I would maintain that that frame provides the overarching motivation for the five stories and their coherence within a single narrative project. The framework appears as a wordless sequence of six pages (nineteen panels) at the beginning of *Cachalote* and an equally wordless sequence of six pages (eighteen panels) as coda to the book. The image of the *cachalote* (cachalot = sperm whale) appears in both introit and coda and appears in the third version of the central narrative thread (i.e., the one that appears third in the initial sequence of the five), the one dealing with the bad-boy Rique. This frame and the dominant image of the sperm whale deserve elaboration, in order to demonstrate how they are key to all five human stories being told.

In the introit, we see an older woman moving around her large mansion: she plays the piano, watches a romance story, and goes for a swim in her luxurious private pool. She is noticeably pregnant, while also notably aged, although no explanation is provided for this circumstance. The one additional frame in the introit, which disrupts the 18/18 distribution between introit and coda, is the image of a fetus floating in the amoebic fluid of the womb (by narrative juxtaposition, we suppose it is that of the pregnant older woman). When the woman, in the final half of the introit and after consulting her watch as though to determine it is time for this part of a daily routine, goes swimming, she and her fetus descend into the depths of the waters of the pool. As the woman surfaces, she comes face to face with a sperm whale, and she pats or strokes its snout. In a fashion characteristic of the non-continuity between the five narrative threads, there is no formal marker of transition from one segment to the other, and we turn the page from this image to see a man urinating in a toilet, the only sign that we have left the introit and entered the story of the first of the five main characters—in this case, the wreck of a Chinese action-film star.

The coda appears at the end of the final sequence of the hardware store clerk and his erotic companion, in which turning on the lights during intense lovemaking leads to the conceit of a black page that is blank, except for the word "CLIC" and, in a circle in the center, as though an expanding point of light, the question (directed by the woman to the man), "Viu?" Rather than seeing what the man is supposed to see or seeing the nature at this point of their complicated ritual lovemaking, we have the transition, on the next page, to the coda. The older woman sits on a beach chair with a closed book in her lap, watching her son, now about five years old, play on the beach. One of his five toys is a whale, which he is holding in his left hand; there are also a space man, a fishing boat, and a sea horse lying on the beach between his legs, and he holds a toy shark in his right hand. One is tempted to correlate these five toys with the five stories that have come between the introit and the coda. But, except for the fact that the whale appears in the final installment of Rique's story, there is no readily apparent symbology in the four other objects, although the reader, if he notices the presence of the five toys, might affect some sort of tenuous association. But then the boy looks up, stares at the roiling waves, and looks at the whale in his left hand. As though surprised, his mother looks up, squinting at the sea over the edge of her sun glasses. She folds the boy (we now see him naked) in a tight embrace, and, as she lets him go, he walks out into the waves. The mother picks up the toys, folds her chair, and walks up the beach away from the waves.

    This mysterious ending, which involves, we imagine, the disappearance of the boy into the waves—Has he seen a whale? *The* whale? Has he gone to search for it? Is the mother's apparent acceptance of the boy's disappearance into the waves as though it were an event foretold, related in some way to her experience in the introit with the whale in the backyard swimming pool? This would suggest a retroflexive reading grounded in a metaphor for the tenuousness of human life and the inevitability of our individual fall into nothingness. While the little boy is, as our cultural tropes would have it, as yet innocent of the complexities of life, he is also in a proleptic fashion, an icon of each human being's disastrous and often deadly existence. Yet no matter how disastrous or deadly one's existence may be, not only do we vanish into thin air, but much of the so-called living moments of our existence are equally the stuff of nothingness: when the writer's ex-wife, struck by deep anxiety as she waits with several other people at a bus stop, downs some of the psychotropic drugs he has just given her illegally, she literally disappears from the page, leaving a blank space between the waiting passengers on either side of her: the miracle of modern pharmaceuticals has not just anticipated her eventual existential vanishment into thin air, but they have afforded a dry run of that inevitability.

The boy's disappearance into the frothy waves of the ocean is the inverse of the appearance of the cachalot. The sperm-whale, the cachalot, is characteristically one of a group of large whales that beach themselves, typically a couple of thousand a year; sometimes they are already dead, while sometimes they die as a consequence of the beaching, often from dehydration or because high tide covers over their blow hole, and they drown.[3] There is considerable disagreement as to why this happens. But there is the fact that the group of whales that include the cachalot are among the few great mammals that dwarf human beings and leave them in awe. Also, they tend to belong to close-knit communities that make their separation from their fellow creatures highly suggestive of the way in which human beings can become alienated from the rest of their society, as is the case of several individuals in the Galera-Coutinho novel. Indeed, there is a double transition. First, it is the transition from the whale encountered by the pregnant woman in the introit to the man urinating in the toilet. But it is also the transition from the whale that mysteriously appears in her swimming pool to the "beached whale" (whether in general or in terms of his circumstantial appearance in Brazil) of the Chinese actor in decline, whose bloated body sprawls on his bed in very much a beached fashion. The prostitute who is with him must wonder where his rock-hard action figure body, which likely still prevails in his publicity shots, has gone.

Not only is there the abiding mystery of the beached whale, an image that goes back hundreds of years in artistic representations, but there is also the mystery of how and where it appears. Even if it is drawn ashore by prevailing tides, why is it that this whale has become beached and why is it in this particular location, with the possibility that the locations in which beached whales appear are unlikely sites, given the marine factors involved. To be sure, there are hardly abundant reports of whales appearing in domestic swimming pools, and besides, in the case of this whale, it is not beached, even if it has scant chance of surviving a pool's chlorinated and foodless waters. A more conventionally beached whale is discovered by Rique, as he comes to the end of his rope on an abandoned beach outside Barcelona. At one point, there is some possibility that the animal may be a figment of his imagination, as it seems to have vanished into thin air. Rique, walking alone and, given the blanked-out look on his face, perhaps suffering from sunstroke, is also a likely candidate to disappear into thin air, at least in the sense of disappearing without a trace, since he is severed from family, friends, and society at large. None are likely to take any note of his disappearance.

Clearly, the whale is important in framing the five narrative threads of *Cachalote* and in iconizing the irony of a presence with such enormous bulk (like human life in general, but the strong, reckless, and most careless lives of the five protagonists), only to disappear without a trace in a process of biological but, more importantly, psychological disintegration.[4] As such, it is a controlling magical icon that lends a heavy mystery to the existential commerce of these individuals and articulates a degree of unknowability that renders fevered human lives (from the louche to the exquisitely sensitive) utterly meaningless. If it is our convention to believe that the magical contains within it a human mystery we must strive to decipher in the best cabalistic fashion, there is little in narrative systems of the Galera-Coutinho narrative to make this possible. The proposition of a higher meaning to the existential events of human lives or to such mysterious signs as the key to an alternative reality is not forthcoming. That is, unless we can sustain the hypothesis that the tropological meaning of events is that they have no meaning.

The unbearable weight of human existence here is that it leads to the empty sound stage where the sculptor thought he has been collaborating in making a documentary on his life and work, to the abandoned beach where Rique can hardly strut his final stuff, to the darkened no-tell hotel room where the hardware store clerk and his erotic partner (the masochist who, in the end, pushes the sadist beyond his limits) vanish into the dark produced by the turning on of the bedside lamp. Nothing times the magical still equals nothing, and what realism there is in the universe is neither deepened nor enhanced by the magical. In this fashion, the dense narrative texture of *Cachalote* is a correlative of the dense narrative texture of the universe we perceive: a lot of very heavy-duty things happen, but they leave nothing in their wake. The image of the mother just walking away from the beach after, apparently, her son has walked into the waves and sunk out of sight is certainly a very emphatic conclusion, in which no amount of affective reader anguish, horror, or terror can alter the finality.

None of the foregoing is meant to signal that the dense narrative texture of *Cachalote* is not, in itself, narratively meaningful, only that there are no transcendent metaphysical implications to draw from it, aside from the metaphysical implication that there are no metaphysical implications. When viewed on the level of narrative structure, *Cachalote* is, indeed, a tightly structured semiotic edifice.

As I have noted, the narrative is explicitly divided into three parts, plus the introit and the coda, which are included in the first and third parts, respectively. These parts correspond to the internal narrative movements of classical Greek tragedy. I am speaking of the way in which the three parts of the narrative may be seen as a presentation or postulation of the characters and the situation of their lives. None is exemplary; rather, all seem to be quite screwed up, to put it bluntly, with the possible exception of the hardware store clerk. Yet this depends on how one wants to read his involvement with the practice of highly dangerous and unquestionably sexist Japanese *kinbaku* (the ritual immobilization of women via complex patterns of trussing with thick ropes).[5] It is not a question of whether or not Vitório's sexual practices or Lara's sexual fantasies are also his, or whether or not her participation can, by any definition, be called consensual. It is an erotic spectrum that functions in tandem with that of the lives of the other four characters and, therefore, there is an implied symbiosis, an implied correspondence between their individual destinies, even if not all are as ruinous as, say, that of the loutish and decadent Chinese actor.[6] Thus, while it appears that we can only make a casual connection between the five main characters (again, they never interact in the narrative), only their faintest coloration as somehow damned is forthcoming: they are, in the end, nothing more than a gallery of rather insignificant human beings, each insignificant in his own intimate way. That some may be immoral is only a further coloration beyond their basic parallels.

The second set of narrative developments corresponds to approximately what we can call the *peripeteia*, the reversal of fortune that will lead the main characters inevitably toward their individual forms of demise: the sculptor begins to perceive that the film in which he has agreed to star is going nowhere; the Chinese star appears to be kidnapped by unknown individuals; Rique buys a sports car and sets out on a highway to nowhere, after having been rebuffed in every quarter in Paris; the wannabe writer's wife disappears into thin air after taking a handful of his psychotropics; Vitório discovers, at the hands of someone who appears to be his lover's dark guardian angel, that he has gotten in over his head in his relationship. Perhaps none of these is as culminating an experience as tragic peripeteia, but Greek tragedy is not involved here. Suffice it to underscore how none of these "reversals" of fortune (perhaps the most momentous one might be the case of Vitório because of the intrinsic interest of frustrated sexuality and the deep terror we associate with the possibility of entertaining erotic games that go terribly wrong) augurs well for the personal story of each of the protagonists.

Each of the three sections is progressively shorter than the preceding one, and the third one, then, rushes, so to speak, toward the five individual dénouements. This is the phase of anagnorisis, when the individual comes face-to-face with his own fate, which, in the case of the pathetic rather than tragic world of *Cachalote*, is the mess he has brought about. The second segment, relating to the Chinese actor, ends with someone from a group of young actors who befriends him asking, "O que aconteceu no hotel, Xu?" (Galera & Coutinho n.p.). The answer to the question may or may not resolve the circumstances of the police warrant out for his arrest. One can envision a piteous reply that might provide an Aristotelian catharsis, while a reply that would confirm the police's suspicions would be more momentous. If a moment of anagnorisis is involved, in which the character must come face-to-face with his actions and the fate he has wrought through them, it is not shared with the reader. Anagnorsis becomes more of a narrative tease here, since one assumes the reader might well want to know what the nature of the relationship was between Xu and Jia, and how the latter fell to his death. However, just as there is Deleuzian narrative fragmentation in the development of the three storylines, there is also, in the final section of *Cachalote*, narrative withdrawal and frustration, something like a *relatio interrupta* that correlates the unbearable weight of existence with the vacuousness at its core. One might entertain the proposition that each of the five protagonists here is, in one way or another, a beached whale, and perhaps Xu even more so, given the bloated and decadent condition of his body. But, I would insist, the authors allow for only the most tenuous of associations, for to do so otherwise, would be to freight these individuals with an essentialist meaning that would be quite at odds with the discursive principles at play. Thus, the final segment for Xu involves the arrival of the police and his disappearance into a squad car. The woman who had asked him to explain what happened is left with an empty verbal gesture: "Pô."

The sculptor decides to crash the sound stage with his automobile to find some trace of what has happened to the film crew that had convinced him to allow them to film his life. There is nothing there but a movie poster with the title *A face de mármore*; the police arrive; and he is attempting to make a call to someone from the stationhouse; his wife picks him up; and in the end, we see her studying the poster she takes from his hands after he falls asleep from exhaustion. We are left to wonder what it is he might have understood from the poster, although it would seem fairly clear that it is a less than generous reference to his hard-hearted ways that plays off of the stony nature of his visage and the marble with which a sculptor customarily works.

Fortunes appear to have changed for the better between the writer and his ex-wife, who—although confessing to being pregnant by her current lover—engages in a long and tender embrace with him. But there is no indication what this might mean, as the sequence concludes with their little girl, who has been told to go play with a puppy, following the puppy to the edge of the park's iron fence. The puppy squeezes through the fence and is run over by a passing truck. What does little, the daughter, understand from this event?

The last we see of Rique is that he's stretched out on the beach, smoking a cigar, lying not quite in the shadow of the now very much present beached whale, whose immense size overshadows the insignificant Brazilian wannabe playboy.[7]

Already characterized in this essay is the concluding segment with Vitório and the now very demanding Lara. Suffice it to reinforce the conceit of the conclusion: she insists on their enacting their rituals of kinbaku with the lights on, but the blacked page, overlain by the CLIC of the lamp being turned on, is as though the sought-after illumination only produced the black hole of their passion. The white dot containing the question "Viu" is like an ironic consequence of the failure of illumination.

In a sense, this concluding interrogative can be read as ironic for *Cachalote* as a whole: given the strategies of narrative displacement, what I am facetiously calling *relatio interrupta*, and a symbolism weighted with the nothingness of being, what can it be that the reader might or might not have seen? Now, if readers were following this commentary with the actual graphic narrative in hand, they would see that I, too, can be accused here of a certain amount of narrative displacement. The stories of the five protagonists are not just told three times, corresponding to the three divisions of the book. Rather, the third part of *Cachalote* actually revisits each one of the five narrative threads twice, thereby drawing out the process of anagnorisis—and the concomitant suppression of an accompanying *catharsis*. The reader does not need a commentary to sketch out all of the details, but rather to give the sense of how each individual narrative thread is given final treatment. To be sure, the fact that the final "act" of the novel is a double *reprise* of each story only reinforces the overarching organizational principle of narrative displacement.

Now, it is necessary to focus a bit more emphatically on the concept of narrative displacement. As has been widely recognized, such displacement, which Deleuze originally formulated with reference to film, but which gibes fairly well with the pronounced cinematographic flow of the graphic narrative, is characteristic of the latter type of narrative. It is as though there were an imperative to move away from transparent narratives, both in the sense of motivation and meaning, but also in terms of cause-and-effect narrativity. To be sure, a classic Latin American work, like Héctor Oesterheld and Francisco López Solana's *El eternauta* (1957–59 in its original serial publication) does, in fact—despite the conceit of a highly allegorical narrative within an enveloping proleptic frame grounded in the transcendent potential of art (Foster, "Masculinity")—tell a very straightforward story of an alien invasion of Buenos Aires, its disastrous consequences, and the way a band of heroic men is able to save the day. Traditional or conventional cartoon art amply satisfies readerly demands (I am clearly evoking the legendary Barthian disjunction here between the readerly and the writerly) for narrative transparency. Moreover, it is the view of graphic fiction as edgy, vanguard, experimental that makes it reasonable, if not expected, that it will move toward the writerly end of the spectrum, toward complicating narrative paradigms and introducing audacious conjugations of narrative elements.

It is for this reason that one can find, as one variety of narrative displacement, an interest in certain modalities of the magical realism that equally characterized the innovative, but strictly word-centered, *nueva narrativa latinoamericana* of the 1960s and 1970s.[8] Although one may have little investment in a genre of magical realism in Latin American narrative, it is unquestionable that something like a magical-realist turn in Latin American writing occurred at one point as a rejection of the social-realist, documentary, quasi-sociological mode of so much early twentieth-century Latin American writing. Carlos Fuentes made this point very early in one of the first commentaries on the new Latin American novel. Where it has gone since then has been of considerable controversy, and I am very much in agreement with my colleague Emil Volek as to what he calls *Macondismo*[9] (and I would call the Macondo) factor: the use of quirky, cute, charming, flamboyant, outrageous, magical-fantastic elements in the service of a really quite disadvantageous, Third-Worldly belief in a primitive world more profoundly authentic than the dreary alienations of hegemonic Western capitalist "realities."

I affirm all of this here not to contribute anything significant to the debate, which may only serve to distract from text-centered analyses, but rather to situate Galera's and Coutinho's work. Because when all is said and done, the narrative universe of *Cachalote* is hardly that of Gabriel García Márquez's Macondo, as in his *Cien años de soledad* (1967). Rather, it is very much postmodern, globalized São Paulo, Brazil. By the same token, *Cachalote* has little to recommend it as a screed on the spiritual depravations of late capitalism, although some may want to pick up on useful suggestions (e.g., the commercialism of the sculptor, the crazed-fan pursuit of the iconic international Chinese action star, Rique's playboy ways).

Where, then, do the elements one might wish to associate with magical realism go in *Cachalote*? Certainly, the process of narrative displacement is suggestive of an abstract narrative conjugation of the five story lines that is not in evidence on the level of *sujet*, the actual dynamics of narrative telling, since none of the five intersects with any of the others, except in the vague perception that all five are somehow beached whales of humanity. That this conjugation involves the mysterious cachalot that appears, may disappear, and may be there but unseen (the coda of the novel, involving the little boy's disappearance into the sea), is what propels this narrative beyond what could easily have been the depiction of the nitty-gritty texture of Paulistano daily life, with all its gallery of human possibilities synthesized in five protagonists. Indeed, as this essay has insistently argued, the narrative tension of *Cachalote* rests on the interplay of a densely evoked quality of the mysterious (beginning with deep human emotions and motivations) and the otherworldliness of the iconic whale, especially in the guise in which it first appears, with the novel's deferral and, ultimately, denial of meaning. Such an affirmation is sustained by the way in which none of the five narrative threads is depicted in terms of any dénouement whatsoever, no matter how much one keeps thumbing back in the various segments and despite the best efforts to review each thread on its own. The awe and circumstantially magical nature of these five urban Brazilian lives finally derives from the unbearable weight of unbeing and nonbeing.

Notes

1. "Highly textured in its narrative scaffolding, comics [i.e., graphic narrative] doesn't [*sic*] blend the visual and the verbal—or use one simply to illustrate the other—but is rather prone to present the two nonsynchronically; a reader of comics not only fills in the gaps between panels but also works with the often disjunctive back-and-forth *reading* and *looking* for meaning" (Chute 452).
2. Galera is well established as an important writer of vanguard narratives, which will alert the reader to the so-called high literary contexts for *Cachalote*. Coutinho is the son of the legendary cartoonist Laerte Coutinho, who signs his work with only his first name.
3. The scientific facts relating to beached whales are taken from the "Beached Whale" entry in *Wikipedia*, accessed November 11, 2013.
4. By this time, the reader will have realized that Galera's and Countiho's narrative necessarily evokes the most famous symbolic whale in Western literature, Moby Dick, from Herman Melville's novel, *Moby-Dick* (1851). Melville's whale is steeped in multiple symbolic meanings, befitting the sort of symbolist narrative of the time, and interpretations of the white whale range across multiple interpretational nodes. Yet no matter how many multiple interpretations are associated with Moby Dick, there is little question that Melville means for his reader to see him as a *symbol* of something, something that must be viewed with a deep resonance in the narrative texture of the novel. The reader of *Cachalote* is left to wonder what degree of resonance this white whale might have. For an example of recent critical analysis of the figure of the whale in *Moby-Dick*, see Calkins; see Bouk and Barnett for the importance of leviathans in the nineteenth-century imaginary.

5. As a consequence, one presumes, of the inclusion of the practice of kinbaku in *Cachalote*, my copy, purchased in the São Paulo Livraria Cultura in July 2010, comes with the front cover sticker "Só para adultos!"—although one wonders if the exclamation mark means that the sticker is more of a teasing come-on than a warning. Kinbaku is like other select Japanese erotic practices, such as deep punishment enemas or the representation of sexual activities in the 1976 Japanese film *The Realm of the Senses*, directed by Nagisa Oshima. At least in terms of what is available on the internet, all of this material is masculinist-anchored, with or without willing female sexual partners. I have found the scantest of references to trussed males, no trace of female-male, or same-sex variations. Let me make it clear, I am referring to kinbaku, which is specifically identified in the Galera-Coutinho text, not to other sexualized forms of bodily immobilization. Sado-masochism in Hispanic literature does not yet have much of a bibliography, with the exception of the Argentine Alejandra Pizarnik's lesbian-marked *La condesa sangrienta* (1971) and *Fe en disfraz* (2009) by the Puerto Rican author Mayra Santos-Febres. See the discussion of the sources for Santos-Febres' novel by Arce.

6. Interestingly enough, as another dimension of underdeveloped narrative schemata in *Cachalote*, there is a physical resemblance between Vitório and the little boy at the end of the novel. And at one point, Vitório and Lara end up swimming together in a pool at someone's house party, although they discover no white whale in the pool. Later, they will swim together in the stormy ocean, and Vitório will rescue Lara from drowning by leaning down to pick her up as he rides an imposing black steed, enacting a medieval fantasy of chivalric manhood. But again, no white whale appears.

7. This image, in a light salmon color in place of white and a burnt sienna in place of black, now serves to illustrate the cover of editions of *Cachalote* subsequent to the first one.

8. I examine the relationship of Brazilian culture to what was a more Spanish-language production, the *nueva narrativa hispanoamericana* or the boom in Foster, "Brazil and the Boom." Yet, while not exactly chronologically coterminous with Spanish-language production, Brazil does evince an equivalent experimental production and certainly something as "magically realist" as the Spanish American paradigms.

9. Volek is not the first to use this term (it is customarily attributed to the Chilean scholar José Joaquín Brunner), but Volek can be credited to having discussed the issue at length.

Works Cited

Arce, Chrissy B. "*La Fe disfrazada* y la complicidad del deseo." *Lección errante: Mayra Santos Febres y el Caribe contemporáneo*. Eds. Nadia V. Celis & Juan Pablo Rivera. San Juan, P.R.: Isla Negra Editores. 2011. 226–46.

Barthes, Roland. *S/Z*. Trans. by Richard Miller. Pref. by Richard Howard. 1st American ed. New York, Hill & Wang, 1974.

Bouk, Dan, & D. Graham Burnett. "Knowledge of the Leviathan: Charles W. Morgan Anatomizes his Whale." *Journal of the Early Republic* 28.3 (2008): 433–66.

Calkins, Jennifer. "How is It Then with the Whale? Using Scientific Data to Explore Textual Embodiment." *Configurations* 18 (2010): 31–47.

Chute, Hillary. "Comics as Literature? Reading Graphic Narrative." *PMLA* 123.2 (2008): 452–65.

Deleuze, Gilles. *Cinema*. Trans. Hugh Tomlinson & Barbara Habberjam. Minneapolis: U of Minnesota P, 1986–89.

Foster, David William. "Brazil and the Boom." *Teaching the Latin American Boom*. Eds. Lucile Kerr & Alejandro Herrer-Olaizola. New York: Modern Language Association of America (forthcoming).

_____. "Masculinity of Privileged Human Agency in H. G. Oesterheld's *El eternauta*." *Transmodernity* 3.1 (Fall 2013): 81-101..

Fuentes, Carlos. *La nueva novela hispanoamericana*. México, D.F.: Joaquín Mortiz, 1969.

Galera, Daniel, & Rafael Coutinho. *Cachalote*. São Paulo: Quadrinhos na Cia, 2010.

Volek, Emil. "Introduction: Changing Reality, Changing Paradigm: Who Is Afraid of Postmodernity?" *Latin American Writes Back: Postmodernity in the Periphery*. Ed. Emil Volek. New York: Routledge, 2002. xi–xxviii.

Underdogs and Beautiful Lies: Magical Realism in the Second World

Nicholas Birns

Magical Realism in the Second World

Canada, Australia, and New Zealand occupy an ambiguous place in the English–speaking world. Though most of their population has historically been white and descended from British settlers, they have, unlike the United States, never been large enough to exercise substantial cultural power. This has led the Canadian critic Stephen Slemon to call these countries "Second World," neither the First World of the United States and Britain nor the Third World of India, Nigeria, and aspects of Latin America and the Caribbean. In other words, despite their seeming cultural proximity to Europe, these countries had a sense of marginality analogous to that of elsewhere, concomitant with the popularity of a magical realist mode of representation.

For most of their post-settlement history, these countries were not particularly noticed in world literary discussion. This changed in the 1970s and after, and, as in Latin America, magical realism played a substantial role. It should be stressed that the influence of Latin American writers was direct: writers from the English–speaking countries read and were affected by such Latin American writers as Borges, García Márquez, Carpentier, and Asturias. Despite reasonable geographic proximity, relations between Latin America and the Anglophone settler colonies had, historically, never been strong. Canada, with its residual ties to Britain, did not even join most inter-American institutions until late in the twentieth century. The very noun "norteamericano" is always applied, in Latin American parlance, to mean just the United States, leaving Canada symbolically dangling in the Arctic. Australia and New Zealand initially had considerable trade ties to South America via the whaling industry. Yet, once the British Empire was formally organized, they entered a far more economically protectionist mode, in which trade and cultural exchange was anchored within the English-speaking world. Australia, for instance, did not even have diplomatic relations with Brazil until 1945.

It was thus only when Latin American literature, and in particular magical realism, became prominent in wider English–speaking literary discussion that magical realist modes became relevant to the former settler colonies; there was no special pipeline. But a book like *One Hundred Years of Solitude* (1967) spoke with particular pertinence to Australia, New Zealand, and Canada. The novel, in these nations, had been dominated by formal realism. Modernism, despite a few attempts, had not taken root, its experimentalism being tacitly seen as a recondite luxury that societies still struggling for literary recognition and self-worth could not afford. Magical realism appealed as a way in which the stories of these countries could be told on a human level, allowing fiction to exercise its inherent imagination, creativity, and ingenuity.

The appeal of magical realism even inflected the work of these countries' most senior writers. In Australia, the Nobel prize-winner Patrick White, most of whose oeuvre, though often visionary and symbolical in import, had adhered to the representational canons of realism, turned more towards fantasy as his later novels *The Twyborn Affair* (1979) and *Memoirs of Many in One* (1986) dealt with people who shift identity, gender, and national origin amid the chaotic flux of the twentieth century. In Canada, Robertson Davies (1913–1995), the leading writer of his generation, turned even more overtly to mysticism and magic in the final of his three completed sets of trilogies, The Cornish Trilogy. In New Zealand, *Smith's Dream* (1971) by the noted poet and critic C. K. Stead (b. 1934) depicted a fictional future New Zealand as a country of dictatorships and resistance movements not unlike Latin America at the time, and Janet Frame 1924-2004), in her final novel, *The Carpathians* (1979), turned from her emphasis on subjective mental states to a world where the very categories of space and time are variable.

Peter Carey and Australian Magical Realism

But it was the writers born in the 1930s and 1940s who fully embraced magical realism. In Australia, Peter Carey emerged in the 1980s as a writer of world stature, a novelist who intrigued and provoked. In *Illywhacker* (1985), Carey used magical realism to knit together traditional oral aspects of Australian life—the yarn, the ballad, the tall tale—with the paradoxes of Australian identity in the wake of British colonization, American economic domination, and the increasingly relevant proximity of Asia. Carey's initial literary production was largely in the form of short stories, and it reflected the parabolic and sometimes apocalyptic preoccupations of Jorge Luis Borges, of whose influence Carey once said "it cannot *not* be there" (Ross 44). In *Illywhacker*, Carey turned to García Márquez as a model, both in terms of characters who have unusually long life spans (its protagonist, Herbert Badgery lives until the age of 139) and can become invisible and in the use of magical realist techniques to comment on the unfulfilled potential of Australia as a nation, how it has prepared over its contradictions and repressed the eccentrics and outsiders—racial, ethnic, sexual—who, in fact, provide much of the flavor and diversity of Australian life. Carey also takes advantage of magical realism's ability to convey large themes through images, in order to construct (to use Frederic R. Jameson's phrase) a "national allegory" of Australia in terms that the Australian realist novel—even at its most experimental in the hands of a homegrown genius like the early twentieth-century writer Joseph Furphy—never could quite do.

Herbert Badgery is not wholly likable; he is a con man, failed husband, indifferent wage earner, and truth-teller. But he is also endearing and adorable in his garrulousness and indefatigability. The permeable barriers between the roles of fraud, liar, and charmer are used by Carey not just to create an unforgettable character, but also to attest to the possibilities inherent in fiction itself, the way something outrageously untrue on the literal level can nonetheless be true in an imaginative sense. The fundamental contract that magical realism makes with the reader—that any departure from plausibility will not infringe on the book's moral impact—is incarnated in the way Badgery, irritating yet admirable, shows us the unofficial Australia, one excluded from superficial national narratives. Like the great Latin American magical realists, Carey celebrates both the power of fiction and the outsiders to social consensus, whose stories magical realism can affirm.

Illywhacker, though, is far more comic in tone than most Latin American magical realist novels. *Oscar and Lucinda* (1988), which won Carey the first of his two Booker Prizes, is darker, as the two title characters converge in a doomed love story whose emblem—the glass church that is supposed to be transported to the Outback—represents the inevitable failure of an attempt to sow European ideals wholesale on Australian soil. That the odd-looking Oscar Hopkins and the misunderstood heiress Lucinda Le Plastrier are both outsiders who are drawn to each other by their shared representation of possibilities that the Australia of their time would not permit. Here, magical realism merges with another genre with which Carey has become associated, the historical novel. Whereas straight realism had tended to concentrate on the present-day or near past, the warrant of magical realism to depart from strict fidelity to observed circumstances enabled Carey to depict a past that was not literally accurate, but was nonetheless eloquently imaginative. In both *Illywhacker* and *Oscar and Lucinda*, Carey was influenced by Günter Grass' *The Tin Drum* (1959), who used magical realist techniques to depict protagonists injured by history. Carey's early books depicted Australians injured by history, who either chose to opt out of society entirely—as in *Bliss* (1981), where Harry Joy leaves his advertising job to join a rural commune—or, as in *Oscar and Lucinda*, bear witness to how structures of domination are so demeaned to maintain control that they end up injuring those who strive for an alternate outcome. Carey was also fascinated by the quirky and unusual, extending this even to his own background in *The Tax Inspector* (1992), set in a car dealership in Bacchus Marsh, Victoria, the community in which he grew up.

In the early 1990s, Carey moved to New York and began a career as a professor of writing at American universities. *The Unusual Life of Tristan Smith* (1994) is an amalgam of startlingly disparate influences: postcolonial theory, the Dutch heritage of New York, the phantasmal animal imagery of Disney World, *apartheid* in South Africa and its comparability to the white Australian treatment of Aborigines, and Carey's awareness of how United States foreign policy had, despite its professions of idealism, often used Australia in an instrumental and exploitative way. Using two fictional South Pacific states, Efica and Voorstand, as examples of the oppressed and the oppressor, Carey paints his protagonist—a young, misshapen boy with no less than three possible fathers—as a naïve, yet perceptive, observer, a subaltern figure seeking recognition in a court stacked in favor of the oppressor. Carey, in his later work, emphasized first the historical, then the constitutive inauthenticity of the narrative act, over the magical realism that had formed a third pillar with these other two traits in books, such as *Illywhacker*. Yet, as late as 2012's brilliant *The Chemistry of Tears*—featuring a complex machine in the shape of a mechanical duck—Carey's work was still characterized by an ingenious braiding of the real and the fantastic.

Another Australian, Rodney Hall, received recognition in both his home country and worldwide for *Just Relations* (1982), a book that seemingly incarnated the ideal of the "total novel" as espoused by Mario Vargas Llosa. Huge in size and scope and attempting to describe an entire community, *Just Relations* tells the story of Whitey's Fell, a community much like García Márquez's region of Macondo: different from the mainstream. Whitey's Fell, threatened by the capitalist economic plans of a mining company, is both traumatized by this difference and determined to preserve it. *Just Relations* tells the story of an entire community in a more panoramic style than the realist novel could ever attempt. Realism can portray a specific tableau, or even patch together several of these as in the "camera eye" technique of the US novelist John Dos Passos. But Hall's creation of a local religion called Remembering, which attracts devotees of extreme old age, evokes the contrast of old and young, of the contrasting allures of past and present, more vividly than a heap of realistic details could by themselves manage. Another trait of Hall's that is reminiscent of some Latin American magical realism is the seemingly contradictory dynamic between the sharp critique of corporate modernity mounted by Hall and the way the novel clearly wants to appeal internationally, to present Australia as somewhat of a commodity to what Pascale Casanova has termed "the world republic of letters." Similarly, *Woman of the Future* (1979) by David Ireland (b. 1927) threads in science-fiction elements with psychological realism. Ireland's *The Chosen* (1997), as in *Just Relations*, uses a small town in rural Australia to write the nation in symbolic form. Barbara Hanrahan (1939–1991), whose half-whimsical, half-bitter novels are at once keenly felt evocations of the life of a creative, yet physically and emotionally vulnerable woman and a challenging examination of what it is to feel embodied, yet not be satisfied with that condition. The "discontinuous narratives" of Frank Moorhouse (b. 1939) were not, strictly speaking, magical realist, but they operated through a similar sense of the continuity of meaning made representational disruption, as did the standard view of magical realism.

Several of the novelists mentioned above were examined in Helen Daniel's breakthrough critical book *Liars* (1988). Here, we once again see, as in Carey, the conflation of the three not inherently related strands of magical realism, metafiction, and national identity. In the United States, magical realism was seen as a political mode appropriate for peoples who had been subordinated and traumatized; metafiction—fiction that foregrounded its own fictiveness—was a First World luxury of writers with the time and social privilege to write fiction about fiction; and nationalism was something vestigial. But in Australia, these three discourses were able to cohabit culturally for a while. Even an overtly metafictional book discussed by Daniel, *The Plains* (1982) by Gerald Murnane (b. 1939), pointed, through a combination of writerly games and alternate realities, to scrutinize the ideal of an Inner Australia. Though not all the writers described above had nationalist agendas—Hanrahan certainly did not—the magical realist techniques they used were most visible in expressing an Australian national identity that had emerged from colonialism. In inheriting the tradition of Australians cooking up, as Mark Twain once said "the most beautiful lies," magical realism was able to affirm imagination and history, inventiveness and national advocacy. All this was to change in the 1990s.

Canada: Magical Realism Reinvents the World

Though Canadian magical realism did not produce a single writer with the magnitude of Peter Carey, if anything, the mode sunk in more deeply in the great white North than in the great Southern land. The first name most Canadian literary scholars would mention with respect to the term "magical realism" is Jack Hodgins. Hodgins wrote on and off Vancouver Island, just off the coast of the province of British Columbia, a region that—while retaining real-world nomenclature—he made into his own Northern, forested Macondo. In *The Invention of the World* (1986), Hodgins exhibits both the good and the bad side of regional distinctiveness. A group of people once domineered over by the charismatic Donal Keneally, a cult leader who segregates his community from the rest of the world. A generation after Keneally's death, the descendants of this group are shepherded by Maggie Kyle, who, in contrast, seeks to succor and sustain the remnants of these renegades, now shambling and marginalized. There is also Becker, an old eccentric who seeks to piece together the community's history, including the deeds of the outsized Keneally. This last element is an example of what Linda Hutcheon later termed "historiographic metaficiton," i.e., fiction that existed simultaneously on past and present levels where the present level functioned as a narrative and perceptual window upon the past. This category could also include works that rewrote earlier texts or cultural legends, as Peter Carey did in *Jack Maggs* (1998), which recast Dickens' *Great Expectations* and *True History of the Kelly Gang* (2001), which represented the tale of Ned Kelly, the iconic Australian outlaw. Historiographic metaficiton, although not inherently magical realist, was, in the work of Carey and Hodgins, compatible with magical realism in that the contrast between present and past could parallel the contrast between realistic and magical. This is how Hodgins operates in *The Invention of the World*, where Becker's research is not just archival striving after the tangible, but an attempt to glimpse into the mystical and sacred. Much like

Illywhacker in Carey's oeuvre, *The Invention of the World* is more rollicking than subsequent books written by Hodgins. Hodgins' later novel, *Broken Ground* (1999), concerns the legacy of the First World War in Canadian culture and examines how a group of traumatized soldiers perseveres through memory and mutual caring. Vancouver Island emerges as an outcasts' sanctuary, a place where "Underdogs of every description, right across the landscape, people fed up with being kicked around somewhere else" (Hodgins 45).

Canada is a country of distinct regional identities, and Canadian magical realist novels tended to come from remote or secluded regions. Very few emerged from Toronto itself, unless they were by those born elsewhere, such as the Sri Lankan-born Michael Ondaatje, whose *In the Skin of a Lion* (1987) manages to make magical the building of a Toronto bridge, or the Argentine-born Alberto Manguel, whose fantastic novels and anthologies of fantastic literature helped turn Canadian literature away from a realistic orientation. Among native-born Anglo-Canadian writing (the Francophone tradition has used magical realism much less, although aspects of Marie-Claire Blais' work have been seen as magical realist), magical realism has flourished most regionally or as an expression of regionalism. Susan Swan, from southwestern Ontario, in *The Biggest Modern Woman in the World* (1988), writes about a giant woman from the nineteenth century who uses size, as Jonathan Swift did in *Gulliver's Travels*, as a way to examine aesthetic issues of disproportion and incongruity. Susan Kerslake, a longtime resident of Nova Scotia, combined fantasy and realism in *Middlewatch* (1976) and *Penumbra* (1984), both of which deal with the mistreatment of women and with insanity and the rival scenarios of perception it foregrounds. *Seasoning Fever* (2002) moves to a very different region, the prairies, and is Kerslake's version of a total regionalist novel, using magical realist techniques to conjure a community. Ann-Marie McDonald, in *Fall On Your Knees* (1996), combines regionalist elements—much of the novel is set on Cape Breton island, a largely Celtic and Francophone part of Nova Scotia—while also reaching out to encompass the turbulent events of the twentieth century as well as dissident identities and modes of perception within family and community. These women writers used magical realism to tell previously unheard stories of women and, often, to pursue a tacitly or explicitly feminist agenda. Robert Kroetsch (1927–2011) possessed a much more philosophic take on these issues. A scholar of Heidegger and of continental thought in general, Kroetsch's tales of hijinks on the Canadian prairies were laced with speculation and a recurrent sense of life as a cosmic joke.

New Zealand and the South Pacific: Islands and Legends

The most famous New Zealand book to feature magical realist techniques is Keri Hulme's *The Bone People* (1985). This was the first novel from New Zealand to win the Booker Prize and it exemplified a new international visibility for New Zealand literature. As with Australia, magical realism served to give the image of New Zealand literature abroad a new start, and it offered a way to present the nation *in toto* that earlier social and psychological novels had not been able to do. Hulme tells the story of a proud, introspective writer, whose name, Kerewin Holmes, marked her as comparable to the author, and her discovery of a mute child, Simon. The novel took up issues of imagination and identity, of art and life, which magical realist novels often seek to braid and suture. That Hulme herself was of partially Maori ancestry, like her alter-ego Holmes, served to tie these issues of art and life with New Zealand's ongoing consolation of its bicultural heritage. When Hulme's Maori descent was called into question by C. K. Stead, he also included a tacit attack on the book's closing scene of spiritual harmony, calling middlebrow and pseudo-uplifting.

Two writers of unquestioned Maori descent, Patricia Grace and Witi Ihimaera, also employed magical realism. In Ihimaera's *The Matriarch* (1986), Maori legends exist side-by-side with a realistic chronicle of a Maori family. In Grace's *Potiki* (1986), chapters alternate between mythic and representational levels. Critics have noted, though, that this technique differs from the way magical realism is used by writers like, say, Carey or Hodgins, where fantasy is used to redress or re-inspire reality. For Maori, with their sense of the continuity of real and spiritual experience, a non-Cartesian, monistic worldview is inherent in their very conception of being.

Polynesian writers, such as Sia Figiel and Albert Wendt, used magical realist techniques in ways that were legible to Western readers as such, but were also expressions of their own cultures' conceptual and spiritual practices. Wendt's *Leaves of the Banyan Tree* (1979) adheres to several magical realist markers: the action takes place over a series of generations and mythic and referential elements are mixed. The novel aspires to present a national allegory of the South Pacific, or at least Samoa. Wendt's work, however, is deliberately difficult, and cannot be readily ingested by the Western reader; its thick implication in the interstices of Samoan lore and memory grants the book a sense of fracture and resistance that pushes back against the complacent harmony, which Stead so criticized in Hulme's work.

Epeli Hau'ofa (1939–2009), a Tongan writer, was inclined more to the short story than the novel. In *Tales of the Tikongs* (1982), Hau'ofa provides the reader with various yarns and tall tales of island life, mixing invention and adaptation, cultural consensus with his own writerly sensibility. Unlike the Australian writers and Keri Hulme, however, South Pacific writing by Polynesians and Melanesians did not reach an international audience outside of academia. Whereas other modes of magical realism could be seen as conveniently literary, South Pacific island writing required a degree of cross-cultural insight that did not simply package the places under discussion in a palatable way for the metropolitan reader.

The 1990s and after: Magical Realism at Bay

What both made and unmade magical realism as an international mode was its formulaic quality. Much like the romantic historical fiction of Sir Walter Scott, which despite the very specific Scottish setting of most of Scott's work acquired imitators worldwide, from Poland's Henryk Sienkiewicz to Australia's Rolf Boldrewood, who basically took the Scott formula and plugged it into their own histories, it was both inspired and opportune for Anglophone writers in the 1980s to take Macondo and plug it into a landscape they were from or to which they had a perceived relation. Thus magical realism (ironically in light of García Márquez's indictment of the United Fruit Company in *One Hundred Years of Solitude*) acquired a corporate quality, where a Hall or a Hodgins was read as the national headquarters of the multinational magical realist corporation. As we have seen in the case of Carey, a truly first-rank authorial career could outgrow this once-beneficial straitjacket.

However, just as occurred in Latin America with the emergence of the McOndo and Crack groups of writers in the 1990s, magical realism quickly became old-hat, and writers reacted against it generationally. Australian writers born in the 1960s, like Christos Tsiolkas or A. L. McCann, looked to or resembled the visceral-realist disillusionment of a Roberto Bolaño rather than the representational panoply of a García Márquez. The gritty naturalism of Alan Duff in *Once Were Warriors* (1990) represented Maori life in circumstances of urban poverty in a very different way from the mythic and rural settings of Grace and Ihimaera. Furthermore, as foreshadowed in Stead's critique of Hulme, magical realism became perceived as middlebrow, the kind of books one's mother or aunt read, which were accepted by a polite literary opinion whose circle of approval younger writers inevitably strove to rupture.

Yet even in the 1990s and 2000s, vestiges of magical realism remained. The interest in out-of-the-way regions of Canada and Australia crested in this decade, as two offshore islands, Tasmania and Newfoundland, received world literary exposure. Tasmania, in the writing of Richard Flanagan, emerged as a wilderness region, filled with convict remnants and strange species of animals, which had its own rules of representation, and the genre of "Tasmanian Gothic" flourished. Flanagan's *Gould's Book of Fish* (2002) reflected magical realist tropes in its intermixture between the human and animal kingdoms and its sharp critique of Enlightenment rationality, raising the question of whether magical realism was a more contemporary and socially responsible form of Romanticism. With respect to Newfoundland, Wayne Johnston's *The Colony of Unrequited Dreams* (1998) used the life of Joey Smallwood, the

Newfoundland politician who brought the island into confederation with Canada in 1949, as the frame for a flagrantly inventive total novel about Newfoundland's multifarious identities and quirky inhabitants. Ironically, Johnston represents Smallwood's drive towards Confederation as a tragic fall from grace, and there is a sense of elegy for the island's lost independence. Yet Johnston's book was successful not just in a national, but also in an international frame, raising the same question as did Hall's *Just Relations*—do magical-realist novels encourage locality on the level of representation, but the metropolitan in terms of audience and reach?

This became even more vexed in the 1990s and 2000s, as previously national institutions of publishing and distribution in Canada and Australia became global. The popularity of Tasmania and Newfoundland in London and New York could be seen as circumventing entirely the intermediate space of the nation. Metropolitans looked for out-of-the-way islands to travel to, in literary terms, precisely because their idiosyncrasy was so opposite from the interchangeable maw of neoliberalism, digital culture, and global exchange. Even in books not set on islands, such as *Eucalyptus* (1998) by Murray Bail, the presentation was at once above and below the national, as not a place but a species of tree became the focal point of the novel's imaginary.

Magical realism thus retained its exotic allure. In some contexts, such as the work of Asian Canadian writers Hiromi Goto and Larissa Lai, it intertwined with diasporic and subaltern discourses. But it forfeited any ability to function as a national allegory, as the very idea of the nation seemed to be under erasure in an era exalting the global as universal norm. This arguably contributed to its loss of literary esteem, as the mode became a ready target for jest and castigation. In Gerald Murnane's acclaimed *A History of Books*, for instance, a narrator resembling, in stance and life-history, Murnane himself states, in the novel's second paragraph:

> At some time during the 1970s, or it may have been earlier, the phrase magical realism became fashionable among the sorts of person who are paid to write comments on published works of fiction. Those

persons mostly used the phrase when commenting on works of fiction from the region known as Latin America. (Murnane 3)

Murnane later mentions the image of a jaguar, clearly alluding to the Guatemalan novelist (and Nobelist) Miguel Ángel Asturias' *Men of Maize* (1949). Though the relationship between the jaguar-image and the images in Murnane's own book is complicated, the overall effect is to dismiss the idea that magical realism represents a quantum innovation over other approaches. True literary pleasures, Murnane suggests, are less contrived, more nuanced. This was in tandem with the increasing desire of Australian and Canadian writers to join in international literary conversation and the international marketplace. The exoticism and instant branding provided by magical realism was, many judged, no longer needed.

And yet, in 2013, the young New Zealand writer Eleanor Catton won that year's Man Booker Prize, the first won by a writer from New Zealand since Hulme's, with *The Luminaries*. This book, huge in size and scope, included astrology, mysticism, characters representing all aspects of New Zealand, including Chinese and Maori. For a book from the Anglophone "Second World" to make it big in the First World, the prodigious, synthesizing qualities of magical realism were apparently still prerequisites.

Magical Realism and Indigenous Imagination
It was fairly seamless for Maori themes and writers, as we have seen in the cases of Hulme, Grace, and Ihimaera, to make their way into the New Zealand magical realist mainstream in the 1980s. Though Maori are still not yet fully enfranchised, they have always had enumerated rights under the 1840 Treaty of Waitangi, and a bicultural (Pakeha-Maori) order is the norm in New Zealand, much the same way English and French identities strive to cohabit in Canada. Indigenous (or "First nations") writing in Canada also moved forward in cultural prominence in the later twentieth century, particularly in the novels of Thomas King and the plays of Tomson Highway. Australian indigenous people, though, long had a very different situation: the object of numerous racist attempts

at extermination and then assimilation, their not being granted citizenship until 1967, and the fundamental principle of land rights not being affirmed until the landmark *Mabo* court decision of 1992. The civic and representational gulf between white and black Australians was much wider than the comparable situation in New Zealand.

Magical realist representations helped suture this gulf in ways that were more than false synthesis. Admittedly, this project got off to a shaky start as B. Wongar, a Serbian national who adopted an Aboriginal name, was revealed as non-indigenous after his nuclear trilogy had gained wide popularity. Even more shockingly, Mudrooroo (formerly Colin Johnson), who had coined the term "maban reality" as an Australian equivalent of magical realism, was revealed to be not of indigenous Australian but African American ancestry. Similarly, Archie Weller, who had openly taken up genres of science fiction and fantasy as an Aboriginal writer, had his ancestry similarly disputed. Far from achieving coalescence between fantasy and reality, magical realism among indigenous Australians seemed to be symptomized by hoaxes and fakery. But the work of Alexis Wright changed all this. Wright's *Carpentaria* (2006) was the first work by an indigenous Australian to receive wide exposure on the Australian literary scene. The plot of Wright's novel, of a small community resisting the hegemonic effort of a mining company, resembles that of *Just Relations*. But unlike Hall's book, where the people of Whitey's Fell (a name singularly inappropriate to be applied to the people Wright features) are unified, the indigenous people of the community of Desperance are divided between the Eastside and Westside Pricklebush mobs, animated by different beliefs and aspirations, as signified by the surnames of their leaders, Midnight and Phantom.

Whereas in a clichéd magical realist novel by a white Australian, the name of one of the book's major figures, "Normal Phantom," might be seen as a middle way between realism and fantasy, in Wright's novel the name signals the necessity to accept what the Western mind might style the fantastic as part of the lived, everyday reality of the indigenous community. Nor, as the very name Desperance connotes, is the presence of indigenous lore mean to be inspirational and repopulate the empty spiritual plenum of jaded metropolitan whites. Thus, as Maria Takolander points out, the term magical realism is both apposite and inapposite for Wright's work. Wright admittedly has read and learned from Latin American authors, but she is repurposing and, in many respects, inverting the readerly expectations that might be brought to her book via accustomed magical realist paradigms. However, Wright could not have done this had magical realism not been available to her as a tool in the first place.

Long after the fashion of magical realism in the Second World became outdated, the legacy of the mode of magical realism might be to have taken a small role in partially healing the national structures of Second World countries and the indigenous inhabitants who have suffered from and persevered under those structures. Magical realism occupied a middle space and made long-unventilated issues more negotiable, within and outside the national space of Second World countries.

Works Cited

Fee, Margery. "Why C. K. Stead Didn't Like Keri Hulme's The Bone People: Who Can Write as Other?" *Australian and New Zealand Studies in Canada* 1 (1989): 11–32.

Hancock, Geoff. "Magic or Realism: The Marvellous in Canadian Fiction." *Magic Realism and Canadian Literature: Essays and Stories*. Eds. Peter Hinchcliffe & Ed Jewinski. Waterloo: U of Waterloo P, 1986. 30–48.

Hodgins, Jack. *Broken Ground*. Toronto: McClelland and Stewart, 1998.

Hutcheon, Linda. *A Poetics of Postmodernism*. New York: Routledge, 1990.

Murnane, Gerald. *A History of Books*. Artarmon: Giramondo, 2012.

Ross, Robert. "'It Cannot *Not* Be There': Borges and Australia's Peter Carey." *Borges and His Successors: The Borgesian Impact on Literature and the Arts*. Ed. Edna Aizenberg. Columbia: U of Missouri P, 1990. 44–58.

Slemon, Stephen. "Unsettling the Empire: Resistance Theory for the Second World." *World Literatures Written in English.* 30.2 (1990): 30–42.

Takolander, Maria, *Catching Butterflies: Bringing Magical Realism to Ground.* Geneva: Peter Lang, 2007.

Proliferation: The Case for Magical Realisms from Oyeyemi's *The Icarus Girl*
Kim Anderson Sasser

Helen Oyeyemi's *The Icarus Girl* (2005), a novel published to critical acclaim when the author was not yet out of her teens, is steeped in suspense due to the malevolent TillyTilly (Tilly)—a character who repeatedly "gets" other characters (to use *Icarus Girl*'s terminology) and whose ontological status remains ambiguous throughout the narrative. On one hand, readers might understand her to be a symptom of child protagonist Jessamy (Jess) Harrison's mental illness, a dangerous alter ego: this is the diagnosis of Jess' British psychologist. On the other hand, Tilly may be the displeased spirit of Jess' twin, who died at birth, Oyeyemi's fictional rendering of Yoruba beliefs in the *ibeji*, or twin lore, and *abiku*, or spirit-child. This is the interpretation of Jess' traditional Nigerian grandfather. Neither possibility is ever given the final word, so that Tilly remains in a state of multiple possibilities. While either rendering of Tilly is equally real to Jess, Tilly must actually exist—apart from Jess—in order for the novel to be positioned within the domain of magical realism, a literary mode that requires a magical phenomenon that cannot be explained away by a natural process, such as human psychology. Because Tilly simultaneously is and is not *super*natural, *Icarus Girl* itself teeters among multiple (literary) registers.

Since magical realist narratives most often present their magical phenomena unequivocally, thereby expecting readers to accept them as occurring, *Icarus Girl*'s multi-positioning of Tilly is important for the way it enriches the ambit of the magical realist narrative mode. With *Icarus Girl*, Oyeyemi handles the mode playfully, experimentally. If the author's treatment of magical realism positions her in a liminal space, though, she is not alone there. Cuban Alejo Carpentier, one of the most significant figures in the development of the seminal Latin American phase of magical realism, employed a similar technique in *El reino de este mundo* (*The Kingdom of this World*, 1949), when Haitian slave Macandal's execution is interpreted in two divergent ways: as a supernatural escape by the other slaves whose worldview is informed by Afro-Haitian voodoo and as a successful punishment by the white slave owners who watch him burn. Oyeyemi's use of this technique, then, connects her to a foundational magical realist predecessor, while also, as this essay will show, revealing the distinct concerns of an author who inhabits a different position on the magical realist timeline.

Rather than debate these novels' magical realist status, I will suggest that we more productively consider *Icarus Girl* and *Kingdom* as comprising a unique strain of magical realism, one characterized by a double-framing, or positioning, of magic. What is more, I will convey this strain as indicative of a broader tendency within magical realism: it is one of many types that have emerged throughout the literary mode's history. Magical realism might be ethnographic or formalist; postcolonial or metropolitan; territorial or global; magically saturated or sparse; Latin American, African, or British. Due to its diverse manifestations, we would do well now to discuss magical realism in the plural, as magical realism*s*. Besides making sense of the proliferating types just mentioned, pluralizing the term responds to recent and increasing critical arguments for a broader understanding of magical realism, one that values the mode's Latin American and postcolonial usages, but offers a more nuanced understanding of what that crucial phase, as well as subsequent phases, are doing with the integration of narrative magic and literary realism. Finally, to discuss a multiplying magical realisms is to participate in a re-visioning of the mode, one that makes ample space for innovative ways of conveying current, twenty-first century concerns, as has been achieved by Oyeyemi, one of the youngest in the new generation of magical realist authors.

Icarus Girl's Double Frame

At eight years old, Jess flies with her Nigerian mother, Sarah, and English father, Daniel, from their home in Cranbrook, England, to Ibadan, Nigeria, where Jess meets her Nigerian family. While Jess is initially excited about the trip, the narrator, looking back on this journey, informs readers that if Jess had known the "trouble" this visit would precipitate—"it all STARTED in Nigeria"—she would have refused to go (7). What trouble started there? On the compound of Jess' grandfather, Baba Gbenga, Jess meets Tilly, a character who appears to be a young Nigerian girl about Jess' age. Tilly becomes the introverted and lonely Jess' first friend, so that Jess is upset upon her departure from Ibadan. However, Tilly inexplicably reappears in Cranbrook in a British school uniform after Jess has returned home, claiming her parents have moved close by. As the narrative progresses, Tilly becomes ever more mystifying and ever more terrifying as Jess realizes Tilly can perform impossible feats, like becoming invisible and falling through stairs and, especially, when she reveals that she intends to displace Jess permanently from her own body, as she does twice. Neither Jess nor readers can pin Tilly down: who and what is she? Is she Jess' imaginary friend? An alter ego? An actual existing spirit?

The narrative offers two explanations for Tilly. Psychologist Dr. McKenzie, the professional to whom Jess is taken because of her unexplained screaming fits, diagnoses Tilly as Jess' alter ego. As he explains to Jess, "It's possible that all TillyTilly means is that part of your mind—say, the part of you that can show you're angry in a reasonable way—hasn't developed as quickly as other parts, like the part of you that likes reading lots of books" (Oyeyemi, *Icarus Girl* 300). In contrast, Baba Gbenga, Jess' Nigerian grandfather, is convinced that Tilly is the spirit of Jess' deceased twin, who must be appeased through the use of an *ibeji* statue, the prescription given by Yoruba culture. Jess' mother describes this tradition to Jess this way: "[I]f one twin died in childhood before the other, the family of the twins would make a carving to Ibeji, the god of twins, so that the dead twin would be . . . happy'" (Oyeyemi, *Icarus Girl* 207).

Within critical treatments of the novel, there is no consensus over Tilly's identity and ontological status; rather, critics tend to bifurcate along the two options the novel offers. Some furnish a rationalist explanation for her, as does reviewer Bruce King: "The way the novel is told, through Jessie's perspective, makes the supernatural appear real, although there are implied natural explanations" (73).

While at one point, King hints at two possible readings, he himself recommends a singular one, suggesting that Tilly is not real, but that Jess merely "feels" her to be so (73). Alternatively, those who emphasize the narrative's filiation with Yoruba mythology (and, by extension, Nigerian culture and the African Diaspora) are more inclined to read Tilly as supernatural. Victoria R. Arana exemplifies this category. She locates the novel entirely within a Yoruba context and, by extension, reads Tilly exclusively as a "seductive and deadly abiku spirit" (Arana 291). While performing important critical work in drawing attention to the Yoruba contexts for the narrative, Arana does not account for the additional alter ego reading furnished for Tilly as well as additional, non-Yoruba cultural resources from which Tilly is drawn, such as the uncanny doppelgänger.

While arguments might be marshaled on both sides (Tilly as ontologically real and unreal), it can be argued that the narrative does not recommend or even allow a conclusive interpretation. Instead, it intertwines the two possibilities without ever bringing closure to their simultaneity. Both interpretations of Tilly sit side by side throughout the story's duration: as soon as the narrative leads the reader to one possibility, that reading is called into question for its alternative. Gail Low, one of the few critics who allows the prospect of two readings (though she hints at the possibility only briefly), draws attention to the way the novel's employment of third-person voice creates a distancing effect that "allows Oyeyemi to preserve a fine balance between the gothic," or supernatural explanation for Tilly "and realist elements of the novel, thus preventing readers from simply labeling the main character as merely mad" (Low 226).

In addition to voice, the narrative itself sets up Tilly's duality in scene after scene, wherein evidence for her ontological status see-saws back and forth, causing readers to continually teeter as well. Consider the fact that Jess is the only person who ever sees Tilly, the implications of which Jess realizes uneasily one day in the park, when Tilly has just disappeared once Jess' classmate spots Jess:

> [Jess] had just realized with stunning clarity that she was the only person who saw TillyTilly. . . . TillyTilly had not met anyone in her

family, no one had met her, and she refused to meet anyone. And even when Jess was with TillyTilly, they couldn't see TillyTilly. She suddenly felt very small and a little bit scared.
Is TillyTilly . . . real? (Oyeyemi, *Icarus Girl* 170)

Lest we begin to doubt Tilly's reality too much, thus tipping her back to the side of alter ego, Tilly finally reveals herself to someone, Jess' friend Siobhan, or Shivs. While Shivs must promise to keep her eyes shut during her encounter with Tilly (tipping readers back over to the Tilly-as-unreal side), she has an experience with Tilly that is deeply convincing, not only to Shivs, but also to readers. Tilly seems to prove herself beyond doubt by doing things that would have been impossible for Jess to fabricate, like emitting a coldness into the air and opening and shutting Jess' bedroom door while Jess is sitting on the bed beside Shivs (Oyeyemi, *Icarus Girl* 294). Of course, readers are not allowed to sit comfortably with Tilly's independent existence. The morning after Shivs has met Tilly, Shivs denies the experience as a good trick, one that "was almost convincing, but only almost" (Oyeyemi, *Icarus Girl* 295). And so it goes in *Icarus Girl*. This kind of wavering between Tilly's two ontological possibilities is representative of her treatment throughout the narrative.

As with Tilly's multiple possible identities, or rather because of them, the novel itself encompasses myriad literary registers: (postcolonial) *Bildungsroman*, (postcolonial) gothic, the uncanny, realism, horror, ghost story, myth (the Greek myth of Icarus and Yoruba mythology), and African oral literatures. In addition to these, can we also fruitfully read *Icarus Girl* through the lens of magical realism? A term that has, by now, slipped into common parlance, magical realism has been affiliated with Oyeyemi by several reviewers and critics, including this author, but one must proceed with caution when linking this particular, formally prismatic novel with what Anita Sethie describes as the author's "trademark magic realism" ("Mr. Fox" n.p.). Tilly's ambiguous status—or, more accurately, her multi-status—challenges this classificatory link because, according to the alter ego reading, Tilly is a creation of Jess' mind. Within this frame, the novel retains gothic features, such as the abandoned Boys' Quarters, blood, Jess' screaming fits, and the profuse number of generally terrifying scenes. However, it ceases to be magical realism.

While magical realism has been notoriously difficult to conclusively define—critics are still working to delimit the mode—most would agree that this is a narrative mode that must include what David Young and Keith Hollaman call an "irreducible element," a phenomenon "that cannot be explained by logic, familiar knowledge, or received belief" (4). Hallucinations, dreams, and alter egos are not irreducible elements, since they can be explained as products of human psychology and, therefore, do not constitute magical realism. Young and Hollaman illustrate their concept of the irreducible element with a short story by Gabriel García Márquez: "How is the angel in 'A Very Old Man with Enormous Wings' to be accounted for? We learn that he is a phenomenon beyond the ken of the church. . . . Few of us would write him off as the joint hallucination of the whole populace. We must take him as a given, accepted but not explained" (5). In *Icarus Girl*, by extension, Tilly "cannot be explained by logic" offered by the scientific domain of psychology. She must exist in her own (unexplainable) right, if we are to discuss the narrative as magical realism. As I have already described, Tilly does and does not objectively exist at the same time. If the view of Tilly as psychological creation prevents the link with magical realism, the alternative view as supernatural being sustains it.

Icarus Girl's complex treatment of literary form both mirrors and enacts one of its most significant thematic threads. Just as the novel is suspended between multiple formal categories, Jess is suspended between multiple identity categories, a situation she experiences as a perplexing conflict. Most saliently, Jess is bi-racial and bi-cultural—thus the reason for the pejorative term "half-and-half child" by which she is repeatedly described. Her simultaneously split and multiple identity causes her to feel like an outsider in Nigeria and at home. Jess is called an *oyinbo*, or stranger, outright upon arriving in Nigeria by a Nigerian man, whom she has never met; he makes this pronouncement by virtue of her visible (racial) difference (18). Similarly, at school in England, the class bully, Colleen McLain, taunts Jess: "'Maybe Jessamy has all these 'attacks' because she can't make up her mind whether she's black or white!'" (92).

The confusion and isolation Jess encounters as a result of her suspension amidst these competing categories is very different from the celebratory treatment of migrant identity found in Salman Rushdie's well-known essay "Imaginary Homelands," wherein Rushdie underscores the benefits afforded him by having proliferating roots, or multiple cultural heritages. Rushdie memorably dramatizes the possibility of resolving the inheritance of numerous sources of identity in his short story "The Courter," wherein his (strongly autobiographical) young migrant protagonist feels intense pressure to adhere either to his Indian heritage or Western home, until finally having the liberating epiphany that he does not have to side with one against the other, but can instead embrace both. In the protagonist's words, ". . . I have ropes around my neck . . . pulling me this way and that, East and West, . . . *choose, choose.* . . . Ropes, I do not choose between you. . . . I choose neither of you, and both. Do you hear? I refuse to choose" (Rushdie 211). As a mixed race, multi-cultural/-national child, Jess never achieves such harmonious resolution, and her inability to arrive at a settled conclusion corresponds with readers' inability to resolve *Icarus Girl*'s formal identity.

Not only do thematics and form reflect one another meaningfully in this way, then, but *Icarus Girl* also enacts Jess' predicament on the level of narrative form. Its formal rehearsal of vexing, multiple identities causes readers to experience a deferred uncertainty akin to its protagonist, perhaps fostering a richer empathy than would have transpired without this formal correspondence.

Kingdom's (Anterior) Double Frame

Besides constructing a telling thematic parallel, *Icarus Girl*'s proliferating formal identity affords additional benefits. By teetering in and out of magical realism, the novel exemplifies a use of the magical realism that pushes at the mode's formal borders, asking the mode to work in unusual—and, therefore, intriguing—ways. In thus toying with magical realism, Oyeyemi is in good company:

Carpentier deployed the form in a strikingly similar manner over six decades prior to his influential novel *Kingdom*. The latter sets a precedent for the dual positioning of narrative magic.[1] In Carpentier's narrative, set in the historical milieu of the Haitian Revolution and its aftermath, the execution of Afro-Haitian slave Macandal is witnessed by onlookers as having two diametrically opposed outcomes. On one hand, the other slaves see him shapeshift and fly away: "The fire began to rise towards the Mandingue, licking his legs. . . . The bonds fell off and the body of the Negro rose in the air, flying overhead, until it plunged into the black waves of the sea of slaves. A single cry filled the square: 'Macandal saved!'" (Carpentier, *Kingdom* 52). On the other hand, the French colonial executioners and onlookers see Macandal burn to death in the fire, so that the response of M. Lenormand de Mézy, inflected with irony by Carpentier, is dismay at "the Negroes' lack of feeling at the torture of one of their own—drawing there from a number of philosophical considerations on the inequality of the human races" (*Kingdom* 52). As in Oyeyemi's novel, neither view is ever privileged over the other, so that the veracity of what happened to Macandal cannot be conclusively determined. Both are allowed to coexist, as indeed the worldviews and cultures of these two groups historically did coexist in the colonial Caribbean and elsewhere.

With Oyeyemi's and Carpentier's narratives, we might posit a particular strain of magical realism, one characterized by the double-framing of narrative magic, so that the magical phenomenon is suspended between two unresolved possibilities.[2] Perhaps Carpentier's unconventional magical realism is the result of his writing *Kingdom* at a time when literary magical realism was still relatively young, so just being forged, while Oyeyemi's can be attributed to her recent appropriation of it, so a time when authors are inclined to reconfigure this now established literary mode. Magical realism's timeline gives context to this possible explanation.

The term *magical realism* is most frequently traced within the twentieth century to Franz Roh's use of it to refer to German post-expressionist painting in his 1925 publication *Nach-Expressionismus, Magischer Realismus*. Subsequently, it was applied to European literature during the second quarter of the century: Irene Guenther notes its application within literary contexts in Germany, Italy, the Netherlands, and Belgium (59–61), and Kenneth Reeds underscores that Latin Americans, having read a translation of Roh's work when José Ortega y Gasset published it in 1927 in his magazine *Revista de Occidente*, also connected the term and concept with European literature during this time (180). Beginning in the mid-twentieth century with Arturo Uslar Pietri's *Letras y hombres de Venezuela* (1949), however, the term became intimately linked with Latin American literature, Reeds explains (181), and it is during this phase that magical realism was most significantly developed and perceived as a cohesive literary phenomenon, gaining global attention upon the publication of García Márquez's *Cien años de soledad* (*One Hundred Years of Solitude,* 1967). Carpentier's *Kingdom*, as well as its seminal preface theorizing a distinctly Latin American vision of magical realism, which Carpentier dubbed *lo real maravilloso americano* (the marvelous American reality), were crucial in this point of literary magical realism's early development.

Following the Latin American Boom, magical realism was globally disseminated. Initially, it was most closely affiliated with postcolonial authors and themes—in the writing of Indo-British Salman Rushdie; Nigerians Ben Okri and B. Kojo Laing; New Zealanders Keri Hulme and Janet Frame; and North Americans Toni Morrison, Louise Erdrich, and Thomas King, for instance—but later was applied by critics, such as Wendy B. Faris, Lois Parkinson Zamora, and Anne Hegerfeldt to authors closely affiliated with the so-called First World, too.

Nigerian-British Oyeyemi might be situated somewhere in between these last two phases (the postcolonial and First World): an author of the African Diaspora who grew up in greater London, she describes her relationship to Africa as vexed in, for example, an editorial piece tellingly titled "Home, Strange Home." Moreover, her young age, spent largely within the twenty-first century, means that many of her concerns will be obliquely positioned to those of her earlier postcolonial predecessors, even if they stem from them. Hence, Oyeyemi's role within the most recent generation of magical realists means that she will likely—by virtue of her recent arrival upon magical realism's timeline—be disposed towards re-visioning the mode, in order to engage it in unexpected ways. While this is speculation, *Icarus Girl*'s unorthodox use of magical realism indicates that she has already effected this outcome, regardless of her self-conscious intentions.

Proliferation Within Double-Framing

Thus far, this essay has considered correlations among Oyeyemi's and Carpentier's narratives in their common double-framing of narrative magic. Now, we will view them from an opposing perspective, exploring how their uses of a similar technique are employed towards divergent ends, thus revealing a shift in the purposes for which magical realism has historically been deployed. *Kingdom* creates a situation in which narrative magic bifurcates along the lines of historical identity categories, which include cultural and geo-political factors, as devised within Carpentier's Latin Americanist postcolonial political ideology: the French colonial regime and slave owners on the one hand and Afro-Haitian slaves on the other. The double-positioning of narrative magic in *Kingdom* is in keeping with the author's territorialization of magic. As Amaryll Chanady has described, this feature of Carpentier's magical realism, the Cuban author positioned Latin America and the Caribbean as the exclusive home to a marvelous reality by virtue of its topography, history, and cultural heritage—fostered by the beliefs of indigenous Amerindian peoples and African Diaspora—whereas Europe(ans) had to fabricate surrealist pyrotechnics. In Chanday's words:

> Carpentier . . . used the concept of the marvelous real as a marker of difference in a Latin American discourse of identity rejecting European influence. . . . [T]he Surrealist quest for the marvelous is portrayed by Carpentier as artificial, while the authentic marvelous is presented as one of the main characteristics of the Latin American continent. ("Territorialization" 137–38)

In *Kingdom*, it is the slaves who witness Macadal's phenomenal escape, while the French elite are excluded from this supernatural experience because it is the former who have a connection with a marvelous reality by way of their belief in Afro-Haitian voodoo.

Icarus Girl's magic also cleaves along cultural lines, but it does so in a way that is unexpected, in light of Carpentier's usage. We may be tempted, initially, to see the opposing views of Tilly as splitting along Western/African worldviews, since British Dr. McKenzie explains her in rationalist, psychiatric terms, while Baba Gbenga treats her in traditional Yoruba terms. But that division is blurred insofar as Shivs, the Anglo daughter of Dr. McKenzie, believes that Tilly is a magical, but actual, person (whether or not she believes she met Tilly), while conversely, Jess' Nigerian mother alternately sides with Dr. McKenzie's account and a traditional Yoruba explanation, perhaps indicating her own conflicted cultural duality. Like *Kingdom*, *Icarus Girl* does demarcate believers from non-believers, allowing its narrative magic to mean different things within different frameworks. But, by establishing a ring of believers that incorporates both Baba Gbenga and Shivs, the narrative draws Anglo-British believers into its magical territory.

Icarus Girl and its literary relative, *Kingdom*, crisscross in their literary projects, merging and diverging at various points. Seen side by side, it seems apparent that Oyeyemi's narrative is not after the same kind of postcolonial agenda as was Carpentier's in its dual positioning of magic. It does not work towards distinguishing the New World and its inhabitants as other than/superior to the Old due to the former's intrinsic magic. Unlike the implicit confidence in identity classifications intimated by Carpentier's territorialization of magic, *Icarus Girl* appears unwilling to craft such categorical distinctions in that its believers include an eclectic mixture—Baba Gbenga; Shivs; and, sometimes, Sarah—who cannot, as a group, be located within any traditional ideological mapping. Instead, the narrative is after something else: it employs its double-framing of narrative magic, along with other devices (characterization, motif, and cultural resources), to convey how identity-related binaries (black/white, Nigerian/English, insider/outsider) are detrimental to Jess' ability to locate a self among proliferating oppositions. Paradoxically, then, while their common use of double-framing can be explained by their polar positions at early and recent points on the magical realist timeline, those same positions also help explain the divergent ends toward which they put this technique, as those positions engender differing perspectives and concerns.

Magical Realisms

If the double-positioning of narrative magic comprises a particular strand within magical realism, it is one of many. As Christopher Warnes explains, "The idea that there might be different types of magical realism is one that has been around for some time—at least since Roberto Gonzalez Echevarría's study of Alejo Carpentier, published in 1974" (13). I have already mentioned some key strains that have surfaced within the various formative phases of magical realism's history: Latin American magical realism, including *lo real maravilloso americano*; postcolonial magical realism; First-World magical realism; and global magical realism. In addition to these, Ato Quayson has theorized a distinct African branch of magical realism, while Anne Hegerfeldt analyzes British magical realism. Perhaps, as Faris has wondered, particular geographical locations stimulate particular strains of magical realism: "[O]ne might speculate about the existence of a tropical lush and a northerly spare variety of this plant" ("Scheherazade's" 165). Continuing with the idea of distinct geographical branches, Lyn Di Iorio Sandín and Richard Perez have recently underscored a specific usage of magical realism that they refer to as "the magical realist moment," or a sparse use of magical realism, in the work of US ethnic writers (1).

Warnes outlines two predominant types of magical realism, within which are encompassed authors from diverse geographical locales: first, what he calls "faith-based" magical realism, wherein authors use the mode towards "legitimizing alternative, participatory realities" (12 and n.8 on 156), and second, "irreverent" usages, wherein authors "deliberately elevate the non-real to the status of the real in order to cast the epistemological status of both into doubt" (14). Prior to Warnes, Jeanne Delbaere-Garant suggested three differing types of magical realism—psychic, mythic, and grotesque realism—in an effort to "leave more room for border-cases and help to situate any contemporary magic realist text, or part of a text, more accurately in a larger conceptual and terminological constellation" (250). And before Delbaere-Garant, Emir Rodríguez Monegal distinguished between the phenomenological magical realism of Roh and the ontological magical realism of Carpentier; Roh's brand of magical realism entails the experience of the marvelous, while Carpentier's indicates a marvelousness that exists objectively in the world, or at least in certain parts of it.

We might see all of these critical efforts at detailing differing types of magical realism as scratches trying to get at the same itch, so to speak, as efforts to understand that magical realism has appeared—and continues to appear—in many different guises. A solution to this effort, and to any impossible hope for a conclusive list of particular strains, is to pluralize the term—to designate the mode as magical realisms, thus creating a visual signification of its proliferating and diverse incarnations. Besides serving a merely descriptive function, the pluralization of the term entails a particular theoretical approach, one that understands the mode as able to be employed towards diverse ends. This approach reflects the recent work of numerous critics such as Faris, Warnes, Wen-Chin Ouyang, Sara Upstone, and the present author, all of whom have recently advocated a critical methodology that enables a more expansive understanding of magical realism's potential.

Not all critics view the mode this way. Instead, many have taken a prototype approach to magical realism, using particular incarnations of the mode as prototypes that define all other instances.[3] Most often, magical realism's Latin American and subsequent postcolonial usages are the original points from which all other texts are judged, and magical realism thereby becomes closely affiliated with indigenous cultures and ethnography. These stages' influence is undeniable. They have been crucial within magical realism's literary history and development as well as in the historical world: they can be credited for having created a viable and highly visible space for silenced peoples, as well as for recuperated indigenous cultures and buried histories; they have brought so-called Third World authors into the global limelight; and they have foregrounded divergent postcolonial concerns. Still, as this reader has argued elsewhere, if magical realism is defined by its formal features rather than through a prototype approach, critics are free to recognize the divergent strains of the multiplex magical realisms, including the formative Latin American and postcolonial brands.

Oyeyemi's *Icarus Girl* performs a significant set of functions within the magical realist timeline. Forming a bridge, it reaches back to one of the foundational magical realist novels, *Kingdom*, with its similar, experimental double-positioning of narrative magic. At the same time, it distinguishes itself from Carpentier and a territorialized Latin American magical realism in that it deploys this particular usage to divergent ends. Whereas Carpentier's narrative magic is crucial for his development of an authentic, unique, and ontological American marvelous reality, Oyeyemi's narrative magic works to trouble distinctions based on geography, identity, and political agendas—and to show the trouble such distinctions engender. Here, we seem to have a branch of magical realism stemming from another branch. Magical realism's propensity to proliferate continues.

To shift our conceptions of this literary mode to one that is plural is to enable the magical realist tree to continue to bear new branches. We make space for future Oyeyemis, authors who will ask the mode's dual codes of magic and realism to craft narrative concerns that merge and depart from previous usages, who will tease at the edges of the form, who will invent it anew.

Notes
1. Zamora and Reeds have also discussed *Kingdom*'s double-positioning of its narrative magic (Zamora 28, Reeds 187–88).
2. In *Magical Realism and Cosmopolitanism* (forthcoming), I posit three different applications of magical realism, or divergent ways the two codes of magic and realism have been understood to interact: subversion, suspension, and summation. While in *Magical Realism and Cosmopolitanism* I do not discuss suspension as I do here, treating it instead according to Stephen Slemon's description of it as the result of magical realism's two "incompatible" codes wherein the narrative reflects "gaps, absences, and silences" that correspond with postcolonial concerns, the kind of suspension Oyeyemi and

Carpentier enact might be added to that category, expanding and enriching it (Slemon 409).
3. I derive the term "prototype" as it is applies to magical realist criticism from *Mimesis, Genres and Post-Colonial Discourse,* wherein Jean-Pierre Durix uses Rushdie and García Márquez as prototypes to delimit other magical realist narratives.

Works Cited

Arana, R. Victoria. "Fresh 'Cultural Critiques': The Ethnographic Fabulations of Achichie and Oyeyemi." *Emerging African Voices: A Study of Contemporary African Literature.* Ed. Walter P. Collins, III. Amherst, NY: Cambria P, 2010. 269–313.

Carpentier, Alejo. *The Kingdom of This World.* Trans. Harriet de Onís. New York: Farrar, 1989.

Chanady, Amaryll. "The Origins and Development of Magic Realism in Latin American Fiction." *Magic Realism and Canadian Literature: Essays and Stories.* Proceedings of the Conference of Magic Realist Writing in Canada, May 1985. Eds. Peter Hinchcliffe & Ed Jewinski. Ontario: U of Waterloo P, 1986. 49–60.

_____. "The Territorialization of the Imaginary in Latin American Fiction: Self-Affirmation and Resistance to Metropolitan Paradigms." Eds. Lois Parkinson Zamora & Wendy B. Faris. *Magical Realism: Theory, History, Community.* Durham, NC: Duke UP, 1995. 125–44.

Delbaere-Garant, Jeanne. "Psychic Realism, Mythic Realism, Grotesque Realism: Variations on Magic Realism in Contemporary Literature in English." Eds. Lois Parkinson Zamora & Wendy B. Faris. *Magical Realism: Theory, History, Community.* Durham, NC: Duke UP, 1995. 249–63.

Durix, Jean-Pierre. *Mimesis, Genres and Post-Colonial Discourse: Deconstructing Magic Realism.* Basingstoke, UK: Palgrave, 1998.

Faris, Wendy B. "Scheherazade's Children: Magical Realism and Postmodern Fiction." Eds. Lois Parkinson Zamora & Wendy B. Faris. *Magical Realism: Theory, History, Community.* Durham, NC: Duke UP, 1995. 163–90.

Guenther, Irene. "Magic Realism, New Objectivity, and the Arts during the Weimar Republic." Eds. Lois Parkinson Zamora & Wendy B. Faris. *Magical Realism: Theory, History, Community.* Durham, NC: Duke UP, 1995. 33–73.

King, Bruce. "Review of *The Icarus Girl* by Helen Oyeyemi." *Wasafiri* 20.45 (2005): 72–4.

Low, Gail. "Helen Oyeyemi." *British Writers: Supplement XVIII*. Ed. Jay Parnini. Farmington Hills: Scribner's, 2012. 223–36.

Oyeyemi, Helen. "Home, Strange Home." *The Guardian*. Web. 2 Feb. 2005.

───. *The Icarus Girl*. Chippenham: Paragon, 2005.

Quayson, Ato. "Magical Realism and the African Novel." Ed. F. Abiola Irele. *The Cambridge Companion to the African Novel*. Cambridge: Harvard UP, 2009. 159–76.

Reeds, Kenneth. "Magical Realism: A Problem of Definition." *Neophilologus* 90.2 (2006): 175–96.

Rodríguez Monegal, Emir. "Surrealism, Magical Realism, Magical Fiction: A Study in Confusion." *Surrealism/Surrealismo: Latinoamérica y España*. Eds. Earle Peter G. & Gullón German. Philadelphia: U of Pennsylvania P, 1977. 25–32.

Rushdie, Salman. *East, West*. London: Vintage, 1994.

Sandín, Lyn Di Iorio, & Richard Perez. "Tracing Magical Irruptions in US Ethnic Literatures." *Moments of Magical Realism in US Ethnic Literatures*. Eds. Lyn Di Iorio Sandín & Richard Perez. New York: Palgrave, 2012. 1–15.

Sethie, Anita. "Mr. Fox by Helen Oyeyemi—Review." *The Guardian*. Guardian News and Media Limited, 12 May 2012. Web. 7 March 2014.

Slemon, Stephen. "Magic Realism as Postcolonial Discourse." Eds. Lois Parkinson Zamora & Wendy Faris. *Magical Realism: Theory, History, Community*. Durham, NC: Duke UP, 1995. 407–26.

Warnes, Christopher. *Magical Realism and the Postcolonial Novel: Between Faith and Irreverence*. Basingstoke: Palgrave, 2009.

Zamora, Lois Parkinson. "Swords and Silver Rings: Magical Objects in the Work of Jorge Luis

Borges and Gabriel García Márquez." *A Companion to Magical Realism*. Eds. Stephen Hart & Wen-chin Ouyang. Woodbridge: Tamesis, 2005. 28–45.

Zamora, Lois Parkinson & Wendy B. Faris, eds. *Magical Realism: Theory, History, Community*. Durham, NC: Duke UP, 1995.

Panthers and Jaguars: Realism and Responsibility in Salman Rushdie's *Shame*
Rachel Trousdale

Salman Rushdie's fiction is full of miraculous coincidences, characters with magical powers, and fusions of the modern with the mythological. His work draws on the conventions of magical realism to build bridges across several divides: between the individual writer and that writer's possible group identities (local, national, or transnational); between the factual and the mythic; and between the personal and the political. His novels examine the different ways that realistic and fantastic fiction deal with moral and political responsibility within and beyond the text. Fantastic fiction, Rushdie suggests, gives writers a kind of freedom of speech impossible in strictly realist works. This freedom does not simply mean that writers who describe magic are not constrained by the laws of physics. According to Rushdie, realism misrepresents its own statements of "truth," which, no matter how based in fact, are inevitably colored by their placement in a narrative, which makes certain elements "compulsory" (Rushdie, *Shame* 67). Fantastic literature, on the other hand, by foregrounding its own unreality, forces authors to take moral responsibility for the content of their texts, and readers to take responsibility for interpreting them. With this freedom comes a moral obligation to tell the most difficult truths.

Rushdie's description of realist fiction—a term he uses to mean fiction containing only events that are scientifically and socially possible in the world as understood by educated rationalists—borders on journalism: realist writers, in his view, are limited to immediate, verifiable facts. This involves a moral burden: realist writers are responsible for reporting political abuses and injustice. But literal reportage, for Rushdie, is also suspect. A realist writer describing an abusive regime may criticize the government's authority, but she may implicitly support an authoritarian structure. In Rushdie's account of realist novels, there is a single person who gets to decide what is true: the novelist, who presents the book's facts as objective (a claim which deliberately and counter-intuitively allies postmodern indeterminacy with the fantastic, rather than the realist). Fantastic literature, by contrast, reminds readers that writers are responsible for the contents of their books. This emphasis on responsibility challenges writers of fantastic literature to do justice to the moral complexity of their novels' events and challenges readers to interpret their work skeptically. Where a realist novel may lead us to criticize a particular political system, the fantastic novel leads us to criticize the ideologies that make the system work, and to identify our own complicity with it.

Rushdie distinguishes between realistic and fantastic fiction, but that distinction can be misleading: magical realist fiction is, by definition, both. Wendy Faris suggests that magical realist texts are characterized by continuity between descriptions of the familiar "phenomenal world"—the world we experience through our senses—and "magical elements [that] grow organically out of the reality portrayed" (170, 163). This is the first of Faris' five "primary characteristics of magical realist fiction" (167): the others are "an 'irreducible element' of magic," which cannot be explained away; ambiguity in describing that "irreducible" magic, so that "the reader may hesitate . . . between two contradictory understandings of events" (171); "the closeness or near-merging of two realms, two worlds," which "stresses the magic *of* fiction rather than the magic *in* it" (172–73); and the tendency of such fictions to "question received ideas about time, space, and identity" (173).

Faris uses Rushdie's 1981 novel *Midnight's Children* as one of her main examples. *Midnight's Children*'s narrator, Saleem, is magically "handcuffed to history" by his birth at the hour of India's independence (3), and the novel is full of sensory descriptions, which give way to fantastical events; elements of magic that, while "irreducible," cause the reader to doubt the narrator's accuracy;[1] and considerations of the origins of identity. *Midnight's Children* also suggests another important characteristic of magical realist fiction: the tendency of magic to literalize metaphor, a phenomenon Saleem calls the "active-metaphorical" (286).[2]

Rushdie clearly enjoys fantastic stories for their own sake. His novels draw on supernatural tales as varied as the Arabic *Thousand and One Nights*; the Hindu *Ramayana*; Greek myths; Günter Grass' *The Tin Drum* (German); Mikhail Bulgakov's *The Master and Margarita* and Nikolai Gogol's stories (Russian); the works of Franz Kafka (German–speaking Czech Jew); and the comic book *Superman* (American). In this context, Rushdie's interest in Gabriel García Márquez and other Latin American magical realist writers hardly needs explaining. But the political elements of magical realist writing are central to the ethical project Rushdie undertakes in his novels.

Rushdie says that Indian and Latin American writers share the experience of life in a postcolonial country—an experience he identifies, in his 1983 essay "'Commonwealth Literature' Does Not Exist," as more important than shared language or even shared membership in the former British Empire. In his first nonfiction book, *The Jaguar Smile*, which describes a three-week trip Rushdie took to Nicaragua in 1986, he explains the affinity he feels with other postcolonial writers, regardless of the language they write in or the continent they come from. Rushdie was born in India a few months before the country achieved independence from the British Empire (his family later immigrated to Pakistan, while he was educated in England). His childhood in the newly independent country makes him sympathetic with Nicaragua:

> When the Reagan administration began its war against Nicaragua, I recognized a deeper affinity with that small country in a continent (Central America) upon which I had never set foot . . . I was myself the child of a successful revolt against a great power, my consciousness the product of the triumph of the Indian revolution. It was perhaps also true that those of us who did not have our origins in the countries of the mighty West, or North, had something in common—not, certainly, anything as simplistic as a unified 'third world' outlook, but at least some knowledge of what weakness was like, some awareness of the view from underneath, and of how it felt to be there, on the bottom, looking up at the descending heel. (Rushdie, *The Jaguar Smile* 4)

This claim of common experience has drawn some criticism. Kim Sasser, influenced by Timothy Brennan and Aijaz Ahmad, argues that *The Jaguar Smile* underplays the difference between the kind of hardships faced by well-to-do migrants and those faced by the poor. But Rushdie's description of his "affinity" with Nicaraguans in *The Jaguar Smile* contains some subtle self-undercuttings: readers are prompted to doubt his authority when he reminds us that the conversations he reports are mediated by a translator; when he reveals that he is the only person in a group afraid that the Contras may attack; or when he expresses doubts about his increasing sympathy with the Sandinista government.

In the midst of this subtly self-critical account of real-world Nicaragua, *The Jaguar Smile* raises a question that is also central to his fictional texts. In *Haroun and the Sea of Stories* (1990), the main character asks, "What's the use of stories that aren't even true?" (22). In *The Jaguar Smile*, Rushdie implicitly asks, what's the use of stories that aren't even possible? At a party celebrating the seventh anniversary of the Sandinista rebellion, Rushdie has a conversation about the importance of realism in postcolonial writing:

> I turned to find a small, elderly gentleman with a cane nodding meaningfully at me. He was, of course, a poet. 'I greatly admire,' he said to me, 'your Indian poet, Tagoré.'
>
> I was taken aback. What was old Rabindranath doing here, with this accent on his final e? 'Is he translated here?' I asked.
>
> 'Victoria Ocampo, the great Argentine editor and intellectual, fell in love with the work, and with the man. . . Victoria Ocampo was determined that Latin America should discover this great genius, and she published many excellent translations.'
>
> 'Then Tagore is better read in Latin America than in India,' I said. 'There, many of the translations are very bad indeed.'
>
> 'Tagoré,' he corrected me. 'I admire him for his spiritual qualities, and also his realism.'

'Many people think of Latin America as the home of anti-realism,' I said. He looked disgusted. 'Fantasy?' he cried. 'No, sir. You must not write fantasy. It is the worst thing. Take a tip from your great Tagoré. Realism, realism, that is the only thing.' (*The Jaguar Smile* 40–41)

This conversation stages a competition between fantasy and realism. The poet identifies realism—"the only thing"—as the center of a global postcolonial literary union connecting Indian and Latin American literature, and he is not alone. Almost everyone Rushdie meets in Nicaragua, including the country's president, Daniel Ortega, is a poet (hence the "of course"), and the Nicaraguan poetry Rushdie quotes is realistic and politically charged. Seven years after the overthrow of the dictator Somoza, in the middle of a war against the right-wing, US-backed Contras, the old poet believes that realism is a moral and political necessity: the job of literature, he and his Nicaraguan colleagues imply, is to testify to urgent real-world struggle.

In his account of this conversation, Rushdie has the elderly poet explain something which, it turns out, Rushdie himself already knows: in "Commonwealth Literature Does Not Exist," published three years before *The Jaguar Smile*, Rushdie mentions Tagore's Latin American readership as part of his evidence that the "postcolonial" is a more meaningful category than "Commonwealth." He writes, "The works of Rabindranath Tagore . . . have long been widely available in Spanish–speaking America, thanks to his close friendship with the Argentinian intellectual Victoria Ocampo" (Rushdie, *Imaginary Homelands* 69). Rushdie's repetition of this fact in almost exactly the same words in *The Jaguar Smile* suggests that the "elderly poet"—whose name, uncharacteristically, he does not mention—may not be a real person at all, but a made-up character inserted into an otherwise true story to dramatize the argument between "realism" and "fantasy." The peculiarity of the conversation— Rushdie's dismissive phrase "old Rabindranath," the old poet's (mis) correction of Rushdie's pronunciation—places Rushdie squarely on one side, and the "realist" Tagore on the other. In "Commonwealth Literature Does Not Exist," Rushdie uses Tagore to show the common experience of postcoloniality, but in *The Jaguar Smile*,

Tagore becomes part of a debate within postcolonial literature about how best to represent that experience.

A complete discussion of Rushdie's shifting uses of the fantastic, particularly as it has changed in what Robert Eaglestone calls the "Po-Fa" (post-*fatwa*) period, is beyond the scope of any single essay. But Rushdie's examination of the value of the fantastic in his early novels is perhaps clearest in *Shame* (1983). *Shame* is based on real events in Pakistan: it recounts the rivalry between Iskander Harappa (based on Zulfikar Ali Bhutto, who became prime minister of Pakistan) and Raza Hyder (based on Muhammad Zia-ul-Haq, who overthrew Bhutto in a military coup and had him executed). The novel tells their story and that of the women in their lives, particularly Raza Hyder's daughter, Sufiya Zinobia Hyder. Over the course of the novel, Sufiya Zinobia, who has been rendered mentally disabled by a fever, slowly succumbs to something like demonic possession. She turns into "the Beast," an avatar of the shame her family and her country repress, and embarks on a wave of brutal, magical murders, culminating in the death of her husband.

While Iskander Harappa and Raza Hyder are based on real people, Rushdie makes clear that *Shame* is set in an alternate world. The book opens in a conventionally fictionalized setting, "In the remote border town of Q." (Rushdie, *Shame* 3). Readers familiar with Pakistan will have no difficulty identifying "Q" as the city of Quetta, but in the second chapter, this disguise becomes both more and less transparent, with the sudden interruption of a first-person narrator who appears to be very like the author himself:

> The country in this story is not Pakistan, or not quite. There are two countries, real and fictional, occupying the same space, or almost the same space. My story, my fictional country exists, like myself, at a slight angle to reality. I have found this off-centering to be necessary; but its value is, of course, open to debate. My view is that I am not writing only about Pakistan.
>
> I have not given the country a name. And Q. is not really Quetta at all. But I don't want to be precious about this: when I arrive at the big city, I shall call it Karachi. (Rushdie, *Shame* 22)

By flagging that his novel is set in a fictional world, Rushdie places *Shame* at a greater distance from reality than, for example, Jane Austen does when she sets a novel in "—shire," a technique which lets us imagine that the events in the story really happened, and that the blank name keeps us from knowing where. Rushdie's discussion of his novel's fictionality makes the placement of his story not just less familiar geographically (by saying we are "not quite" in Pakistan), but less familiar *fictionally* (by emphasizing his story's "off-center" relationship with reality).

Further complicating the story's partial reality, the narrator, who speaks this aside, closely resembles Salman Rushdie. All the attributes we learn about the speaker—he writes; his family lives in Pakistan, but he has "never lived there for longer than six months at a stretch" (66); his younger sister is "a Pakistani citizen," but he is not (65)—are also true about the real Rushdie. *Shame*, then, does not just exist "at a slight angle to reality;" it exists at a clearly marked intersection with reality, with the author himself standing at the crossroads. The narrative asides emphasize that the rest of the novel is imaginary, prompt us to look for the novel's roots in real-world Pakistan, and suggest that we should think carefully what the author is doing when he makes things up.

At least one reason Rushdie gives for setting his story in an imaginary country should provoke some skepticism. He claims that fictionalizing events will help avoid censorship because a realist book about Pakistani politics "would have been banned, dumped in the rubbish bin, burned. All that effort for nothing! Realism can break a writer's heart" (Rushdie, *Shame* 68). This claim is deliberately naïve: no one familiar with Pakistan would miss the book's real-world political content, and a censor inclined to ban a realist novel about Bhutto would have plenty of provocation to ban *Shame*, too. As Rushdie's work would demonstrate all too thoroughly following the publication of *The Satanic Verses* (1988), fantastic fiction can be just as politically provocative as realism.

The more compelling reason for writing "at a slight angle to reality" is not to avoid prescriptions on writing imposed by the government, but those imposed by genre:

> But suppose this were a realistic novel! Just think what else I might have to put in it. . . . would I also have to describe the Sind Club in Karachi where there is still a sign reading 'Woman and Dogs Not Allowed Beyond This Point'? Or to analyse the subtle logic of an industrial programme that builds nuclear reactors but cannot develop a refrigerator? (Rushdie, *Shame* 66)

Like the Nicaraguan poet, the narrator believes that realist writing has political power. But where the poet's claim that realism is "the only thing" implies that realist fiction affects its readers, the narrator's list of what he "might have to put in" to a realist novel emphasizes the constraints it places on its author. Realist fiction, Rushdie's narrator claims, would force him to describe a list of abuses:

> How much real-life material might become compulsory!—About, for example, the longago Deputy Speaker who was killed in the National Assembly when the furniture was flung at him by elected representatives; or about the film censor who took his red pencil to each frame of the scene in the film *Night of the Generals* in which General Peter O'Toole visits an art gallery, and scratched out all the paintings of naked ladies hanging on the walls, so that audiences were dazzled by the surreal spectacle of General Peter strolling through a gallery of dancing red blobs; or about the TV chief who once told me solemnly that pork was a four-letter word; or about the issue of *Time* magazine (or was it *Newsweek*?) which never got into the country because it carried an article about President Ayub Khan's alleged Swiss bank account . . . Imagine my difficulties! (Rushdie, *Shame* 67)

Of course, these events do make it into the novel, whether via this list or (like the *Time* or *Newsweek* article) as part of the plot. Others elements, including the TV chief who bans the word "pork," appear in Rushdie's essays (Rushdie, *Imaginary Homelands* 38). The problem, then, is not that he is unwilling to discuss politics. On the contrary, this list shows what he considers the absurd combination in Pakistan of corruption, censorship, artistic insensitivity, and sexism. His objection is that "realism" renders these events "compulsory," prescribing not just that these particular events be mentioned, but that they be discussed in precisely this way. "Realism can break a writer's heart" not only because it can get his novel banned, but because it infringes upon his freedom of speech by forcing him to include these details whether he wants to or not.

Fantasy, on the other hand, makes no such demands:

> Fortunately however, I am only telling a sort of modern fairy-tale, so that's all right; nobody need get upset, or take anything I say too seriously. No drastic action need be taken, either.
> What a relief! (Rushdie, *Shame* 68)

The one-sentence paragraph "What a relief!" is obviously a joke: clearly Rushdie intends his critique of Pakistan in *Shame* to be "taken seriously." The fact that he does not mean it to be taken *literally*, however, empowers him to choose what material he includes. This freedom is morally suspect: choosing one's story, he says, is "a kind of censorship," too (Rushdie, *Shame* 68). But fantastic literature places the burden of choice on the storyteller.

The narrator of *Shame* defends the fantastic in these asides, but he repeatedly chooses realism over fantasy during the course of the book. Passages that appear magical frequently end up with realist explanations. Babar Shakil's death, for example, is heralded by the advent of golden archangels who surround him in the mountains, but this image turns out to be supplied not by the narrative voice, but by his mothers Chhunni, Munnee, and Bunny Shakil, who acknowledge that their story is fantastic:

> Of course his death was not described in any notebook; it was enacted within the grieving imaginations of his three mothers, because as they told Omar while recounting the tale of their son's transformation into an angel, 'We have the right to present him with a good death, a death with which the living can live.' (Rushdie, *Shame* 136)

Unlike things "described in [a] notebook," the presence of angels is not a verifiable fact; in this context, fantastic stories produced by the imaginations of grieving parents become a form of denial. Similarly, Raza and Bilquìs Hyder's "distracted imaginations" endow their stillborn son with "an air of . . . solid actuality," which leads them to believe that he will be reincarnated (Rushdie, *Shame* 81); this belief helps cause the novel's final catastrophe, when their next child is not a boy, but the doomed Sufiya Zinobia. Unlike *Midnight's Children*, *Shame* literalizes metaphors as jokes, not as magic: "our government . . . has made our sex-drive the top national priority . . . this government is happy to go on screwing us from now till doomsday" (Rushdie, *Shame* 134). What the narrator of *Midnight's Children* calls the "active-metaphorical," the irreducible action of metaphor on real-world events, becomes, in *Shame*, merely word play. Despite its defense of the fantastic, *Shame* repeatedly sides, if not with realism, at least with physical plausibility.

Sufiya Zinobia's transformation into the Beast, however, remains irreducibly magical. Her magical properties, like Babar's archangels, are described via other characters' perspectives, but the plot demands that we believe the magic described. This is partly a result of whose perspective describes her. Her husband, Omar Khayyam, is a rationalist, a doctor who has no supernatural beliefs, but:

> he began to learn that science was not enough, that even though he rejected possession-by-devils as a way of denying human responsibility for human actions, even though God had never meant much to him, still his reason could not erase the evidence of those eyes, could not blind him to that unearthly glow, the smouldering fire of the Beast. (Rushdie, *Shame* 248–49)

Unlike Raza and Bilquìs Hyder, Omar Khayyam's detection of the supernatural contradicts both his desires and his own beliefs. Instead, Sufiya Zinobia's "possession-by-devils" echoes the "two countries . . . occupying the same space" construction of *Shame*'s fictional world: Omar thinks she looks "as if there were two beings occupying that air-space" (Rushdie, *Shame* 248). The meaningful fantastic is not, Rushdie suggests, a form of wish-fulfillment, but a form of double exposure.

The narrator, too, treats Sufiya Zinobia in a kind of double exposure, giving her two origin stories. The first is the story of her birth to Raza and Bilquìs Hyder, made tragic by her parents' fantasies about reincarnating her stillborn brother. This origin story begins as fantasy and becomes realism: her parents' supernatural beliefs are the basis for tragic disappointment. But Rushdie also tells the story of the character's composition by her author. In this account, too, Sufiya Zinobia is a substitute for a different imagined person: instead of a dead brother, the narrator says that he first imagined her as a British girl of Pakistani descent named Anna Muhammad. Anna has a clear, real-world origin: she is to be the main character in a novel about the real-world killing of an East London girl murdered by her father for sleeping with a white boy.

Where Bilquìs and Raza's fantasy resolves into realism, the narrator's realism gives way to the fantastic. His initial plan is gruesomely detailed:

> Wanting to write about shame, I was at first haunted by the imagined spectre of that dead body, its throat slit like a halal chicken, lying in a London night across a zebra crossing, slumped across black and white, black and white, while above her a Belisha beacon blinked, orange, not-orange, orange. I thought of the crime as having been committed right there, publicly, ritually, while at the windows eyes. And no mouth opened in protest. And when the police knocked on doors, what hope of assistance had they? Inscrutability of the 'Asian' face under the eyes of the foe. It seems even the insomniacs at their windows closed their eyelids and saw nothing. And the father left with blood-cleansed name and grief. (Rushdie, *Shame* 118)

Despite the narrator's comparison of the image of Anna's dead body to a "spectre," his description of her murder is couched in realist terms: the "haunting" is only a simile, whereas the physical circumstances of the "London night" are unarguably real. The "zebra crossing" and "Belisha beacon," which mark pedestrian road crossings in Britain, are described in stark, accurate visual terms. But this lurid passage also draws on the conventions of crime fiction and the tabloid press—genres that claim to be realistic but significantly distort facts. Rushdie's description of Anna's death invokes British racism ("Inscrutability of the 'Asian' face") and fear of immigrant communities (suggested by the unwillingness to assist the police). At the same time, he implicitly critiques the murderer's beliefs ("throat slit like a halal chicken"). The novel Rushdie first wants to write is not fantastic, but its attempts at accurate physical description cause it to deviate from the truth.

Unable to do justice to Anna, Rushdie shifts the scene of his novel to Pakistan:

> I would have to go back East, to let the idea breathe its favorite air. Anna, deported, repatriated to a country she had never seen, caught brain-fever and turned into a sort of idiot. Why did I do that to her?—Or maybe the fever was a lie, a figment of Bilquìs Hyder's imagination, intended to cover up the damage done by repeated blows to the head: hate can turn a miracle-gone-wrong into a basket case . . . How hard to pin down the truth, especially when one is obliged to see the world in slices; snapshots conceal as much as they make plain. (Rushdie, *Shame* 118–19)

In describing how Anna becomes Sufiya Zinobia, the narrator does something none of his characters can: he considers the possibility of his own guilt. Fiction, for Rushdie, is more morally demanding than reality because in the fictional world, we know that there is someone to blame for suffering. While the narrator instantly backs away from his admission of guilt, suggesting that Sufiya Zinobia's mother is "really" responsible for her state, Bilquìs' possible responsibility is secondary to the author's, since he controls her actions as much as he controls Sufiya Zinobia's brain-fever.

Fantastic fiction, then, alters our perception of moral responsibility. In a realist novel, what is "compulsory" is the inclusion of a given set of facts: these novels, Rushdie says, have their content dictated by circumstances beyond the novelist's control. Failure to include major political abuses, acts of censorship, or instances of corruption would be a moral lapse. Fantastic novels, by contrast, make their authors responsible not for representing *facts* but representing *causality*. Since Rushdie's subject in *Shame* is the emotion that drives people to harm their offspring, he is forced by his relationship to the text to confront not just Bilquìs' possible guilt, but his own.

Once Sufiya Zinobia is transformed into the Beast, reports reach Omar Khayyam describing her as a "panther . . . Black head, pale hairless body, awkward gait" (Rushdie, *Shame* 268). Finally, at the end of the novel, she returns to kill him: "then she was there, on all fours, naked, coated in mud and blood and shit, with twigs sticking to her back and beetles in her hair. She saw him and shuddered; then she rose up on her hind legs with her forepaws outstretched and he had just enough time to say, 'Well, wife, so here you are at last,' before her eyes forced him to look (Rushdie, *Shame* 304). Although she is described here in terms of "blood and shit," Sufiya Zinobia's most grotesque change is not physical. The "black head" is merely her hair, grown matted and unkempt; she has had the "awkward gait" since childhood. The use of the word "forepaws" to describe her hands does not indicate that her body has literally become a panther's; rather, it shows the transformation of her mind. Unlike the account of Babar Shakil's death, there is real magic here—Sufiya Zinobia hypnotizes Omar Khayyam, rips his head off, and then explodes—but it is magic which transforms who she is, not what her body is.

This description of Sufiya Zinobia conveys truths that the description of Anna's death cannot because its double vision of magical beast and real woman is not dictated by generic demands. Sufiya Zinobia is the "avatar" (Rushdie, *Shame* 210) not only of shame, but of the real power of the fantastic. Rushdie uses her to show that realism, far from representing objective truth, distorts our perceptions by conforming to predetermined narratives. The realist account of Anna Muhammad's murder leaves room for misreadings because what we take to be "reality" is framed by the perspective of the onlooker. Sufiya Zinobia's story, by contrast, resists our efforts "to ignore the reality of her" (Rushdie, *Shame* 210) through its bizarre unreality. For Rushdie, the fantastic forces us into awareness of fiction's rhetorical modes. Fantastic fiction, he suggests, reminds us through its very impossibility of the choices made by its author, making us aware of the author's responsibility for representing truth and of our own responsibility for understanding it.

Notes

1. See Rushdie, *Imaginary Homelands* 22–25; Ten Kortenaar 197–98, and Noor.
2. See also Trousdale, 107.

Works Cited

Ahmad, Aijaz. *In Theory: Classes, Nations, Literatures.* London: Verso, 1992.

Balasubramanian, Radha. "The Similarities Between Mikhail Bulgakov's *The Master and Margarita* and Salman Rushdie's *The Satanic Verses.*" *International Fiction Review* 22.1–2 (1995): 37–46.

Brennan, Timothy. *Salman Rushdie and the Third World: Myths of the Nation.* New York: St. Martin's, 1989.

Clark, Roger Y. *Stranger Gods: Salman Rushdie's Other Worlds.* Montreal: McGill-Queen's UP, 2001.

Cornwell, Neil. "Masters of the Satanic: Mikhail Bulgakov, Salman Rushdie and Umberto Eco." *Bulgakov: The Novelist-Playwright.* Ed. Lesley Milne. Luxembourg: Harwood, 1995. 225–31.

Eaglestone, Robert. "Po-fa: *Joseph Anton.*" *Salman Rushdie.* Eds. Robert Eaglestone & Martin McQuillan. Foreword by Kenan Malik. New York: Bloomsbury, 2013. 115–23.

Faris, Wendy B. "Sheherazade's Children: Magical Realism and Postmodern Fiction." *Magical Realism: Theory, History, Community.* Eds. Lois Parkinson Zamora & Wendy B. Faris. Durham, NC: Duke UP, 1995.

McMillin, Arnold. "*The Satanic Verses* and *Master i Margarita.*" *Bulgakov: The Novelist-Playwright.* Ed. Lesley Milne. Luxembourg: Harwood, 1995. 232–43.

Merivale, Patricia. "Saleem Fathered by Oskar: *Midnight's Children*, Magic Realism, and *The Tin Drum.*" *Magical Realism: Theory, History, Community.* Eds. Lois Parkinson Zamora & Wendy B. Faris. Durham, NC: Duke UP, 1995. 329–45.

Monti, Alessandro. "A Hoarding of Goats and Rumours of Mermaids: Puzzling out Myth in *The Ground Beneath Her Feet.*" *The Great Work of Making Real: Salman Rushdie's* The Ground Beneath Her Feet. Eds. Elsa Linguanti & Viktoria Tchernichova. Pisa, Italy: Edizioni ETS, 2003. 43–53.

Noor, Ronny. "Misrepresentation of History in Salman Rushdie's *Midnight's Children*." *Notes on Comparative Literature* 26 (1996): 7–8.

Rushdie, Salman. *Haroun and the Sea of Stories*. London: Granta, 1990.

_____. *Imaginary Homelands: Essays and Criticism 1981–1991*. New York: Penguin, 1991.

_____. *The Jaguar Smile: A Nicaraguan Journey, with a New Preface by the Author*. New York: Henry Holt, 1997.

_____. *Midnight's Children*. New York: Penguin, 1981.

_____. *The Satanic Verses*. Dover, Delaware: The Consortium, 1988.

_____. *Shame*. New York: Henry Holt, 1983.

Sasser, Kim. "Solidarity through Difference: Rushdie's Anti-Example in *The Jaguar Smile*." *Symbiosis* 13.1 (2009): 61–80.

Thompson, Jon. "Superman and Salman Rushdie: *Midnight's Children* and the Disillusionment of History." *Journal of Commonwealth and Postcolonial Studies* 3 (1995): 1–23.

The Shadow of Magical Realism in José Luis Cuerda's 1980s films

Ignacio López-Calvo

> My style, this is my firm belief, is not surrealism, as has been said, but throwing logic on the floor, fighting it one on one, and twisting its neck until it vomits its last arguments.[1]
> (José Luis Cuerda)

In three of his works, *Neguijón* (2005), *Mi poncho es un kimono flamenco* (*My Poncho Is a Flamenco Kimono*, 2005), and *España, aparta de mí estos premios* (*Spain, Take These Awards from Me*, 2009), Peruvian author Fernando Iwasaki argues that there is a *sui generis* magical realist tradition in Spain that pre-dates the Latin American one all the way to the Middle Ages. Thus, in *"Die kartoffelblüte* o la flor de papa," an essay from *Mi poncho es un kimono flamenco*, he explains:

> Not even magical realism has a Latin American copyright, since we find it in Spanish authors such as Valle Inclán, Álvaro Cunqueiro and Juan Perucho. Why does the ghost in Manuel Rivas novel *El lápiz del carpintero* (The Carpenter's Pencil, 1998) have to come from the specter of Prudencio Aguilar in *Cien años de soledad* (1967), when the ghosts were already alive in Wenceslao Fernández Flórez *El bosque animado* (*The Living Forest*, 1943)? Why can't the apocryphal adventure in the Cave of Montesions be the first "real marvelous" episode in the history of literature in Spanish? Anyone who knows minimally this delirious culture that engendered lives of saints, chronicles of the Indies, and Golden Century novels, would agree with me that in the Latin American butterfly of magical realism there was once a Spanish Baroque worm.[2]

Iwasaki goes on to remind the reader that there is a greater number of necromancers, fortune tellers, and charlatans on Spanish public television than either scientists or researchers. I would add that, as early as 1928, Wenceslao Fernández Flórez included a scene with the apparition of a lost soul interacting with the protagonist, Anselmo Varona, in the novel *Relato inmoral* (*Immoral Account*): "A ghost?" "It would be more appropriate to say a lost soul. That's what I am, to my dismay."[3]

The former washerwoman with whom he interacts, who is followed by her five children, also lost souls, eventually explains to Anselmo that she became a lost soul after the local priest refused to bury her in the cemetery as punishment for not marrying the father of her children. In the end, the bored protagonist politely tells the lost soul of the washerwomans that her story is interesting and then asks her to help him find his hotel room. In this case, Fernández Flórez resorts to magical realism to mock the prudish morality of Spain at the time and to denounce the resulting sexual repression.

Iwasaki, in these paragraphs, does not present Spanish magical realism as a sort of corrective to the mystification of Latin American magical realism. Instead, he demonstrates that, much like Latin American writers, Spanish writers also drew from pre-Christian and pre-Cartesian (mostly Celtic) worldviews. Instead of acknowledging the Afro-Caribbean or Amerindian knowledge that informs Latin American writers, such as Miguel Ángel Asturias, Alejo Carpetier, or Gabriel García Márquez, they looked at the Celtic societies of Galicia, Asturias, and Cantabria, where people had traditionally believed in the cult of nature and the existence of lost souls, witches, and the Galician Santa Compaña (also known as Huéspeda or Estantigua in other Spanish regions). The oeuvre of Galician poet and novelist Rosalía de Castro (1837–1885), with her "black shadows" (ghosts) of existential *saudade*, is a good example of this worldview, as seen in the poem written in Galician "Negra sombra" (Black Shadow), included in the collection *Follas novas* (New Leaves, 1880).[4]

The influence of magical realism can be found in three films directed by José Luis Cuerda in the 1980s: *Total* (1983), and *El bosque animado* (1987), and *Amanece que no es poco* (*Dawn is Breaking and That Is Something*, 1988). This essay shall consider the influence of Spanish and Latin American literary magical realism on the absurdist humor with touches of sarcastic "surruralism" (a neologism that blends the words "surreal" and "rural" and was created by the Italian Gianni Toti specifically to describe *Amanece que no es poco*) that makes Cuerda's comedies so unique. In many ways, it is precisely this trait that separates Cuerda's witty, grotesque, and delirious humor from the typically easy, and often clumsy, humor of the so-called *españoladas* of the 1970s and 1980s. I shall also compare the "surrural" magical realism that appears in *Total* and *Amanece que no es poco* with the more conventional one in Cuerda's comedy *El bosque animado*. Perhaps influenced by Latin American literary magical realism, in the fifty-two minute comedy *Total*, the first in the trilogy completed by *Amanece* and *Así en el cielo como en la tierra* (*On Earth As It Is in Heaven*, 1995), Cuerda creates a less conventional version of this narrative mode, which leans toward the creation of an absurdist, incoherent humor. Although it flirts in some scenes with social criticism, in *Total*, magical realism serves mostly as a tool to create a new type of humor. As the filmmaker has explained in interviews, he was disappointed in Spanish National Television (TVE), which kept asking him to write comedies, when, in fact, he had several dramas already written and ready to be filmed. Cuerda recalls having to stop his car in order to cry, unable to repress his rage, because his true genre of choice was drama. Therefore, the absurdist humor in *Total* and *Amanece* seemingly emerged from the filmmaker's desire to protest what he deemed as an unfair identification of his filmmaking career with only comedy.

Another driving force behind his creation of an absurdist filmic version of magical realism was his "anxiety of influence" (to use Harold Bloom's term): "Then, I decided that, if they wanted laughter, they were going to have my kind of laughter. It would be a comedy, but a weird one. In Spain, it was absurd to film comedies in Berlanga's style, because he was already filming them and no one could do it better."[5] The end result was the medium-length film *Total*, Cuerda's first film after the filmic adaptation of Ernesto Sábato's novel *El túnel* in 1975. Cuerda's absurd humor in his trilogy, his own version of Spanish comedic magical realism, was the outcome of his desire to avoid repeating the films of Spanish director and scriptwriter

Luis García Berlanga (1921–2010) and the scripts of Rafael Azcona (1926–2008), even though he recruited many of the same actors that appear in their films. Despite these precautions, some of Cuerda's scenes still display intertextualities with Berlanga's choral films, such as the rural comedy *Bienvenido, Mister Marshall* (1953). For example, there is a portrait of former US president Dwight David "Ike" Eisenhower by the mayor, played by Rafael Alonso, when he announces the results of the local elections in *Amanece*. Similarly, the mayor's reception when he returns from the capital city is reminiscent of the reception for Eisenhower in Berlanga's film (as well as of Christ's arrival on a donkey in Jerusalem, where he is received by the masses who are bearing palm leaves). But there is no doubt that the humor in *Total* and *Amanece* is Cuerda's own unique brand, as he had planned before filming.

Made for television and based on a script written by Cuerda himself, *Total* was very poorly received by Spanish film critics, but it won the International Critics' Award and a Jury Award's Special Mention, both at the 1983 Montercarlo Film Festival. Its first-person narrator, a shepherd named Lorenzo (played by Agustín González), opens the film by looking straight at the camera and pointing at a small hamlet while stating: "Londres." What we see on the screen, a Castilian hamlet in the province of Soria, is supposed to be London in the middle of the twenty-sixth century. Toward the end of the film, we learn that three days earlier, the narrator had escaped the apocalypse that destroyed London and most of its citizens by outrunning it (we also find out that Álvarez, a local woman [played by Chus Lampreave; her character reappears in *Amanece*], had survived thanks to psychoanalysis). Then, stating the obvious and playing with the boundaries between fiction and reality, Lorenzo, the narrator and apocalypse survivor, points at a sheep while uttering the word "oveja" (sheep). Later in the film, he clarifies that the little town we see on the screen is actually not London, but Paris, which may explain why, from time to time, two of the characters speak in French. Speaking from the future, the narrator explains the situation to the audience, who is still back in the 1980s.

As in *Amanece*, in *Total* the filmmaker's childhood memories of being educated by priests and spending three years in a seminary pervade the film, hence the prominence of the Biblical theme of the apocalypse, which links all of the film's gags. And as can be noticed in Cuerda's book *Amanece que no es poco*, memories regarding the demeanor of these Piarist fathers—who are also known as Escolapios, or Poor Clerics of the Mother of God—are full of justified resentment:

> The only thing I can say about the Piarists with whom I had to live is that their unjustifiable acts are barely redeemed by the fact that, as I learned later, the Pious Schools of Albacete were for the Piarist order the penitentiary of the Valencian region, the origin of most of those poor devils, whose destiny ended up in a nest of maggots—like everybody else's—instead of—according their apparent beliefs--in the hell they so deserved. Whoever wants to learn more about this matter may ask those of us who were students in that center in the 1950 and 1960s, and went through the hands of such preceptors. No one who was not there knows how literal what I have just written is.[6]

Incidentally, the mockery of religious vocabulary and theological concepts, such as free will, charity, the mystic body of Christ and the Holy Trinity, is reminiscent of the light-hearted representation of priestly worldviews and formalities present in García Márquez's 1955 short story "Un señor muy viejo con unas alas enormes" ("A Very Old Man with Enormous Wings").

In a long flashback in *Total*, Lorenzo recalls the extraordinary events that, in his view, undeniably announced the end of the world: cows were trying to enter the local school building, walls and houses kept collapsing, the narrator's son became forty years older overnight (this idea reappears in *Amanece*), and a woman named Doña Paquita kept appearing and disappearing. In line with the tenets of magical realism, neither of these events is seen with particular surprise by the locals, who walk by collapsing walls as if nothing were happening. Along these lines, upon realizing the failure of her beatification process, Doña Paquita decides to make a living out of her apparitions and puts on a show crossing walls; an unimpressed member of the audience asks her if she also cures the blind. *Total* is, therefore, full of delirious and impossibly absurd scenes that, ironically, were inspired by what a young Cuerda saw every day in Calle Albaderos, a street in an Albacete neighborhood. Inspired by one of his former neighbors, for example, a character named Sabina keeps asking her husband Pascual (played by Luis Ciges) to jump, in order to avoid stepping on nonexistent puddles (a scene reminiscent of the picaresque text *Lazarillo de Tormes*) or to bend down in order to avoid hitting the branch of a tree when, in fact, there are none. Later, she serves nonexistent fried eggs to him for lunch and blames him for not seeing them. In another scene, the teacher's wife strikes him, insults the students, and makes daily public scenes, just like the wife of one of Cuerda's teachers did when the filmmaker was a child. Likewise, all the scenes in *Amanece* and *Así en el cielo* where children sing in school to learn about the apocalypse, European rivers, the human heart, or multiplication are inspired by the way Cuerda was taught as a child. Overall, there is no attempt in the film to make viewers suspend their disbelief. That verisimilitude is not one of the director's goals is made apparent in the monologue, during which Lorenzo, belying Álvarez's previous comments praising cows, claims that sheep are better "and provide more milk. This, in spite of their smaller size, and against all logic and reality."[7] Later, he points out that a local boy became a famous meteorologist and then a fictional being. It is precisely this irrationality and denial of logical arguments that elicits the viewers' laughter.

The recurring theme of the apocalypse resurfaces in the third comedy in Cuerda's trilogy, *Así en el cielo*, which José María Caparrós Lera, in his negative review of the film, has defined as "the most unusual film in the history of Spanish film."[8] This time, it is a very human Christ (played by Jesús Bonilla) who suggests the apocalypse as a solution to his father (God is played by Fernando Fernán Gómez), while eating breakfast in a Heaven that looks very much like a post-Civil War, little Castilian town. Having failed as his father's messenger to humans, a Christ with very low self-esteem (he has to confess his psychological traumas to a psychoanalyst) convinces God not to send a second son to Earth, suggesting instead the apocalypse and final judgment as the only possible ways to correct humans' wrongdoings since Biblical times. Although he fears that his current budget is too small to stage an apocalypse, in the end, God the father agrees. Saint Peter, dressed as a Spanish civil guard and played by Francisco Rabal, has to raise funds by asking local ladies to donate their jewelry for the construction of the New Jerusalem.

Beyond Cuerda's trilogy of absurdist comedies, a type of *avant-la-lettre* Spanish magical realism that is more akin to Latin American literary magical realism can be found in his film *El bosque animado*, based on Wenceslao Fernández Flórez's 1943 novel of the same title and adapted to the screen by Rafael Azcona. In it, we find Cuerda's unique blend of humor and harsh social criticism in the contrasts between the presumptuous world of local oligarchy and that of the poor and exploited, between the snobbishness of the summer visitors from Madrid who do not know how a dog "works" and the simplicity of the town's people. Among the latter is an impoverished peasant, who becomes a thief known as Fendetestas (played by Alfredo Landa). When he tries to rob a man in the forest, unaware that he is facing the lost soul of Fiz de Cotovelo, the latter avers:[9] "I am Fiz de Cotovelo's soul who walks along these paths in torment, looking for a Christian."[10] Subsequently, a scared Fendetestas runs away, to the lost soul's dismay. We learn that Fiz the Cotovelo became a lost soul after being unable to fulfill his promise of visiting San Andrés de Teixido. According to one of the characters, Señor D'Abondo (played by Fernando Rey), the only thing that can stop this lost soul is holy water. Besides the lost soul, other characters see the Santa Compaña, a nocturnal procession of dead people from the purgatory or lost souls, always dressed in white, who visit homes where someone will soon die. The ghosts, after midnight, carry candles through the forest, smelling like wax. According to popular Galician mythology, whenever a person sees the procession, he or she automatically joins them, sometimes liberating the first soul that was seen, as a young girl in the film explains. Adding to the otherworldly cast, the film boasts witches and soothsayers who read one's future with decks of cards, and characters who know remedies against the evil eye. In the last scene, we learn that the lost soul of Fiz the Cotovelo never left the forest and that a local young girl who had recently passed away has also become another lost soul. As is typical in magical realism, characters see these bizarre events emerging from a mundane reality as just another aspect of everyday life. Thus, the well digger who walks by her in the forest, simply greets her, showing no surprise at all. One can also find the absurdist humor that is present (albeit more exaggerated) in *Total* and *Amanece*: the kind-hearted Fendetestas bargains with the people he robs, since they are his former neighbors and friends, and during a robbery of the local priest's house, he ends up helping his domestic servants who are worried about a cow that is delivering a calf.

In Cuerda's most celebrated comedy, *Amanece*, which has become a cult film and is often considered a classic in Spanish filmography, he returns to the *sui generis*, absurdist version of magical realism that was present in *Total*. *Amanece*'s outstanding collection of Spanish comedians, witty social criticism, off-color political incorrectness,[11] and peculiar "surruralist" humor turned it into an unexpected landmark in Spanish film. After its debut, Spanish critics reviewed it in very negative terms, often pointing out the lack of an organically unified and coherent script. They did not understand, unlike Spanish viewers decades later, the collage of eccentric scenes that make up the storyline of this choral film. Perhaps, after the great success of Cuerda's previous film, *El bosque animado*, they expected a sequel or a similar one. Yet today, *Amanece* is as popular as it has ever been. Its numerous fans—often referred to as *amanecistas*—still know entire dialogues by heart, and some sentences from the film have been incorporated into the Spanish vernacular. In several interviews, Cuerda has proudly associated *Amanece* with the Spanish picaresque tradition, along with *costumbrismo* and expressionism. Several critics have also associated the film with surrealism and consider the intertextuality with Luis Buñuel's surrealist films. However, as seen in the epigraph, Cuerda (while admitting the influence of Buñuel, as well as those of Berlanga and Azcona, Fernando Fernán Gómez, and Marco Ferreri), insists that there is nothing surrealist in the film, since every scene was very well reasoned and consciously prepared, leaving nothing to the mechanical and free association of ideas.

The case can be made that some viewers will associate the levitation scenes, the rain of Calasparra rice dropped by angels, and other related scenes with the Latin American literary tradition universally popularized by Gabriel García Márquez's *Cien años de soledad* (*One Hundred Years of Solitude,* 1967). Even if the comedic outlook of the film may distance it from the everyday-occurrence atmosphere of the magical realist scenes in García Márquez's novel, the common denominator is still there. Tellingly, in the third scene of the original script written by Cuerda in 1984 for a television series and titled "Ab urbe condita," we read:[12] "A flood of people rushes toward the church. The ones who run faster are a couple of men who levitate. Their legs cross the air at large strides. This levitation *does not surprise anyone*" (my italics).[13] Therefore, as is typical of Latin American literary magical realism, in this scene (as in many others in the film), we have something extraordinary, unreal, and magical that takes place in an otherwise realistic, everyday setting, blending organically with it and to no one's surprise. Throughout the film, characters strike up the most outrageous dialogs, which they deliver with complete seriousness and in realist settings in a remote, mountainous, small town (Lampreave and Ciges are particularly successful in their scenes). They unproblematically continue with their routines after witnessing marvelous, extravagant, and bizarre occurrences, which include, among others, a sunrise that takes place in the wrong place; a mayor who hangs himself to protest the fact that local men want his girlfriend to be "communal," yet he never dies[14] (and the local priest senses the scene from far away through the "mystic body of Christ"); a drunkard with a sober *doppelgänger*; a woman who reaches puberty at age sixty and is older than her own mother;[15] and an adulterous woman who delivers twins—without a nine-month pregnancy—only ten minutes after having sex with Morencos, a local farmer and "intellectual," who produces fiery flatulence upon seeing a women he finds desirable. According to Lois Parkinson Zamora, contemporary magical realists "undermine the credibility of narrative realism by flaunting the relative incredibility of their own texts" (501). This is obviously the case in *Total* and *Amanece*, where we even have a character, Cascales (played by Quique San Franscisco), who tries to exchange his role for others' throughout the film.

As stated, the humor in *Amanece* is blended with subtle social criticism of Spanish idiosyncrasies, institutional perpetuation of power, and backward sociocultural customs. Thus, the elections are always won by the same people: the mayor continues to be the mayor, and the secret police beat the civil guards . . . but they happen to be the same people. The Church is also mocked and criticized: Paquito (played by Manuel Alexandre) asks his son, the priest, if instead of fasting, it would not be better to give that food to the poor, and the only black man in town, Ngé Ndomo, is not allowed to go to mass because he is a catechumen. Mocking empty political correctness, several characters remind Ngé that he is not "black," but an "ethnic minority." Yet racism persists and, after decades living under the same roof, his uncle continues to be scared of Ngé every time they run into each other at home. American imperialism is also parodied when the mayor expels students of the Nonexistent University of Eaton from town, and they latter threaten him with retaliation once they attain absolute power. And the civil guard does not arrest Jimmy for killing his wife, since in the capital city, civil guards did not think he deserved to be arrested, but they do imprison a Latin American writer for plagiarizing William Faulkner. Civil guards also exert control over how alcoholics get inebriated and even over local sexual habits.

Moving back to the topic of magical realism, in the three films, *Total*, *Amanece*, and *El bosque animado,* we find levitation scenes, *doppelgängers,* apparitions, and other fantastical events that are associated with magical realism, whenever they emerge naturally from everyday social interactions and characters conceive of them as just another aspect of their mundane life. As in García Márquez's magical realist texts, these scenes are, for the most part, an exaggeration or parody of real events witnessed by the author (or in this case, the scriptwriter and director) during his childhood. In the case of *Amanece*, even the atemporal nature of the plot and its indefinite location—together with the fact that the setting is associated with a seemingly pre-modern, rural Spain, full of donkeys and lacking any sort of technology—is reminiscent of magical realism's tendency to include non-Western cultural traditions that challenge hegemonic, Western modernity. In Zamora's words, magical realist texts "seem to pulsate with proliferations and conflations of worlds, with appearances and disappearances and multiplications of selves and societies" (501). This is clearly the case in Cuerda's trilogy of comedies.

While peripheral, the settings in *Total* and *Amanece* still belong to a Western society. Yet they share the subversive nature of many magical realist texts written in the so-called Third Word in that there is also a subtle undercurrent of satirical political messages. Thus, as mentioned, during local elections (which include the election of the local prostitute, the adulterous women, the butch, and the town fool) in *Amanece*, institutions and their leaders barely change. We also find the sad social reality of Latin American exiles, who try to make a living as novelists, but, as expected, it is tempered with humor: one of them, Bruno, ends up plagiarizing Faulkner, who happens to be the town residents' favorite writer. In fact, this source of absurdist humor is perhaps the biggest risk in the film: the contrast between the *costumbrista*, rural, pre-modern setting and the locals' fascination with Faulkner, Fyodor Dostoyevski, renaissance Castilian madrigals, and George Frederick Handel's arias, or the sophisticated vocabulary used in certain scenes. As Juan A. Ríos Carratalá points out, "The dialogs and situations in *Amanece que no es poco* do not try to mock highbrow, and therefore extraordinary, culture inserted in a rural ambience that is supposedly ignorant and even provincial . . . Our smile is more joyous than satirical upon realizing how naturally an apparently logical order is subverted."[16] In this way, the filmmaker contributes to breaking down new barriers. In the words of Steven Marsh, et al., "Cuerda's work of the 1980s and early 1990s, in its exploitation of the comic possibilities of the conjunction of surrealism and the everyday, helps to break down the traditional critical dichotomy between arthouse cinema and popular film" (198). Cuerda's preference for these pre-modern settings, seemingly in a post-civil war deep (and rancid) Spain, also goes against the grain of 1980s Spanish cinema, which was beginning to be celebrated abroad: the cosmopolitan, urban, and modern Spain of Pedro Almodóvar's and Fernando Trueba's films.

Cuerda's comments in several interviews reveal that his childhood in post-civil war Albacete, Castile-La Mancha, and his education at a Catholic school and then in a seminary provided him with a rich source of inspiration for the odd stories he would later satirize in his films. After all, in *Amanece*, American students of the Nonexistent University of Eaton, Belgian meteorologists, and dissidents of the Soviet Army Choirs travel all the way to this town just to see Don Andrés (played by Cassen), a world-renowned local priest and devout admirer of free will, deliver the liturgy and dramatically elevate the holy host during the Eucharist. A standing ovation of the locals, who attend mass every day of the year and conceive of it as a sort of theatrical performance, together with the American students' singing of the traditional folk song "The Yellow Rose of Texas," follow the sacrament. Therefore, rather than pure imagination, as the viewer might think, the humorous scenes in Cuerda's 1980s films build on his own perplexity, as a child, when trying to rationalize the odd things (including cultural, religious, and sociopolitical conventions) that he saw every day. He recalls, for example, how one day the second floor of an apartment gave in, leaving his mother hanging from the neck, with only her head visible. This strange episode ended up being the source for the scenes, in *Amanece*, where men grow in an agricultural terrace (one of them, Garcinuño, sprouted back in the sixteenth century, but failed to ripen adequately as a result of the lustful life he led).

Regarding these same scenes, the director has also pointed out in interviews that, since he enjoys playing with the literal meaning of words, for him, the best way to represent how deeply a man is rooted to his homeland is to plant him. In his book *Amanece que no es poco*, Cuerda also considers the possibility that the inspiration may have come from the oft-used metaphor of the seedbed in the seminary, where he studied for three years.

To make clear that the outrageous fiction of *Amanece* is not so distant either from the sources that inspired him or from the daily life in the towns of the Sierra del Segura (Molinicos, Aýna, and Liétor, all of them in Albacete province), where he filmed it, Cuerda is quick to point out some locals' reaction to the presence of the filming crew. For example, he recalls that an elderly man who was stopped by civil guards while carrying a rifle in town confessed that he was looking for the actors because "he had had enough of them." Even more surrealistically, the Spanish Civil Guard gave Cuerda the Silver Cross of the Order of Merit, and explained to him that high-ranking officers loved his film (characters playing civil guards have a major role and their headquarters boast the sign "Headquarters and Public Library").[17] Likewise, a local baker, the filmmaker recalls, assured everyone very seriously that he had known those agricultural terraces all his life and that it was impossible that a man would ever grow in them. Even the opening scene in *Amanece* is, according to Cuerda, a literal transcription of the comments of a local man, who solemnly explained to the film crew the reason there was no inn in town: although the place was very cultured and boasted a colorful folklore, visitors had to stay in private homes "to avoid something bad from happening to local women."[18]

Overall, Cuerda's three 1980s films fluctuate between the more conventional magical realism of *El bosque animado* (although inspired by a Spanish novel published before the emergence of Latin American literary magical realism) and a unique version of magical realism in *Total* and *Amanece*, which resorts to absurdist contrasts between the marvelous and the real to elicit laughter. Particularly interesting is the fact that, while *Amanece* was not very successful at the box office when it was first released and received a very negative critical reception, a quarter of a century later, it is more popular than ever. One of the Facebook pages dedicated to the film has over 100,000 followers, many of whom participate in *amanecista* meetings. There is also a tourist route connecting locations where *Amanece* was filmed, along with a museum devoted to the movie's production and a short film contest named *Amanece que no es corto*, which requires that the same locations in the Sierra de Segura be used. Furthermore, contemporary Spanish comedians, such as the protagonists of the television show Muchachada Nui, openly admit the influence of the film *Amanece*. This shows that the initially misunderstood film has struck a chord in the collective subconscious of contemporary Spanish viewers. But why did it become a cult film decades after it was produced? Was Cuerda a visionary who was ahead of his time? Perhaps its current success stems from the uniqueness of its grotesque humor, which is reminiscent of Valle-Inclán's *esperpento* (a literary style invented by Spanish author Ramón María del Valle-Inclán that uses distorted and grotesque descriptions of reality to criticize society sarcastically), but still an original, unique blend of magical realism, absurdism, and social commentary that ignored mainstream cinematic standards. Ultimately, however, Cuerda's hilarious humor hides a sort of repressed rage (also present in his numerous Tweets) caused by the essential absurdity of some traditional religious values and sociopolitical idiosyncrasies that continued to be alive in the Spain of the 1980s, despite the advent and celebration of democracy. Caricature and laughter, therefore, veil a subtle invitation to reflect on the absurdity and incoherence of our own Spanish reality.

Notes

1. "Lo mío, esa es mi firme creencia, no es surrealismo, como se ha dicho, sino pegarle un revolcón a la lógica, fajarse con ella cuerpo a cuerpo y retorcerle el pescuezo hasta que vomite sus últimos argumentos" (n.p.).
2. "Ni siquiera el realismo mágico tiene copy-right latinoamericano, ya que lo encontramos en autores españoles como Valle Inclán, Álvaro Cunqueiro y Juan Perucho. ¿Por qué el fantasma de la novela El lápiz del carpintero (1998) de Manuel Rivas tiene que provenir del espectro de Prudencio Aguilar de Cien años de soledad (1967), si los fantasmas ya hablaban con los vivos en El bosque animado (1943) de Wenceslao Fernández-Flórez? ¿Por qué la apócrifa aventura de la Cueva de Montesinos no puede ser el primer episodio 'real maravilloso' de la historia de la literatura en español? Cualquiera que conozca mínimamente esa delirante cultura que engendró la multitud de Vidas de Santos, Crónicas de Indias y novelas del Siglo de Oro,

estaría de acuerdo conmigo en que la mariposa latinoamericana del realismo mágico alguna vez fue un gusano barroco español. Comprendo que para un lector alemán lo latinoamericano pueda ser 'mágico', 'exótico' y 'sobrenatural', pero cuando escucho semejantes adjetivos dentro de España se me alborota el cóndor que se supone que todos los peruanos escondemos en la jaula del canario. En España los nigromantes, adivinadores y charlatanes tienen más presencia que los científicos e investigadores en la televisión pública, pero eso no es realismo mágico. En numerosas plazas de toros españolas y en diversos aviones de la flota de Iberia no existe la fila de asientos número 13, pero eso no es realismo mágico. Y en Bélmez—un pueblo de la provincia andaluza de Jaén—el ayuntamiento ha declarado monumento local una casa donde aparecen y desaparecen una serie de rostros fantasmagóricos, pero eso tampoco es realismo mágico aunque ese pueblo sea gobernado por Izquierda Unida" (49).

3. "—¿Un fantasma? . . . Estaría más indicado decir un alma en pena. Eso soy, por mi desventura" (182).

4. "Cando penso que te fuches, / negra sombra que me asombras, / ó pé dos meus cabezales / tornas facéndome mofa. // Cando maxino que es ida, / no mesmo sol te me amostras, / i eres a estrela que brila, / i eres o vento que zoa. // Si cantan, es ti que cantas, / si choran, es ti que choras, / i es o marmurio do río / i es a noite i es a aurora. // En todo estás e ti es todo, / pra min i en min mesma moras, / nin me abandonarás nunca, / sombra que sempre me asombras."

5. "Entonces decidí que, si querían risa, iban a tener risa de la mía. Sería una comedia, pero 'raruna'. En España era absurdo hacer comedias al estilo Berlanga, porque ya las hacía él y nadie las iba a hacer mejor" (Tagarro n.p.).

6. "De los escolapios con los que me tocó convivir solo puedo decir que apenas redime sus actos injustificables el hecho de que, como supe después, las Escuelas Pías de Albacete eran para la orden escolapia el penal de la región valenciana, procedencia mayoritaria de aquellos pobres diablos, cuyo destino acabó en la gusanera—como el de todos—en vez de—de seguir sus aparentes creencias—en el infierno, que tanto merecían. Quien desee ampliar estudios sobre este asunto, que pregunte a cuantos cursamos en los años cincuenta y primeros sesenta en ese centro y pasamos por las manos de semejantes preceptores. No sabe nadie que no estuviera allí lo literal que es lo que acabo de escribir" (12).

7. "Y dan más leche. Esto último a pesar de su tamaño más reducido y en contra de la lógica y de la realidad" (n.p).
8. "La película más insólita realizada en toda la Historia del Cine español" (33).
9. With this film, Cuerda won in 1988 six Goya awards: best film, best actor (Alfredo Landa), best script, best costume designs, and best music.
10. "Soy el ánima de Fiz de Cotovelo que anda penando por estos caminos en busca de un cristiano" (n.p.).
11. There are numerous jokes about the character Ngé Ndomo (played by Samuel Claxton) being black. We are told that South American characters some days ride a bicycle, while others they "smell well," and Jimmy (played by Luis Ciges) kills his wife because "she was very bad." Ciges' character, incidentally, also kills his wife in Total.
12. The original script can be found in the recently published book *Amanece que no es poco*, which also includes explanations and anecdotes, scenes that were not filmed or did not appear in the final cut, and photographs of the shooting. As to the title of this manuscript, "Ab urbe condita," it is plausible that Cuerda's three years in a seminary influenced his fondness for Latin terms.
13. "Riadas de gente apresurada se dirigen a la iglesia. Los que más corren son un par de hombres que levitan. Sus piernas cruzan el aire a grandes zancadas. Esta levitación no llama la atención de nadie" (93).
14. A character named Erminio is executed by hanging in Total, but he resurrects.
15. We have a similar situation in Total, where the character played by Manuel Alexandre is older than that of his father, played by Agustín González. Cuerda found the inspiration for this incongruence in the fact that he always considered himself older than his own father, who reportedly died at age eighty with the body of an adolescent.
16. "Los diálogos y las situaciones de Amanece que no es poco no pretenden hacer burla de lo culto, y por eso mismo extraordinario, insertado en un ámbito rural que se supone ignorante y hasta paleto . . . Nuestra sonrisa es más gozosa que satírica al comprobar la naturalidad con la que se subvierte un orden aparentemente lógico" (58).

17. "Casa Cuartel y Biblioteca Pública" (n.p.).
18. "Por lo que les pueda ocurrir a las mujeres" (n.p.).

Works Cited

Amanece que no es poco. Dir. José Luis Cuerda. Perf. Antonio Resines, Luis Ciges, José "Saza" Sazatornil, Chus Lampreave, Gabino Diego. Compañía de Aventuras Comerciales, TVE, Paraíso, 1988.

Así en el cielo como en la tierra. Dir. José Luis Cuerda. Perf. Fernando Fernán Gómez, Francisco Rabal, Jesús Bonilla, Luis Ciges. Atrium Productions, 1995.

Bienvenido, Mister Marshall. Dir. Luis García Berlanga. Perf. José Isbert, Manolo Morá, Lolita Sevilla. Uninci. 1953.

El bosque animado. Dir. José Luis Cuerda. Perf. Alfredo Landa, Tito Valverde, Alejandra Grepi, Fernando Rey, Manuel Alexandre, Luis Cijes. Classic Films Producción, 1987.

Caparrós Lera, José María. *El cine de nuestros días (1994–1998)*. Madrid: Rialp, 1999.

Cuerda, José Luis. *Amanece que no es poco*. Logroño: Pepitas de Calabaza, 2013.

Fernández Flórez, Wenceslao. *Relato inmoral*. Barcelona: Planeta, 1958.

García Márquez, Gabriel. *One Hundred Years of Solitude*. New York: Perennial Classics, 1998.

Marsh, Steven, Chris Perriam, Eva Woods Peiró,& Santos Zunzunegui. "Comedy and Musicals." *A Companion to Spanish Cinema*. Eds. Jo Labanyi & Tatjana Pavlović. Malden, Massachusetts: Wiley-Blackwell, 2013. 193–223.

Ríos Carratalá, Juan A. *La sonrisa del inútil: imágenes de un pasado cercano*. Alicante, Spain: Publicaciones Universidad de Alicante, 2008.

Tagarro, Ana. "Saza, que no es poco." *XL Semanal*. Inversión & Finanzas. 6 Oct. 2013. Web. 22 Jul. 2014.

Total. Dir. José Luis Cuerda. Perf. Miguel Rellán, Manuel Alexandre, Luis Ciges, María Luisa Ponte. TVE, 1983.

Zamora, Lois Parkinson. "Magical Romance/Magical Realism: Ghosts in U.S. and Latin American Fiction." *Magical Realism: Theory,*

History, Community. Eds. Lois Parkinson Zamora & Wendy B. Faris. Durham, NC: Duke UP, 1995. 497–550.

RESOURCES

Additional Works on Magical Realism

Ten Nights of Dreams (1908), by Natsume Sōseki (Japan)
The Living Forest (1943), by Wenceslao Fernández-Flórez (Spain)
The Kingdom of This World (1949), by Alejo Carpentier (Cuba)
The Palm-Wine Drinkard (1952), by Amos Tutuola (Nigeria)
Pedro Páramo (1955), by Juan Rulfo (Mexico)
The Tin Drum (1959), by Günter Grass (Germany)
Palace of the Peacock (1960), by Wilson Harris (Guayana)
Big Mama's Funeral (1962), by Gabriel García Márquez (Colombia)
Aura (1962), by Carlos Fuentes (Mexico)
One Hundred Years of Solitude (1967), by Gabriel García Márquez (Colombia)
One Arm (1969), by Kawabata Yasunari (Japan)
Bless Me, Ultima (1971), by Rudolfo Anaya (United States)
The Autumn of the Patriarch (1975), by Gabriel García Márquez (Colombia)
The Road To Tamazunchale (1975), by Ron Arias (United States)
The Man Who Turned into a Stick (1975), by Kōbō Abe (Japan)
The Woman Warrior (1976), by Maxine Hong Kingston (United States)
Nambé—Year One (1976), by Orlando Romero (United States)
Song of Solomon (1977), by Toni Morrison (United States)
The Incredible and Sad Tale of Innocent Erendira and Her Heartless Grandmother (1978), by Gabriel García Márquez (Colombia)
The Book of Laughter and Forgetting (1979), by Milan Kundera (Czech Republic)
Distant Relations (1982), by Carlos Fuentes (Mexico)
Midnight's Children (1981), by Salman Rushdie (India-United Kingdom)
The White Hotel (1981), by D.M. Thomas (United Kingdom)
The House of the Spirits (1982), by Isabel Allende (Chile)

Ironweed (1983), by William Kennedy (United States)
Pungchuk, Wind Flute (1983), by Sung-Dong Kim (South Korea)
The Diffuse Biography of Sombra Castañeda (1984), by Marcio Veloz Maggiolo (Dominican Republic)
The Year of the Death of Ricardo Reis (1984), by José Saramago (Portugal)
Love in the Time of Cholera (1985), by Gabriel García Márquez (Colombia)
Perfume: The Story of a Murderer (1985), by Patrick Süskind (Germany)
Red Sorghum: A Novel of China (1986), by Mo Yan (China)
Sweet Country (1986), by Kojo Laing (Ghana)
Eva Luna (1987), by Isabel Allende (Chile)
Beloved (1987), by Toni Morrison (United States)
Dance Dance Dance (1988), Haruki Murakami (Japan)
The Satanic Verses (1988), by Salman Rushdie (India-United Kingdom)
Kitchen (1988), by Banana Yoshimoto (Japan)
Woman of the Aeroplanes (1988), by Kojo Laing (Ghana)
The Dream of Santa María de las Piedras (1989), by Miguel Méndez M. (United States)
Like Water for Chocolate (1989), by Laura Esquivel (Mexico)
Sexing the Cherry (1989), by Jeanette Winterson (United Kingdom)
A Thousand Years of Solitude (1989), by Sung-Kee Cho (South Korea)
The Last Harmattan of Alusine Dunbar (1990), by Syl Cheney-Coker (Sierra Leone)
The Famished Road (1991), by Ben Okri (Nigeria)
La Maravilla (1993), by Alfredo Véa, Jr. (United States)
So Far from God (1993), by Ana Castillo (United States)
The Hundred Secret Senses (1995), by Amy Tan (United States)
Pig Tales (1996), by Marie Darrieussecq (France)
DMZ (1997), by Sang-Yeon Park (South Korea)
The Wind-Up Bird Chronicle (1997), by Haruki Murakami (Japan)
The Carpenter's Pencil (1998), by Manuel Rivas (Spain)

Devil's Valley (1998), by André Brink (South Africa)
Hardboiled & Hard Luck (1999), by Banana Yoshimoto (Japan)
The Host (2001), by Suk-Yeong Hwang (South Korea)
Life of Pi (2001), by Yann Martel (Canada)
Kafka on the Shore (2002), by Haruki Murakami (Japan)
Lenin's Kisses (2003), by Yan Lian-ke (China)
Waiting for Snow in Havana. Confessions of a Cuban Boy (2003), by Carlos Eire (Cuba-United States)
The Instant of Eternity (2004), by Zoé Valdés (Cuba)
The Island of Eternal Love (2006), by Daína Chaviano (Cuba)
The Brief Wondrous Life of Oscar Wao (2007), by Junot Díaz (Dominican Republic-United States)

Bibliography

Aldama, Frederick Luis. *Postethnic Narrative Criticism: Magicorealism in Oscar 'Zeta' Acosta, Ana Castillo, Julie Dash, Hanif Kureishi, and Salman Rushdie*. Austin: U of Texas P, 2003.

Aldea, Eva. *Magical Realism and Deleuze: The Indiscernibility of Difference in Postcolonial Literature*. London: Continuum, 2011.

Anderson-Imbert, Enrique. "Magic Realism in Spanish American Fiction." *The International Fiction Review* 1.1 (January 1975): 1–7.

Angulo, María-Elena. *Magic Realism: Social Context and Discourse*. New York: Garland, 1995.

Arva, Euguen L. *The Traumatic Imagination: Histories of Violence in Magical Realist Fiction*. Amherst, NY: Cambia Press, 2011.

Boland, Roy C., & Sally Harvey. *Magical Realism and Beyond: The Contemporary Spanish and Latin American Novel*. Melbourne: Vox/AHS, 1991.

Bowers, Maggie Ann. *Magic(al) Realism*. New York: Routledge, 2004.

Chanady, Amaryll. *Magical Realism and the Fantastic: Resolved Versus Unresolved Antinomy*. New York: Garland, 1985.

Cooper, Brenda. *Magical Realism in West African Fiction: Seeing with a Third Eye*. New York: Routledge, 1998.

Daniel, Lee A. "Realismo Magico: True Realism with a Pinch of Magic." *The South Central Bulletin* 42.4 (1982): 129–30.

Danoe, David K. *Spirit of Carnival: Magical Realism and the Grotesque*. Lexington, Kentucky: UP of Kentucky, 1995.

_____. *The Spirit of Carnival: Magical Realism and the Grotesque*. Lexington, Kentucky: UP of Kentucky, 2004.

De la Campa, Román. "Magical Realism and World Literature: A Genre for the Times?" *Revista Canadiense de Estudios Hispánicos* 23.2 (Winter 1999): 206–19.

Di Iorio Sandín, Lyn, & Richard Perez, eds. *Moments of Magical Realism in U.S. Ethnic Literatures*. New York: Palgrave MacMillan, 2012.

Durix, Jean-Pierre. *Mimesis, Genre, and Post-Colonial Discourse: Deconstructing Magic Realism*. Hampshire: St. Martin's Press, 1998.

Faris, Wendy B. *Ordinary Enchantments: Magical Realism and the Remystification of Narrative.* New York: Vanderbilt UP, 2004.

Flores, Ángel. "Magical Realism in Spanish American Fiction." *Hispania* 38.2 (1955): 187–92.

Hancock, Geoff, ed. *Magic Realism.* Toronto: Aya Press, 1980.

Hart, Patricia. *Narrative Magic in the Fiction of Isabelle Allende.* London & Toronto: Associated U Presses, 1989.

Hart, Stephen M., & Wen-chin Ouyang, eds. *A Companion to Magical Realism.* New York: Tamesis, 2005.

Hegerfeldt, Anne C. *Lies That Tell the Truth: Magic Realism Seen Through Contemporary Fiction from Britain.* Amsterdam: Rodopi, 2005.

Hinchcliffe, Peter, & Ed Jewinski, eds. *Magic Realism and Canadian Literature: Essays and Stories.* Waterloo: U of Waterloo P, 1986.

Kalogeras, Yiorgos, "Magic Realism in American Literature: The Case of Ethnic and Minority Literatures." *Porphyras* 41–42 (1987): 305–09.

Linguanti, Elsa, Franceso Casotti, & Carmen Concilio, eds. *Coterminous Worlds: Magical Realism and Contemporary Post-Colonial Literature in English.* Amsterdam, Atlanta: Rodopi, 1999.

McMurray, George. "Magical Realism in Spanish American Fiction." *Colorado State Review* 8.2 (1981): 3–20.

Menton, Seymour. *Magic Realism Rediscovered, 1918–1981.* London & Toronto: Associated UP, 1983.

Merrell, Floyd. "The Ideal World in Search of its Reference: An Inquiry into the Underlying Nature of Magic Realism." *Chasqui* 4.2 (Feb 1975): 5–17.

Moreiras, Alberto. "The End of Magical Realism: José María Arguedas' Passionate Signifier ('El zorro de arriba y el zorro de abajo')." *The Journal of Narrative Technique* 27.1 (Winter, 1997): 84–112.

Noriega Sánchez, María Ruth. *Challenging Realities: Magic Realism in Contemporary American Women's Fiction.* Valencia, Spain: Departament de Filologia Anglesa i Alemanya, 2002.

Rodríguez Monegal, Emir. "Surrealism, Magical Realism, Magical Fiction: A Study in Confusion." *Surrealismo/ Surrealismos: Latinoamérica y España.* Eds. Peter G. Earle & Germán Gullón. Philadelphia: U of Pennsylvania P, 1977. 25–32.

Schroeder, Shannin. *Rediscovering Magical Realism in the Americas.* Westport, CT: Praeger, 2004.

Simpkins, Scott. "Magical Strategies: The Supplement of Realism." *Twentieth Century Literature* 34.2 (Summer 1988): 140–54.

Slemon, Stephen. "Magic Realism as a Postcolonial Discourse." *Canadian Literature* 116 (Spring 1988): 2–24.

Spindler, William. "Magic Realism: A Typology." *Modern Language Studies* 29.1 (January 1993): 75–85.

Takolander, Maria. *Catching Butterflies: Bringing Magical Realism to Ground.* Bern, Switzerland: Peter Lang AG, European Academic Publishers, 2007.

Warnes, Christopher. *Magical Realism and the Postcolonial Novel: Between Faith and Irreverence.* New York: Palgrave Macmillan, 2009.

Wilson, Robert Rawdon. "On the Boundary of the Magic and the Real: Notes on Inter-American Fiction." *Compass* 6 (Spring 1979): 37–53.

Young, David, & Keith Hagarman, eds. *Magical Realist Fiction: An Anthology.* New York: Longman, 1984.

Zamora, Lois Parkinson, & Wendy B. Faris, eds. *Magical Realism: Theory, History, Community.* Durham, NC: Duke UP, 1995.

Zlotchew, Clark M. *Varieties of Magic Realism.* New Jersey: Academic Press ENE, 2007.

About the Editor

Ignacio López-Calvo is a professor of Latin American literature at the University of California, Merced. He is the author of seven books on Latin American and US Latino literature and culture, including *Dragons in the Land of the Condor: Tusán Literature and Knowledge in Peru*, *The Affinity of the Eye: Writing Nikkei in Peru*, *Latino Los Angeles in Film and Fiction: The Cultural Production of Social Anxiety*, *Imaging the Chinese in Cuban Literature and Culture*, *"Trujillo and God": Literary and Cultural Representations of the Dominican Dictator*, *Religión y militarismo en la obra de Marcos Aguinis 1963–2000*, and *Written in Exile. Chilean Fiction from 1973–Present*. He has also edited the books *Peripheral Transmodernities: South-to-South Dialogues between the Luso-Hispanic World and "the Orient,"* *Alternative Orientalisms in Latin America and Beyond*, and *One World Periphery Reads the Other: Knowing the "Oriental" in the Americas and the Iberian Peninsula*. Additionally, he had co-edited *Caminos para la paz: literatura israelí y árabe en castellano*. López-Calvo is the co-executive director of the academic journal *Transmodernity: Journal of Peripheral Cultural Production of the Luso-Hispanic World*.

Contributors

Rudyard J. Alcocer is the Forrest & Patsy Shumway Chair of Excellence in Romance Languages and associate professor of Latin American literature and culture in the Department of Modern Foreign Languages and Literatures at the University of Tennessee, Knoxville. He is the author of *Time Travel in the Latin American & Caribbean Imagination: Re-reading History* (Palgrave Macmillan, 2011) and *Narrative Mutations: Discourses of Heredity and Caribbean Literature* (Routledge, 2005). His current book-length project examines the intersections between literary and scientific discourses.

Gene H. Bell-Villada is professor of Romance Languages at Williams College. His books on Borges and García Márquez are now in their second editions and are consulted frequently in colleges and high schools. His wide-ranging study, *Art for Art's Sake & Literary Life*, was a finalist for the 1997 National Book Critics Circle Award and has been translated into Chinese and Serbian. The author of two books of fiction, *The Carlos Chadwick Mystery* (1990) and *The Pianist Who Liked Ayn Rand: A Novella & 13 Stories* (1998), he has also published a memoir, *Overseas American: Growing Up Gringo in the Tropics* (2005), and edited a follow-up collection of essays, *Writing out of Limbo: International Childhoods, Global Nomads and Third Culture Kids* (2011). His latest book is *On Nabokov, Ayn Rand and The Libertarian Mind: What the Russian American Odd Pair Can Tell Us about Some Values, Myths and Manias Widely Held Most Dear* (2013).

Nicholas Birns is the editor of *Antipodes: A Global Journal of Australian/NZ Literature* and has given many papers on Australian literature, traveled to Australia frequently, and written for journals, such as *Southerly Westerly, Australian Literature Studies, The Australian Book Review,* and *Australian Humanities Review*. He co-edited (with Robert Dixon) *Reading Across The Pacific Australian-United States Intellectual Histories* (University of Sydney Press, 2010), which contained his essay "Missed Appointments: American Literary Travelers Down Under." In 2012, he published an article on the figuration of the Pacific and Indian

Oceans in *Moby-Dick* in *Leviathan: A Journal of Melville Studies*. He has also published the following books: *Willa Cather* (Salem Press, 2011); *Vargas Llosa and Latin American Politics* (co-edited with Juan E. De Castro, Palgrave Macmillan, 2010); *Theory After Theory. An Overview of Currents in Literary Theory from the 1950s to the Present* (Broadview Press, 2010); *Companion to Twentieth-Century Australian Literature* (co-edited with Rebecca McNeer; Camden House, 2007); and *Understanding Anthony Powell* (University of South Carolina Press, 2004).

Maggie Ann Bowers is a senior lecturer in literatures in English at the University of Portsmouth, United Kingdom. Her research field covers contemporary postcolonial studies, most particularly focusing upon comparative multi-ethnic literatures of North America and Native American Studies. She is the author of *Magic(al) Realism*, part of Routledge's "New Critical Idiom" series. Recent research projects have examined the links between storytelling, ritual, law, and sovereignty in Native American writing.

Erik Camayd-Freixas is professor of Latin American literature at Florida International University. He received his PhD from Harvard University in Romance languages and literatures. Camayd has lectured and published internationally on linguistic, literary, and cultural studies, immigration, labor, ethics, and human rights. The recipient of numerous academic and human rights awards, he has published *Realismo mágico y primitivismo* (University Press of America, 1998); *Primitivism and Identity in Latin America* (University of Arizona Press, 2000); *Postville: La criminalización de los migrantes* (F&G Editores, 2009); *Etnografía imaginaria: Historia y parodia en la literatura hispanoamericana* (F&G Editores, 2012); *Orientalism and Identity in Latin America* (edited, University of Arizona Press, 2013); and *U.S. Immigration Reform and Its Global Impact* (Palgrave Macmillan, 2013); in addition to numerous articles in collective volumes and journals. Dr. Camayd specializes in discourse analysis, cultural studies, literary theory, ethnopoetics, and anthropological approaches to the literature and historiography of the colonial and contemporary periods of Latin America and the Caribbean.

Martín Camps is the author of *Cruces fronterizos: hacia una narrativa del desierto* (University of Ciudad Juarez, 2008) and co-editor of *Aproximaciones a la narrativa de Luis Arturo Ramos* (University of Ciudad Juárez, 2003). He has published four books of poetry and one novel. He is currently an associate professor of Spanish at the University of the Pacific in Stockton, California.

Juan E. De Castro is an associate professor in literary studies at Eugene Lang College, The New School for Liberal Arts, New York. He is the author of *Mestizo Nations: Culture, Race, and Conformity in Latin American Literature* (2002); *The Spaces of Latin American Literature: Tradition, Globalization and Cultural Production* (2008); and *Mario Vargas Llosa: Public Intellectual in Neoliberal Latin America* (2011). He is also the editor of *Vargas Llosa and Latin American Politics* (2010, with Nicholas Birns); *The Contemporary Spanish American Novel: Bolaño and After* (2012, with Will H. Corral and Nicholas Birns); and *Critical Insights: Mario Vargas Llosa*. He is currently working on a book-length study on the pioneer Peruvian Marxist thinker and activist José Carlos Mariátegui.

Ángel L. Estévez is an assistant professor at the CUNY Graduate Center. He is the director of the master's program in Spanish at The City College in New York. His area of research centers on twentieth-century Spanish-American and Caribbean literatures, including Magic Realism and the Fantastic. His most recent publications include *El español y su evolución* (coauthored with Silvia Burunat; Peter Lang, forthcoming); *El español y su estructura* (coauthored with Silvia Burunat and Aleksín Ortega; Peter Lang, 2012); *El español y su sintaxis* (coauthored with Silvia Burunat and Aleksín Ortega; Peter Lang, 2010); and *La modalidad fantástica en el cuento dominicano del siglo XX* (Mellen Press, 2005). Estévez has taught at Lehman College and Fordham University at Lincoln Center Campus.

David William Foster (PhD, University of Washington, 1964 [BA, 1961; MA, 1963 University of Washington]) is Regents' Professor of Spanish, Humanities, and Women's Studies at Arizona State University. He served as chair of the department of languages and literatures from 1997 to 2001. In spring 2009, he served as the Ednagene and Jordan Davidson Eminent Scholar in the Humanities at Florida International University. His research interests focus on urban culture in Latin America, with emphasis on issues of gender construction and sexual identity, as well as Jewish culture. He has written extensively on Argentine narrative and theater, and he has held Fulbright teaching appointments in Argentina, Brazil, and Uruguay. He has also served as an Inter-American Development Bank professor in Chile. McFarland Publishing brought out *Urban Photography in Argentina* in 2007. *São Paulo: Perspectives on the City and Cultural Production* was published in 2011 by the University Press of Florida. *Latin American Documentary Filmmaking: Major Texts* (University of Arizona Press) and *Glimpses of Phoenix: The Desert Metropolis in Written and Visual Media* (McFarland Publishing) both come out in 2013. In June–July 2013, as in June 2010, Foster directed a program in São Paulo on Urban Brazilian Narrative as part of the National Endowment for the Humanities Summer Seminars for College and University Teachers, and he will repeat in July 2014 in Argentina his NEH seminar on "Jewish Buenos Aires."

Kim Anderson Sasser is the author of *Magical Realism and Cosmopolitanism: Strategizing Belonging* (Palgrave Macmillan, 2014). Assistant professor of English at Wheaton College, she has taught courses including "Magical Realism, Modern Global Literature, and West African Literature." Her areas of interest include twentieth- and twenty-first-century Anglophone fiction, magical realism, cosmopolitanism, and postcolonial literature and theory.

Rachel Trousdale is visiting associate professor of English at Northeastern University. She is the author of *Nabokov, Rushdie, and the Transnational Imagination: Novels of Exile and Alternate Worlds*. Her work on twentieth-century fiction, poetry, and comics has appeared in *The Journal of Commonwealth Literature*, *The Journal of Modern Literature*, *Comparative Literature Studies*, *The Yale Review*, and many other places. She also writes poetry. She received her PhD from Yale University.

Fernando Valerio-Holguín is a full professor of Caribbean literature and culture at Colorado State University, where he won the John N. Stern Distinguished Professor Award. Poet, fiction writer, and critic, he has published articles on literature, cinema, music, and culture in journals and has presented papers at national and international conferences. He has been invited to lecture and read poetry at universities and institutions, such as the Julian Samora Research Institute at Michigan State University, the Smithsonian Institution, the University of Newcastle-Upon-Tyne, Oxford University, University of Warsaw, and the Library of Congress, among others. He has published the following books: *Viajantes insomnes* (short stories, 1982); *Poética de la frialdad* (criticism, 1996); *Autorretratos* (poetry, 2002); *Memorias del último cielo* (novel, 2002); *Café Insomnia* (short stories, 2002); *Banalidad posmoderna: Ensayos sobre identidad cultural latinoamericana* (criticism, 2006); and *Rituales de la Bella Pagana* (poetry, 2009). He has edited *Arqueología de las sombras: La narrativa de Marcio Veloz Maggiolo* (2000) and *La novela-bolero en Latinoamérica* (2008).

Index

African Diaspora 165, 170, 171
Afro-Caribbean Religions 129
Aguilar, Prudencio 53, 193, 206
Aguilera-Malta, Demetrio xxv
Ahmad, Aijaz 181
Aizenberg, Edna 160
Alazraki, Jaime 9
Aldea, Eva 35
Alegría, Ciro 27
Alegría, Fernando 12
Alexandre, Manuel 202, 208, 209
Alexis, Jacques Stephen 7
Alfredo, Cernícalo 104
Allende, Isabel xxi, xxiv, xxv, 12, 21, 26, 36, 73, 81, 86, 213, 214
Almodóvar, Pedro 204
Alonso, Rafael 196
Amanece que no es poco xv, 194, 195, 197, 203, 204, 208, 209
Amuleto 30
Anaya, Rudolfo 21, 213
Andrés, Don 204
Anscombe, G. E. M. 17
Arana, R. Victoria 176
Arana, Victoria R. 165
Arce, Chrissy B. 145
Argentino, Carlos 58
Arguedas, José María xxv, xxxi, 16, 27, 218
Arias, Claudia M. Milian xxiii
Arnason, H. H 15
Ashcroft, Bill 48
Así en el cielo 195, 198, 209
Así en el cielo como en la tierra 195, 209
Asturias, Miguel Ángel xvii, 6, 27, 100, 114, 158, 194

Auerbach, Erich 61
Aura 52, 55, 63, 213
Austen, Jane 184
avant-garde 3, 5, 24, 88
Azcona, Rafael 196, 199
Aziz, Adam 39
Aziz, Naseem 39

Babilonia, Mauricio 92
Badgery, Herbert 148
Bail, Murray 157
Balaguer, Joaquín 103, 110
Balasubramanian, Radha 191
Baldeosingh, Kevin 71
Balenyó, Ogún 103
Baroque and the Marvelous Real, The xxi, 15, 128
Barthes, Roland 145
Bayly, Jaime xxii, 18
Beckmann, Max 4
Belcan, Belié 123
Belecou, Toro 123
Beloved 52, 63, 96, 214
Benito, Jesús 25
Benjumea Brito, Paola 95
Bergero, Adriana 73, 81
Berlanga, Luis García 196, 209
Beverley, John 41
Bhutto, Zulfikar Ali 183
Bienvenido, Mister Marshall 196, 209
Blackburn, Paul 62
Blais, Marie-Claire 153
Bloom, Harold 195
Boccaccio 50
Bogin, Magda 47
Bolaño, Robero 30
Boldrewood, Rolf 155

229

Bolosse, Similá 123
Bombal, María Luisa 8
Bonilla, Jesús 198, 209
Bontempelli, Massimo 3, 5
Boom, The xxiv, 19, 20, 21, 22, 28, 73, 86, 101, 144, 145
Borges, Jorge Luis x, xix, xxxi, 101, 148
Bortolin, Celia 34
Bouk, Dan 145
Brennan, Timothy 41, 181
Breton, André 100, 114
Brief Wondrous Life of Oscar Wao, The xvi, xxii, xxix, xxxi, 215
Brito, Benjumea 95
Broken Ground 153, 160
Bromwich, David 63
Brontë 50
Brunner, José Joaquín 145
Bruno 203
Buckley, Christina 21, 33
Buendía, Aureliano 91
Buendía, José Arcadio xii, 53, 89
Buendía, Tim 95
Bulgakov, Mikhail 180, 191
Buñuel, Luis 200
Burgos, Elisabeth 101
Burnett, D. Graham 145

Calkins, Jennifer 145
Candé, Jérémie 123
Caparrós Lera, José María 198
Capellá, María Fernanda Valerio 97
Carey, Peter xiii, 148, 152, 160
Carfú, Papá 123
Carpentier, Alejo ix, xii, xiv, xvii, xxi, 6, 12, 15, 23, 43, 68, 82, 100, 107, 113, 114, 128, 130, 162, 173, 213
Carratalá, Juan A. Ríos 203
Carter, Angela 45
Casanova, Pascale xxvii, 54, 151
Casares, Bioy 8
Castañeda, Ricardo Chávez xxiv, 18, 34
Castañeda, Sombra xii, 97, 98, 102, 103, 104, 105, 106, 110, 112, 214
Castro, Rosalía de 194
Catholicism 24, 117
Catton, Eleanor xiii, 158
Celis, Nadia V. 145
Cendrars, Blaise 5
Cervantes Saavedra, Miguel de 49, 55
Chakrabarty, Dipesh 37
Chanady, Amaryll Beatrice 62, 128
Chatterjee, Partha 47
Chaturvedi, Vinayak 47, 48
Chávez Castañeda, Ricardo xxiv, 18, 34
Chaviano, Daína 71, 215
Cheever, John 56
Cheney Coker, Syl xvi
Chiampi, Irlemar 10
Ching, Erick 33
Christ 196, 197, 198, 201
Chute, Hillary 145
Ciges, Luis 198, 208, 209
Civilization and Its Discontents 16
Clark, Roger Y. 191
Claxton, Samuel 208
Clifford, James 100, 111
Cohen, Sandro 86
Collard, Patrick 112

Collins, Walter P., III 176
Colón, Bartolomé 108
Commonwealth Literature 180, 182, 226
Como agua para chocolate xxv, 12
Compaña, Santa 194, 199
Cooper, Brenda 35, 37
Corngold, Stanley 62
Cornwell, Neil 191
Corral, Wilfrido H. xxiv
Cortázar, Julio xix, 22
Cosentino, Donald J. 129
Cotes, Petra 91
Courter, The 168
Coutinho, Laerte 143
Coutinho, Rafael v, xii, 131, 132, 145
Crack Generation, The xxiv
Crespi, Pietro 90, 95
Cuerda, José Luis v, xiv, 193, 194, 209
Cunqueiro, Álvaro 193, 206

D'Abondo, Señor 199
Daniel, Helen 151
David, Dwight 196
Davies, Robertson 147
Deive, Carlos Esteban 108
Delaura, Cayetano 72
Delbaere-Garant, Jeanne 173
Deleuze, Gilles 145
Delgado, Yolanda 34
Devil, The 50
Diaspora 165, 170, 171
Díaz, Junot xvi, xxii, xxix, xxxi, 215
Dickens, Charles 50, 152
Diego, Gabino 209
Dix, Otto 4
Dobek-Bell, Audrey 49
Domingo, Santo 98, 108, 109, 111, 112, 128, 129
Dos Passos, John 150
Dostoyevski, Fyodor 203
Doubois, Philippe 97
Dreifus, Claudia 33
Dubois, Laurent 128
Duff, Alan 156
Duncan, Cynthia 128
Durix, Jean-Pierre 176, 217

Eaglestone, Robert 183, 191
Earle, Peter G. 218
East, West 177
El bosque animado xv, 193, 194, 195, 199, 200, 202, 205, 206, 209
El etnógrafo 101, 111
El hablador xxv, 12
El hombre del acordeón xii, 97, 98, 108, 112, 123, 130
El lápiz del carpintero 193, 206
El olor de la guayaba 16
El túnel 195
End of the Game and Other Stories 62
Era of Trujillo 103
Erdrich, Louise 170
Erzulie-Freda 122, 123
España, aparta de mí estos premios 193
Esquivel, Laura xxiv, 12, 21, 73, 81, 86, 214
Essay on Blindness 56

fantastic, the xi, xvi, xix, xx, 8, 9, 10, 11, 13, 56, 57, 60, 61,

88, 125, 150, 159, 179, 183, 186, 187, 188, 190
Fantasy 51, 182, 186
Faris, Wendy B. xx, xxx, xxxi, 15, 16, 17, 62, 63, 64, 69, 82, 83, 96, 128, 130, 170, 176, 177, 191, 210, 219
Father Nicanor 18
Faulkner, William 202
Fee, Margery 160
Fendetestas 199, 200
Fernández, Acedonio 125
Fernández Flórez, Wenceslao 193, 194, 199
Fernández Olmos, Margarite 128
Ferreri, Marco 200
Figiel, Sia 155
First World xiv, 87, 146, 151, 153, 158, 170
First World War 153
Fiz the Cotovelo 199, 200
Flanagan, Richard 156
Flores, Ángel xix, xxi, 7, 51, 69
Flórez, Wenceslao Fernández 193, 194, 199
Follas novas 194
Foreign Policy 33
Forster, E. M. 51
Foster Jr., John Burt 63
Fox from Up Above and the Fox from Down Below, The xxv
Frame, Janet 147, 170
Franco Pichardo, Franklin 127
Freud, Sigmund xvii, 9, 99
Friedman, Edward H. 111
Frye, Northrop 51, 52
Fuentes, Carlos xi, 21, 22, 141, 213
Fuguet, Alberto xxx, 33, 96

Furphy, Joseph 148

Galera-Coutinho 135, 136, 144
Galera, Daniel v, xii, 131, 132
Gallagher, David 27
Gallegos, Rómulo 8, 92
Gamboa, Santiago xxii
García Berlanga, Luis 196, 209
García, Cristina xi, 53
García, Mario T. 82
García Márquez, Gabriel v, x, xi, xvi, xix, 18, 33, 36, 38, 63, 67, 76, 81, 82, 84, 142, 167, 177, 180, 194, 201, 213, 214
García, Pedro 44
Gbenga, Baba 164, 172
Geertz, Clifford 105, 111
globalization xxiii, 28, 29, 30, 95
God of Small Things, The 42, 48
God's Script, The 57
Gogh, Van 3
Gogol, Nikolai 180
Gómez, Fernando Fernán 198, 200, 209
Gómez, Sergio xxii, xxx, 18, 19, 33
González, Agustín 196, 208
González Echevarría, Roberto 36, 41, 100
González, José Eduardo 15, 112
Goor, Tim Aan't 95
Gosser Esquilín, Mary Ann 129
Goto, Hiromi 157
Grace, Patricia 154
Gramsci, Antonio 35
graphic narrative 131, 132, 140, 141, 143
Grass, Günter 13, 38, 149, 180, 213

Gray, Dorian 59
Grepi, Alejandra 209
Griffiths, Gareth 48
Grossman, Edith 82, 129
Grosz, George 4
Guenther, Irene 61, 170
Guha, Ranajit 38

Hahn, Óscar 23
Haiti xii, xvii, 23, 24, 71, 115, 118, 121, 124, 128, 129
Haitian Revolution 24, 25
Hall, Rodney 150
Hancock, Geoff 160, 218
Hancock, Joel 63
Handel, George Frederick 203
Hanrahan, Barbara 151
Harappa, Iskander 183
Haroun and the Sea of Stories 181, 192
Harris, Wilson 13, 71, 213
Hartlaub, Gustav 3
Hau'ofa, Epeli 155
Herrasti, Vicente xxiv
Herrer-Olaizola, Alejandro 145
heteroglossia 106, 107, 108
Heureaux, Ulises "Lilís" 103
Highway, Tomson 158
Hinchcliffe, Peter 160, 176
Hispaniola xii, 108, 113, 115, 116, 117
Hodgins, Jack 152
Holguín, Fernando Valerio 112
Hollaman, Keith 167
Holmes, Kerewin 154
Holy Trinity 197
Home, Strange Home 170, 177
Hopkinson, Nalo 149
Hopkins, Oscar 149
Howard, Richard 145

Huéspeda 194
Hulme, Keri 154, 155, 170
Hurley, Andrew 62
Husserl, Edmund 4
Hutcheon, Linda 37, 152
Hyder, Bilquìs 186, 187, 189
Hyder, Raza 183
Hyder, Sufiya Zinobia 183

Icarus Girl, The xiv, 162, 177
Ideas 13, 23, 29, 42, 80, 101, 117, 126, 179, 201
Ihimaera, Witi 154
Imaginary Homelands 41, 48, 168, 182, 185, 191, 192
Inclán, Valle 193, 206
indigenous people xiii, 105, 117, 158, 159
Innocent Eréndira and Other Stories 63
Introduction à la littérature fantastique 57, 64
Iowa International Writer's Workshop 19
Iowa Review xxiii, 19, 20
Ireland, David 151
Irele, F. Abiola 177
Isbert, José 209
Iwasaki, Fernando 193

Jacob, Max 5
Jaguar Smile, The xiv, 180, 181, 182, 192
James, Henry 50
Jameson, Frederic R. 148
Jelloun, Tahar Ben 13
Jérémie 123
Jessamy 162, 168
Jessel 58
Jesus 49

Jewinski, Ed 160, 176, 218
Johnson, Colin 159
Johnston, Wayne 156
Joyce, James 5
Joy, Harry 149

Kafka, Franz 62, 68, 180
Karamazov, Ivan 50
Katukani, Michiko 82
Kelly, Ned 152
Kemp, Lysander 63
Keneally, Donal 152
Kennedy, William xi, 53, 214
Kerr, Lucile 145
Kerslake, Susan 153
Khair, Tabish 78
Khan, Ayub 185
Khayyam, Omar 187, 190
King, Bruce 164
Kingdom of This World, The xii, xiv, xvii, 23, 24, 25, 42, 68, 162
King, Thomas 158, 170
Kirchner, Ernst 4
Kluwick, Ursula 40
Kovalev, Platon 54
Kroetsch, Robert 154
Kundera, Milan 13
Kyle, Maggie 152

Labanyi, Jo 209
La biografía difusa de Sombra Castañeda xii, 98, 112
LaForte, Nicol xxiii
Lai, Larissa 157
Laing, B. Kojo 170
La invención de América mestiza 130
La Isabela 108

La lotería en Babilonia xix
la Menor, Santa María 108
Lampreave, Chus 196, 209
Landa, Alfredo 199, 208, 209
Lautreaumont, Comte de 24
Leal, Luis xix, xxi, 5, 7, 8, 51, 54, 69, 82
Le Plastrier, Lucinda 149
Lera, José María Caparrós 198
Library of Babel, The xix, 60
Linguanti, Elsa 191
Lins, Alavaro 16
Loi, Maman 118, 119
López-Calvo, Ignacio iii, iv, v, ix, xvi, 193, 221
Lora, Honorio 124
lore, Samoan 155
Losada, Basilio 64
Lovecraft, H. P. 50
Low, Gail 165
Lozano-Alonso, Angélica 21
Lucas, George 25
Luperón, Gregorio 103

macondismo xi, 84, 85, 95, 96
Maggiolo, Marcio Veloz v, xii, 97, 112, 113, 123, 227
magic iv, v, xix, xxi, xxx, xxxi, 16, 19, 20, 22, 27, 28, 33, 47, 48, 49, 61, 69, 108, 113, 115, 117, 119, 121, 123, 125, 127, 128, 129, 160, 176, 177, 191, 217, 218, 219, 224, 225
Maldoror 24
Malentendidos alrededor de García Márquez 30, 34
Mandinga, María 72
Manguel, Alberto 153

Manifiesto Crack xxiv, 34
Manzana, Ana María 33
Marcus, George E. 111
Marechal, Leopoldo 27
María, Sierva 72, 73, 74, 75, 78, 80, 81
Marías, Tres 44
market xviii, xxi, 20, 27, 28, 29, 86
Marquis de Casualdero 72
Marsh, Steven 203
Martínez Almánzar, Juan Francisco 129
marvelous ix, xvii, xviii, xx, xxv, 7, 8, 9, 10, 12, 13, 23, 24, 25, 29, 30, 51, 68, 69, 71, 100, 113, 115, 127, 170, 171, 172, 174, 175, 193, 201, 205
McCann, A. L. 156
McDonald, Ann-Marie 153
McHale, Brian 13
McKenzie, Dr. 164, 172
McLain, Colleen 168
McLean, Anne 34
McMillin, Arnold 191
McOndo x, xvi, xxii, xxiii, xxiv, xxvii, xxix, xxx, xxxi, 18, 19, 23, 27, 28, 29, 30, 33, 86, 96, 156
McOndo and Latinidad: An Interview with Edmundo Paz Soldán xxx
McOndo group x, xxii, 86
McQuillan, Martin 191
Me llamo Rigoberta Menchú 111
Melville, Herman 143
Menchú, Rigoberta 101, 111
Menippean satire 55

Men of Maize 12, 100, 158
Menton, Seymour xii, xix, 5, 98
Merivale, Patricia 191
Metamorphosis, The 52, 54, 60, 61, 62
Métraux, Alfred 124
Mezzadra, Sandro 85
Midnight's Children 37, 38, 39, 40, 41, 48, 53, 64, 79, 179, 187, 191, 192, 213
Miguel the Indian 104, 106
Mikics, David 70
Miller, Richard 145
Miller, Scott 34
Milne, Lesley 191
Mi poncho es un kimono flamenco 193
modernity ix, xii, xviii, xxi, xxvi, 22, 28, 32, 38, 39, 40, 89, 91, 95, 151, 203
Monegal, Emir Rodríguez 9, 174
monoglossia xii, 106, 107
monomania 39
Montercarlo Film Festival 196
Montero, Felipe 52
Montero, Mayra xii, 113, 120, 128, 129, 130
Monti, Alessandro 191
Moorhouse, Frank 151
Morales, Ana María 16
Morá, Manolo 209
Morand 58
Moreiras, Alberto xxv
Moretti, Franco 64
Morrison, Toni xi, 13, 21, 53, 68, 86, 170, 213, 214
Morris, Pam 112
Moscote, Don Apolinar 90
Moya Pons, Frank 127

Muhammad, Anna 188, 190
Muir, Edwin 63
Müller-Bergh, Klaus 129
Munch, Edvard 4
Murdock,Fred 101
Murnane, Gerald 151, 157
Murrell, Nathaniel Samuel 129

Ndomo, Ngé 202, 208
Negra sombra 207
Neguijón 193
Neilson, Brett 85, 96
neoliberalism xxiv, 86, 157
New Historical Novel 98, 111, 118, 129
New Zealand xiii, 146, 147, 154, 158, 159, 160
Nicaragua 180, 181, 182
Nights at the Circus 45, 47
Nocturno de Chile 30
Noel,Ti 104, 110
Nolde, Emil 4
Noor, Ronny 192
Nose, The 54, 63

Ocampo, Silvina 8
Ocampo,Victoria 181, 182
Ochoa, Ana María 96
Ōe, Kenzaburō 13
Oesterheld, Héctor 141
Of Love and Other Demons xi, 67, 71, 72, 73, 74, 75, 76, 77, 79, 80, 81, 82
Okri, Ben 13, 21, 170, 214
Olmos, Fernández 121, 128
Omotoso, Kole xvi
Ondaatje, Michael 153
One Hundred Years of Solitude xi, xvi, xviii, xxv, xxx, 12, 18, 21, 22, 23, 26, 29, 30, 31, 42, 47, 51, 52, 59, 61, 63, 70, 72, 74, 84, 87, 96, 100, 104, 147, 156, 170, 201, 209, 213
Ong, Walter 87
On the Marvelous Real in America xxi, xxx, 15, 128
Ortega, Daniel 182
Ortega y Gasset, José 5, 170
Oshima, Nagisa 144
O'Toole, Peter 185
Ouyang, Wen-Chin 129, 130, 174
Oyeyemi, Helen xiv, 162, 177

Pact of Bois Caiman 118
Padilla, Ignacio xxiv, xxv, 18, 34, 86
Pakeha-Maori 158
Palmié, Stephan 129
Palou, Pedro Ángel xxiv, 18
Paquita, Doña 197
Paranagua, Paulo A. 32
Paravisini-Gebert, Lizbeth 128
Parnini, Jay 177
Pavlović, Tatjana 209
Paz Soldán, Edmundo xxii, xxiii, xxx, 18, 86
Pearson, Lon 76
Peden, Margaret Sayers 64
Pedro Paramo 12
Peiró,Eva Woods 209
Perriam, Chris 209
Perucho, Juan 193, 206
Pevear, Richard 63
phantoms 49, 53, 58
Phelan, Francis 53
Pichardo, Franklin Franco 127
Pierre, André 113, 126

Pierre, Roland 129
Pietri, Arturo Uslar 170
Pilar 53
Pizarnik, Alejandra 144
Pollack, Sarah 86
Pons, Frank Moya 127
Ponte, María Luisa 209
popular religion v, 113, 115, 117, 119, 121, 123, 125, 127, 129
Portuondo, José Antonio 17
post-Boom xxiv
Postcolonialism 82
post-expressionist ix, xxi, 3, 4, 88, 169
postmodernity 95, 145
postmodern neoliberalism xxiv
Prakash, Gyan 38
Prakash, Nandy 48
Pratt, Mary Louise 112
Preciado, Juan 53
Prólogo 23, 24, 32, 33
Proust 7
Pynchon, Thomas 13

Quayson, Ato 173
Quint 58

Rabal, Francisco 199, 209
Rabassa, Gregory 47, 63
Rama, Ángel xxvi
Ramírez, Esculapio 103
Realists, The xxi
real marvelous 23, 24, 25, 29, 30, 193
Reati, Fernando 73
Reeds, Kenneth 170
Relato inmoral 194, 209
Rellán, Miguel 209
Rendón, Serapio 103

Rengifo, Alejandra 129
Resines, Antonio 209
Reyes, Alina 58
Rey, Fernando 199, 209
Reyna, Nicanor 90
Rilke, Rainer Maria 5
Ríos Carratalá, Juan A. 203
Rivas, Manuel 193, 206, 214
Rivera, Juan Pablo 145
Rivera Villegas, Carmen M. 129
Rodríguez, Félix Pita 8
Rodríguez, Ileana 38, 47, 48
Roh, Franz xxi, 3, 4, 9, 51, 67, 88, 169
Romero, Joaquín María Aguirre 34
Ross, Robert 160
Roy, Arundahti 42
Rubber Man 131
Ruiz, Labrador 8
Rulfo, Juan 53, 213
Rushdie, Salman xiv, 13, 21, 37, 38, 47, 48, 53, 68, 86, 168, 170, 178, 184, 191, 192, 213, 214, 217

Sábato, Ernesto 195
Sagastume, Camila 93
Saint Peter 199
Saleem 39, 40, 41, 179, 191
Samsa, Gregor 54
Sandín, Lyn Di Iorio 173, 177
San Franscisco, Quique 202
Santana, Pedro 103
Santos-Febres, Mayra 129, 144
Saramago, José xi, 13, 56, 214
Sardiñas, José Miguel 16
Sasser, Kim 181

Satanic Verses, The 184, 191, 192, 214
Schroeder, Shannin 71
Scott, Sir Walte 155
Secret History of Costaguana, The 30, 34
Segundo, Aureliano 91, 93
Segundo, José Arcadio 59, 91
Sethie, Anita 166
Sevilla, Lolita 209
Shadbolt, Maurice xiii
Shakil, Babar 186, 190
Shakil, Bunny 186
Shame xiv, 178, 183, 184, 185, 186, 187, 188, 189, 190, 192
Sheppard, R. Z. 74
Sienkiewicz, Henryk 155
Siete lunas y siete serpientes xxv
Silver Cross of the Order of Merit 205
Simal, Begoña 25, 33
Sinai, Saleem 39
Sklodowska, Elzbieta 105
Slemon, Stephen 53, 146, 175
Smallwood, Joey 156
Sobre cultura dominicana y otras culturas 108, 112
Solana, Francisco López 141
Solidarity through Difference: Rushdie's Anti-Example in The Jaguar Smile 192
Sound of Things Falling, The xxv, xxxi
Spengler, Oswald 105
Spivak, Gayatri Chakrabarty 35, 42
Stavans, Ilan 73, 82
Stead, C. K. 147, 154
Stoker, Bram 50
Strachey, James 16
subaltern studies x, 35, 36, 37, 38, 41, 42, 45
Suburbano Revista Cultural Miami 33
supernatural ix, xi, xix, 4, 6, 9, 10, 11, 49, 50, 51, 52, 53, 55, 57, 60, 61, 69, 70, 74, 78, 87, 91, 92, 113, 119, 122, 125, 162, 163, 164, 165, 167, 171, 180, 187, 188
surrealism ix, xvii, xviii, xxi, 4, 24, 68, 100, 114, 115, 193, 200, 203
surruralism 195
Swanson, Roy Arthur 74
Swan, Susan 153
Swift, Jonathan 153
syncretism ix, 7, 117, 121

Tagarro, Ana 209
Tagore, Rabindranath 182
Takolander, Maria 160
Tchernichova, Viktoria 191
Ten Kortenaar 191
Third Reich 6, 51
third world 180
Thomas, D. M. 13
Thompson, Jon 192
Tientos y diferencias: ensayos 81
Tiffin, Helen 48
Todorov, Tzvetan 57
Tomlinson, Hugh 145
Torgovnick, Marianna 101
Total 98, 116, 119, 150, 153, 157
Toti, Gianni 195
Trask, Willard 62
travel xiv, 85, 89, 92, 126, 157, 204

Treaty of Waitangi 158
Triste, Aureliano 91
Trueba, Esteban 44
Trueba, Fernando 204
Trujillo, Héctor B. 110
Trujillo, Rafael Leónidas 103, 109, 124
Tsiolkas, Christos 156
Tuchman, Barbara 96
Turn of the Screw, The 50, 58, 63
Twain, Mark 151

unreality xiv, 56, 61, 178, 190
Updike, John 68
Upstone, Sara 174
Urroz, Eloy xxiv, 18, 34
Úrsula, Amaranta 94
Usigli, Rodolfo 17
Uslar-Pietri, Arturo xvii, 6

Valdivieso, L. Teresa 111
Valle-Inclán, Ramón María del 206
Valverde, Tito 209
Van Maanen 107
Vargas Llosa, Mario 21, 22, 150, 225
Varona, Anselmo 194
Vásquez, Juan Gabriel xxv, xxxi, 18
Veloz Maggiolo, Marcio v, xii, 97, 112, 113, 123, 227
ventriloquism 36, 37, 41, 42, 46
Verne, Jules 50
Verson, Lidia 123
Viramontes, María Elena 21
Vodou xii, 7, 43, 118
Volek, Emil 95, 142, 145
Volokhonsky, Larissa 63

Volpi, Jorge xxiv, 18, 31, 34, 86
Von Der Walde, Erna 96
von Hardenberg, Friederich Freiherr 88
voodoo 97, 108, 124, 127, 129

Warnes, Christopher 173
Weller, Archie 159
Wells, H. G. 50
Wendt, Albert 155
White, Edmund xxv
White, Patrick 147
Whitey's Fell 150, 159
Wilde, Oscar 59
Wilson, Jason 130
Wittgenstein, Ludwig 17
Wongar, B. 159
Woolf, Virginia 5
World War I 3
Wright, Alexis xiii, 159

Xu 138, 139

Yates, Donald 17
Yoruba 162, 164, 165, 166, 172
Young, David 167

Zakrzewski Brown, Isabel 112
Zamora, Lois Parkinson xix, xx, xxx, xxxi, 15, 16, 17, 62, 63, 64, 69, 82, 83, 128, 170, 176, 177, 191, 201, 210
Zia-ul-Haq, Muhammad 183
Zinobia, Sufiya 183, 187, 188, 189, 190
Zunzunegui, Santos 209

The Manchester Library
The Bishop's School
La Jolla, California
WITHDRAWN